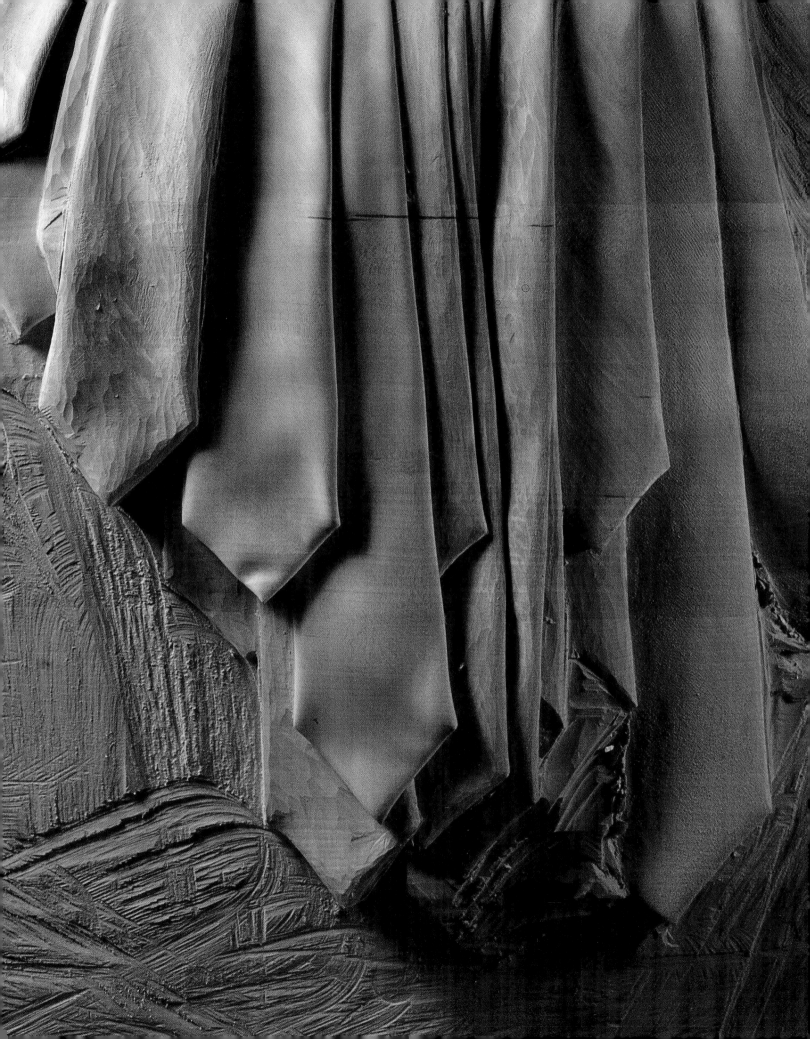

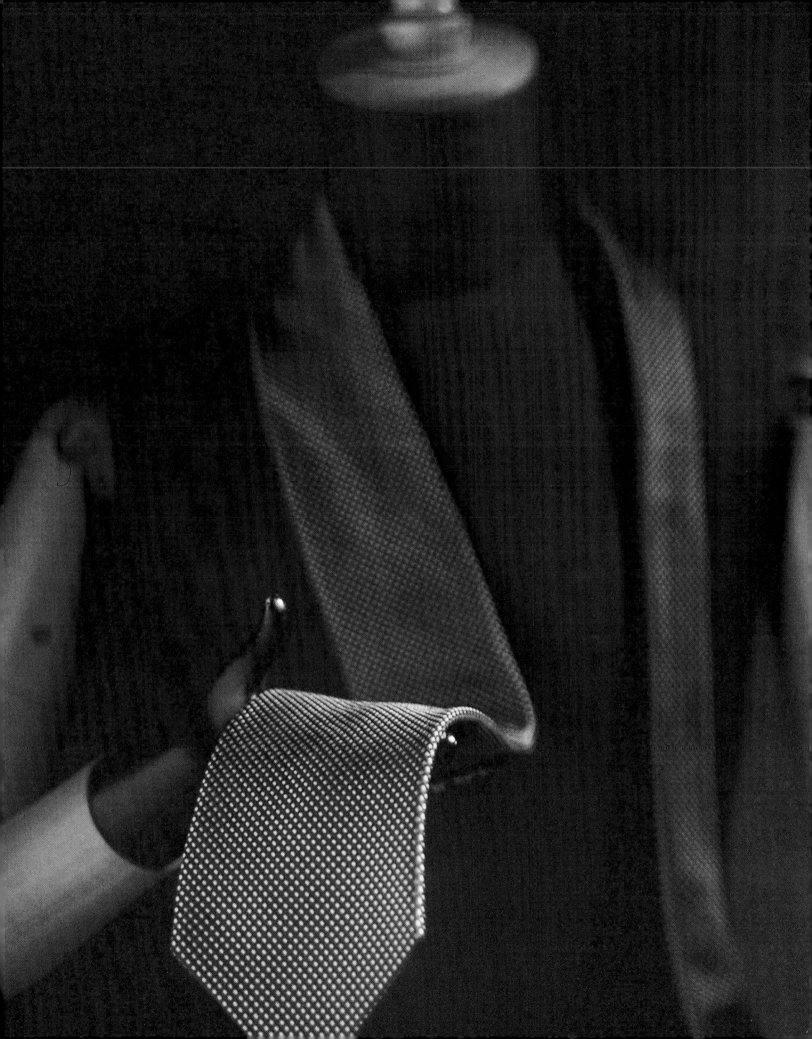

THE BOOK OF
TIES

François Chaille

———

Flammarion
Paris - New York

Editorial Direction
Ghislaine Bavoillot

Design
Marc Walter

Translated from the French
by John Goodman

Copyediting
Christine Schultz-Touge

Typesetting
Octavo Editions, Paris

Photoengraving
Colourscan, France

Printed by Canale

Flammarion
26, rue Racine
75006 Paris

ISBN: 2-08013-568-6
Numéro d'édition: 0820
Dépôt Légal: September 1994
Printed in Italy

CONTENTS

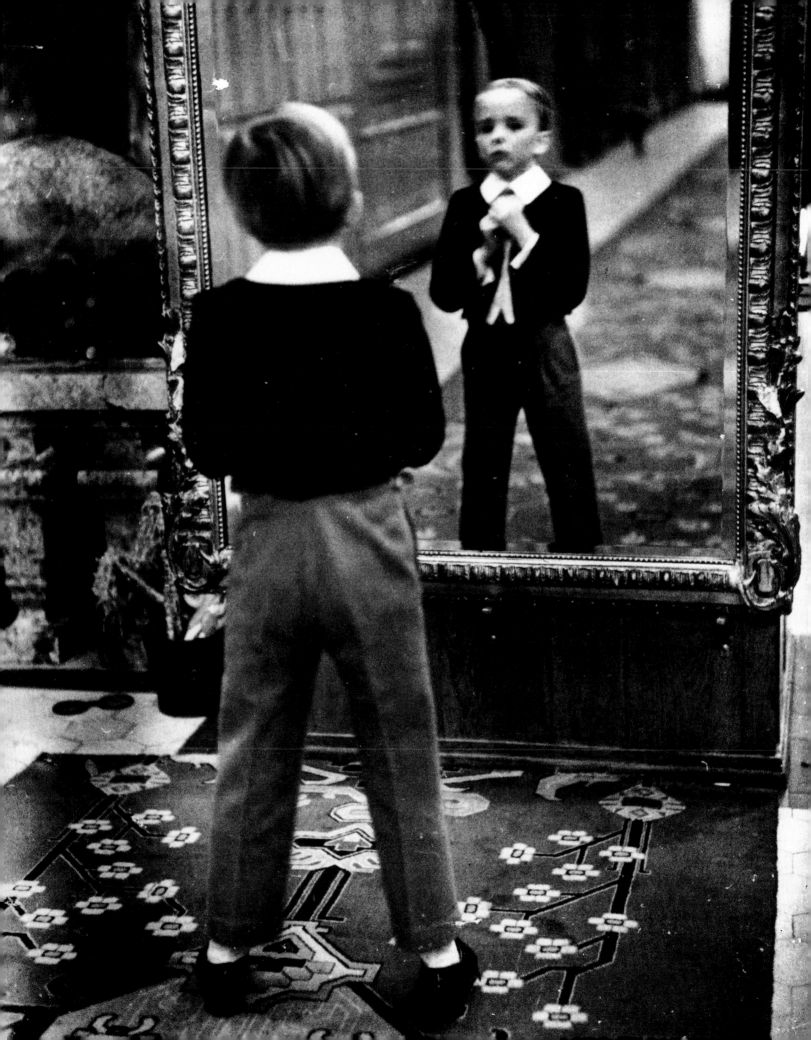

PREFACE

In the burgeoning literature available on men's clothing, there has been a growing need for a beautiful book on ties. A book with lavish illustrations, the better to reveal the great wealth of the subject; a complete book that does more than invoke a few supposed rules of elegance or discuss a single aspect of the field in depth; a book sufficiently well-documented to provide the reader with an overview unencumbered by the author's prejudices. I am pleased to report that this book has been written—not by a specialist, but by a writer who is, in the best sense of the word, an amateur: a man who surveys the world of ties with immense curiosity and passion. François Chaille has filled an especially troubling gap by emphasizing the important contributions of the many skilled artists and craftsmen involved in every step of the tie production process. Tie designers, weavers, printers, and finishers are all part of an extremely rich tradition within which they create contemporary neckwear. Their relationship with this tradition is a complex one, combining reference, adaptation, and even complete opposition. The tie is without doubt the most versatile and sensuous element in the male wardrobe—and, as we say today, it is the one that carries the highest information content. It can convey a feeling, a situation, and above all the elegance of the wearer, since his choice of tie is an expression of his inner self. This proliferation of meaning has been made possible by two hundred years of history and technological advances in the textile arts. The development of patterns and color schemes, which are often based upon earlier models, is continually being enriched by an ever-increasing variety of manufacturing techniques, as the processes of fabric production, dyeing, and weaving are constantly being improved. I invite the reader to share this pleasure, to look into this mirror of history, to explore these complex patterns, and I do so with all the more enthusiasm because the author has managed to avoid confining his subject within normative standards which are fundamentally at odds with the very object of the art of the tie, namely, self-expression.

Jean-Claude COLBAN

A well-tied tie is the first serious step in life, according to Oscar Wilde. An English boy, photographed by Alfred Eisenstaedt for *Life Magazine* at the Grand Hotel, St. Moritz in 1932 (left).

The necktie, in the form either of the four-in-hand or the bow tie, has been an indispensable adjunct to male elegance for the best part of a century. An illustration from *The Tie: a Breviary of Good Taste*, a 1912 guide published in Germany (right).

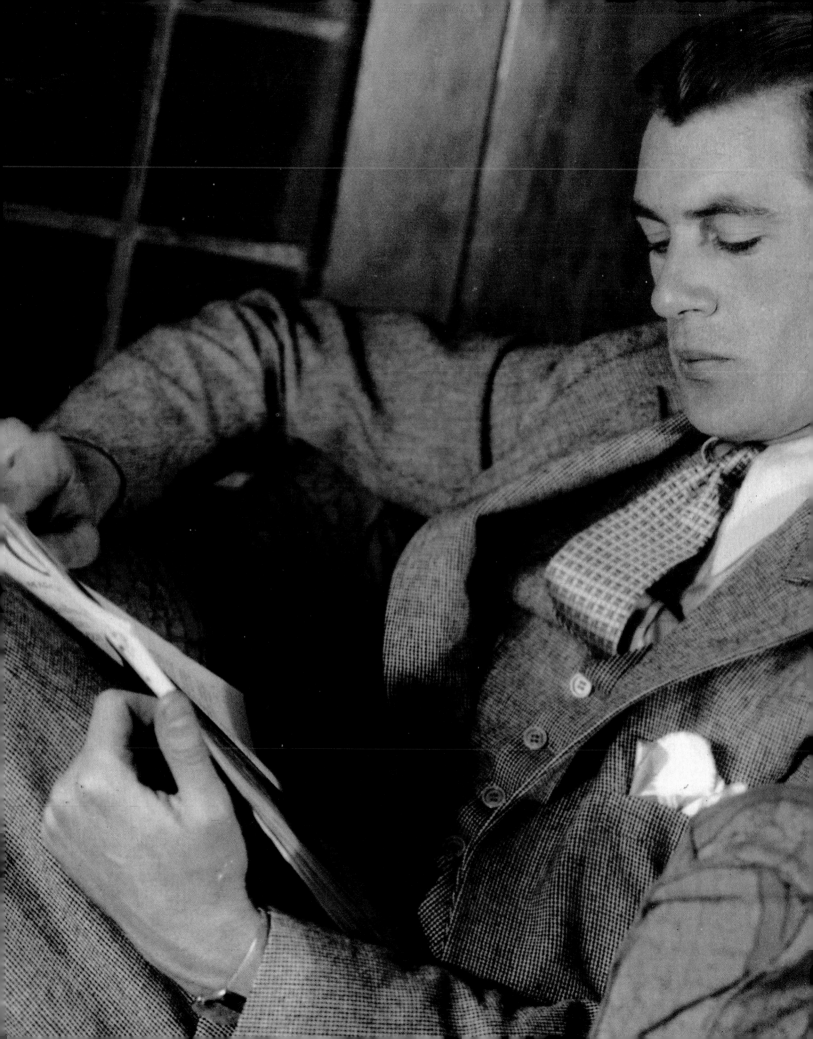

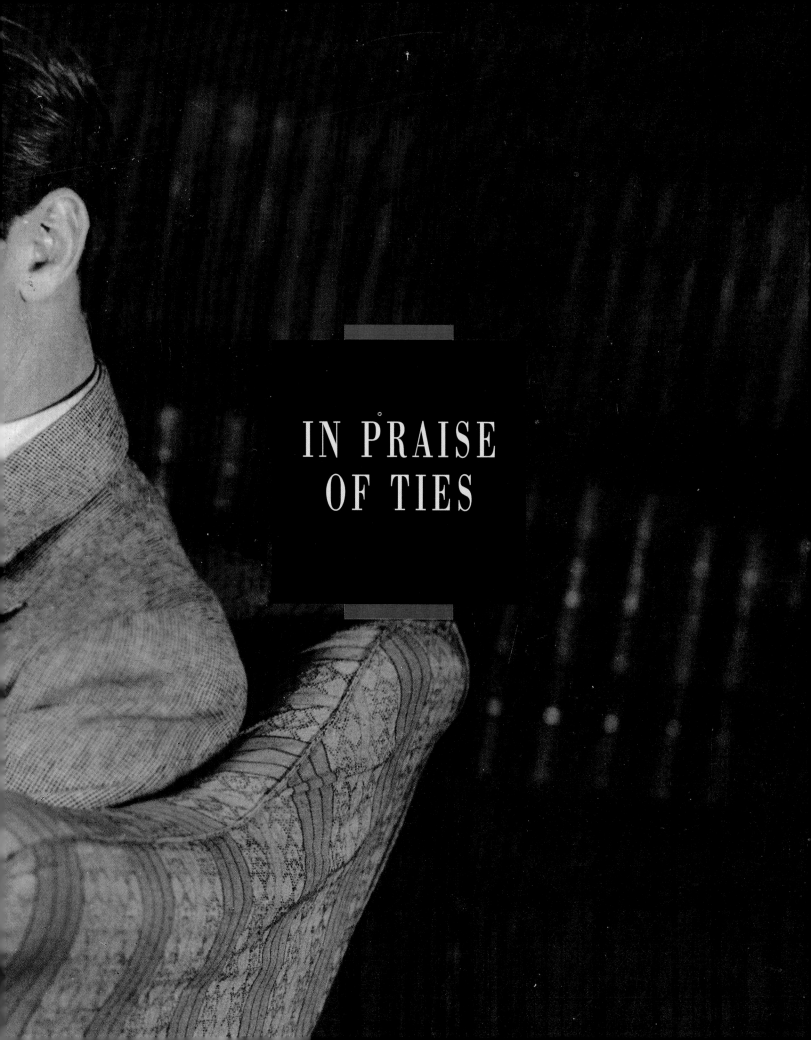

IN PRAISE OF TIES

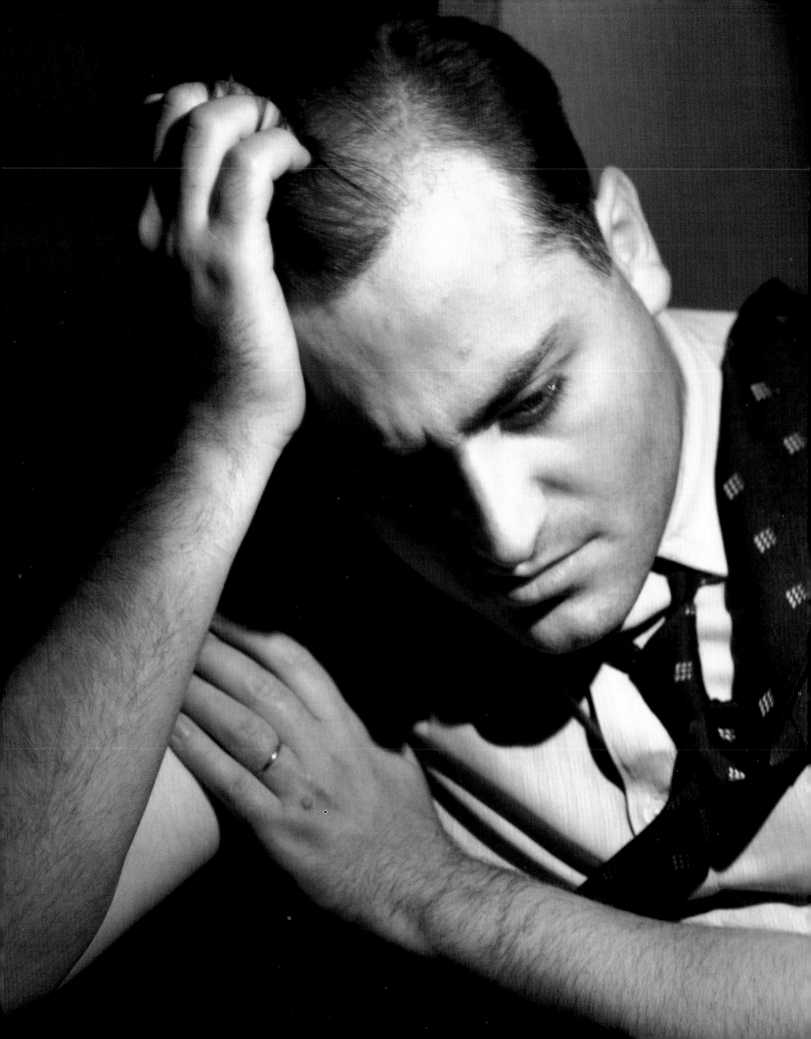

Twenty years ago the idea of writing a book in praise of neckties would have seemed ludicrous. At that time they were widely considered the preeminent symbol of middle-class convention, submission to hierarchical rules, and identification with patriarchal values. Consequently they were worn less and less frequently. I remember people predicting that ties would disappear altogether because they were emblems of a reactionary culture destined to be blown away by the winds of history. In a sense, this profound crisis was salutary. From the late 1950s on, the tie had become a binding obligation, a constraint imposed at the office, on evenings out, and on certain family occasions. Many men wore ties resentfully, viewing them as signs of conformity and social regimentation. Their virtual disappearance in the 1960s outside spheres of politics, business, and finance was a cause for celebration. But ten years later, having survived their moment of ideological vilification, ties again assumed the function ascribed to them upon their invention some three centuries earlier: namely, as purely ornamental articles, worn for the most part without complaint or resistance.

Today, few men wear ties against their will.

Although they are compulsory in many workplaces (the phrase "power ties" conveys the extent to which some of the old social messages retain their force), it is increasingly common to see men in positions of authority

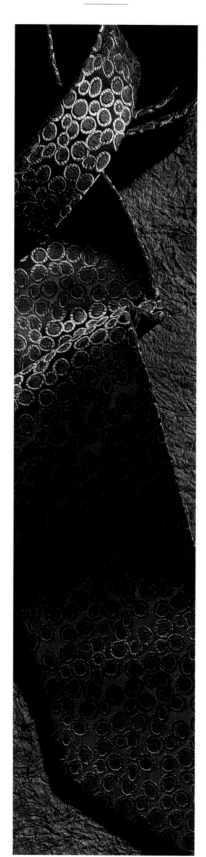

without them. In *Le Nu vêtu et dévêtu*, Jacques Laurent describes their current status as follows: "Ties are of course worn by senators, lawyers, and office workers, but they are also sported by wealthy pleasure seekers, Hollywood types, journalists, and clothing salesmen. They no longer necessarily correspond to one's social aspirations and ambitions; they can also signal the embrace of a certain dressy look." Instead of viewing them as emblems of conformity, many now see wearing ties as proof of a particular fashion statement made with complete freedom of choice. Increasingly, men regard ties as just another accessory from which they can derive pleasure should they so desire. Certainly no one would now predict their imminent demise.

Pleasure must figure prominently in any attempt to size up ties and their role in the current fashion scene. The pleasure associated with self-expression and social communication. The pleasure derived from a certain flair in one's self-presentation. The pleasure derived until early in the present century from the variety of possible knots, and subsequently from the many available colors and patterns. For ties are the sole touch of sartorial fantasy allowed in the masculine wardrobe, and they constitute a veritable stylistic language for users of all ages and backgrounds. Essentially purposeless, and increasingly worn at one's own discretion, ties are now above all statements of the wearer's personality.

"A useful article of clothing, a vest for example, is

Like all dandies inspired by Beau Brummell, Jules Barbey d'Aurevilly (1808–89)—the author of *Diaboliques, Chevalier Des Touches,* and *Du Dandysme et de George Brummell*—made his ties the principle feature of his wardrobe. As shown in this portrait by Émile Lévy (right), he had a preference for lace cravats, in the seventeenth-century style. An eccentricity not shared by the most fashionable of dandies of the Belle Époque, Boni de Castellane, who was noted for his sumptuous receptions and his somewhat garish silk ties. Caricature by Cappiello (below).

insignificant precisely because of its utility," wrote Alberto Moravia in his preface to *188 Ways to Tie One's Tie.* "One can appreciate its elegance, yet one does not ask after its purpose or meaning. But, as with the atrophied parts of certain animals' skeletons (a whale's "paws," for example), ties slowly became useless, not to say absurd, and then, rather like officers' stripes, we started asking what they meant. In other words, in light of their relative superfluity, they ceased to appear to us as what they were, namely strips of fabric run through shirt collars and knotted in various ways, and became symbols fraught with meaning. . . . Modern man is permitted but one accessory allowing him to reveal his vision of the world, to signal his presence in it: the tie."

Pleasure in cutting an original figure, pleasure in expressing oneself not only to seduce, but also to "unfurl," as it were, those motifs and colors most reflective of one's temperament and inner being. Insofar as they elaborate a metaphorical language by means of which a simple design can convey a character or an emotion, today's ties could serve as the basis for a monumental poetic anthology.

In reality, this poetry of the tie began well before the current proliferation of designs and colors. At the beginning of the nineteenth century, the art of the tie—or as it was then called, the cravat—was limited to different types of knotting and so was a function of the individual wearer's ingenuity. Honoré de Balzac, who prefaced a treatise on cravats whose author had pseudonymously styled himself the baron Émile de L'Empesé (in French, *empeser* means "to starch"), enumerated the temperaments evoked by fifteen different knots. According to him, the scientist's objectivity was best conveyed by the sober cross knot of the *cravate mathématique*; the poet's romantic bent by the puffy lyricism of the *cravate Byron*; and the lover's bashfulness by the seductive *cravate sentimentale*, simultaneously gracious and virile. A few years later, the rise of the black cravat, previously worn only by mem-

bers of the military or in periods of mourning (as in 1805, when all England donned black cravats in observing the death of Admiral Nelson), allowed men the opportunity to add a new touch of self-expression in order to convey political and social messages: adoption of this style signified one's embrace of liberal ideas.

There are many accounts of strangely intense relations cultivated by eminent figures with their cravats—for it was not unusual to make a fetish of them, rather like the writer's obsessive quest for the *mot juste.* First there is the well-known example of Beau Brummell, who approached his cravat knots as if they were *haiku,* the classic form of Japanese poetry in which a sentiment of absolute purity is expressed in only three lines: he was determined that they should be given life by a single movement (heaven forbid retying!); the effect he sought was no less than absolute perfection. He sometimes knotted dozens, undoing the failures, dropping them at his feet, and continuing until he attained a satisfactory result. The first dandies were his imitators, and they often betrayed their model. Whereas Brummell sought perfection in

simplicity, attracting attention through his elegant but spare attire, his emulators set out to use their cravats, in the words of Baudelaire, *d'étonner l'olympienne poire* (roughly, "to dazzle mere mortals"). The Belle Époque was richly populated with such poets of the strange and marvelous, like the actor Charles Le Bargy, who according to Léon Paul Fargue sported extravagantly colored cravats that "created more commotion than [the socialist politician] M. Jaures." Barbey d'Aurevilly signaled his extreme delicacy of soul by wearing lace cravats. Boni de Castellane, the fashionable Parisian master of ceremonies, required the most brilliant silks for his cravat-plastrons.

In the world of male elegance, the emblematic figure of George Bryan ("Beau") Brummell still stands as an essential reference. The label from an American tie of the 1940s (bottom, left). The numerous emulators of the world's most famous dandy have sought self-expression in the clothes they wear, most particularly in their neckties. An unusual asymmetrical knot for Charles Baudelaire, who made himself the poet of dandyism in the *Peintre de la vie moderne.* Photographed by Nadar *circa* 1865, (right-hand page, top left). A soft four-in-hand, for Oscar Wilde who would happily parade about in silk stockings, bright red vest and apple-green cravat, *circa* 1890, (right-hand page, top right). A stylish *lavalière* for Rudolph Valentino the legendary "Latin lover" whose ephemeral elegance and good looks fired the passions of a generation (right-hand page, bottom left). A martial four-in-hand with a small knot under a stiff collar, for the Italian writer Gabriele D'Annunzio whose fabulous wardrobe was recently exhibited at the Pitti Palace in Florence (facing page, bottom right).

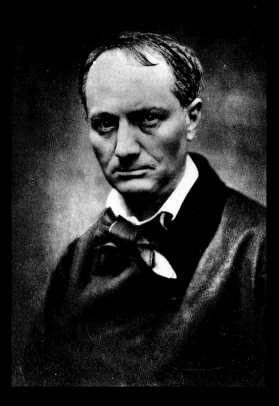
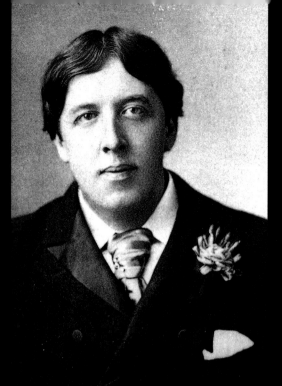
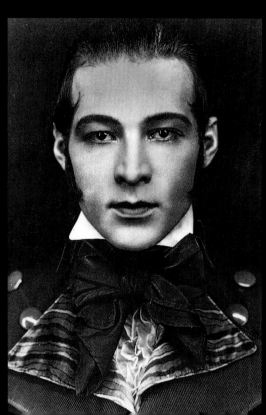
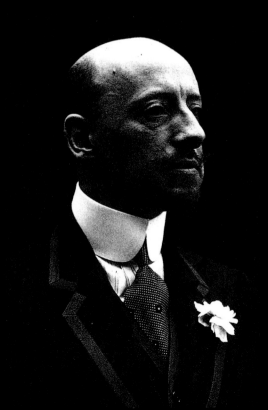

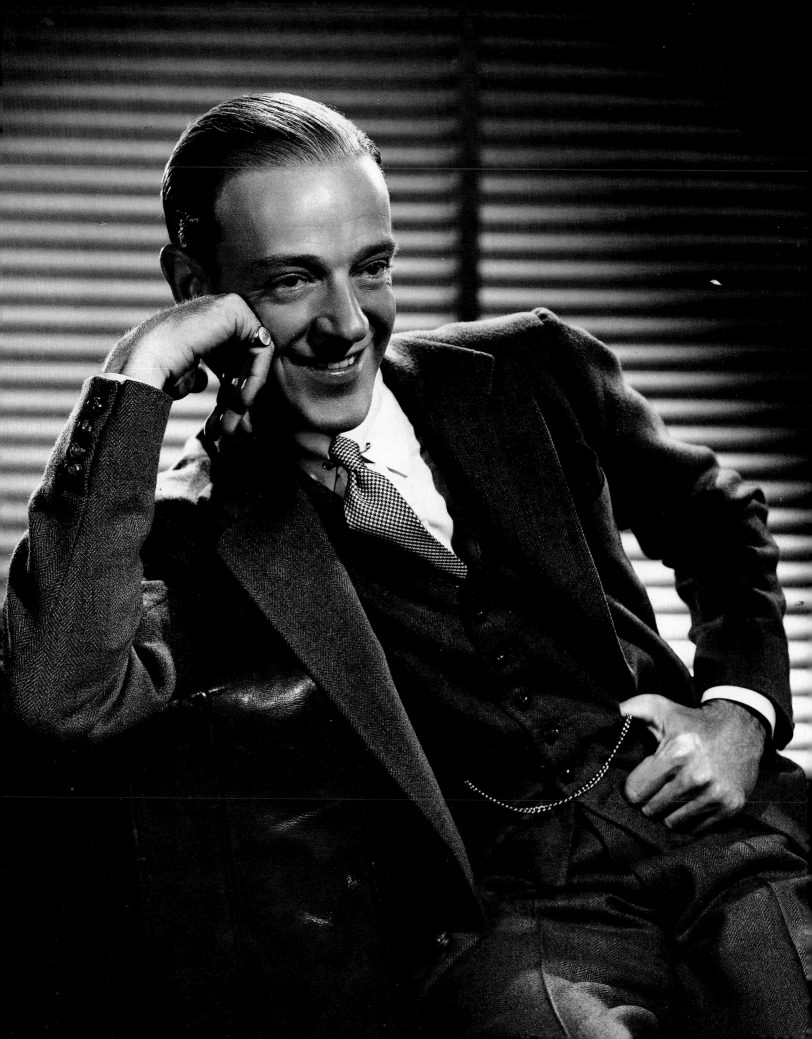

Fred Astaire, who began life as Frederick Austerlitz, had a career as actor and dancer that took him from the age of seven to seventy-seven—from his first appearance in 1907 to part two of *That's Entertainment* in 1976. Several generations have considered him to be the epitome of male elegance. His graceful nonchalance was not in contradiction with his London-tailored suits and the exquisite ties that generally featured classic motifs and light colors. Fred Astaire in 1941, shortly after his great success in the RKO films co-starring Ginger Rogers. Note the way in which his pin collar pushes the knot forward making the tie stand out (left-hand page).

Later, in the 1930s, the Duke of Windsor and Fred Astaire—whose flawless silhouettes were omnipresent on magazine covers and movie screens—set the pace for male fashion on at least two continents. In constructing their images they both availed themselves of the rich resources of the necktie. They shared only one quirk: a penchant for mixing dots and stripes on, respectively, their ties and shirts. Otherwise, the comparison stops there: the duke became identified with the measured audacity of the large knot that now bears his name, while the dancer preferred ties that were of discreet colors and lightweight enough to take flight with him. Another prominent figure of the era, Aristotle Onassis, an empire builder who also succeeded in seducing two legendary women—Maria Callas and Jackie Kennedy—hid the knots of his ties (always black) by wrapping them around his neck a second time, a curious but entirely appropriate gesture if one ponders over the strategies largely responsible for his success: secrecy, dissimulation, and calculated surprise. Women succumbed to his charm, and men to his power—techniques revealed at just the right moment, when least expected. Annually, the insatiable and legendary tycoon ordered forty-eight specially tailored ties (half for winter and half for summer) to be placed in his numerous houses and yachts. The extra circuit and its magical effect required more

than six feet of fabric—one and a half times the usual length. In light of this example, can we have any doubts that ties, like poems, are more or less conscious expressions of character?

"The fact that I arrive at the office every morning wearing an ordinary striped tie is significant, as is my replacing it on a whim with a psychedelic tie, or my attending a business meeting without wearing a tie at all." This is how Umberto Eco, in his *Psychology of Clothes*, sums up the poetic freedom and functionality of ties today. Not only do they "speak," conveying all sorts of messages, but men are now at liberty to use them as they deem appropriate for a given occasion—or to refrain from using them, communicating by means of "silence."

With regard to freedom, we should bear in mind that there are countries in which ties—viewed as symbols of Western ethical and ideological bankruptcy—are prohibited. This was long the case in China, and to a lesser extent in the Soviet Union during its most repressive period under Stalin, a sworn enemy of neckties.

What is this miracle that matches the appearance of a tie to its wearer's state of mind? This is the tie of a desperate man, which, like the man himself, lets itself go, gives in, gives up. A still from *The Miracle Man*, a film by George Loane Tucker, 1919 (left).

The Duke of Windsor—formerly Edward VIII—became the darling of the United States when he arrived on a visit and initiated a new "English chic" that was more comfortable and more relaxed than its predecessor. It is still an internationally popular style. He became Duke of Windsor after his abdication in 1936, and his habitual knot was subsequently named after him. The Windsor knot calls for a broad, spread collar. The Duke of Windsor, photographed by Cecil Beaton in 1939 (below).

It is still the case in certain countries controlled by Islamic fundamentalists. In Turkey, by contrast, ties—being symbols of a secular state—are compulsory wear for members of the legislative assembly. To shift registers, they were also symbols of freedom for the first feminists: George Sand and Flora Tristan, for example, wore men's ties as emblems of emancipation.

The freedom of expression offered by ties was recently evoked by Christian Dior's menswear designer Patrick Lavoix in the magazine *Jet Society*: "Ties are like banners. They are tools of cultural revolution, which is simply not the case with suits." The enormous variety of patterns on today's ties offers a striking contrast with the endless uniformity of men's suits and facilitates a wide range of personal statements. Only a psychologist or semiologist is equipped to produce an analysis of the universe of contemporary ties which could encompass it in all its variegated splendor. A few such attempts have already been made—but they tend to be confusing, and their penchant for crude symbolism is a distinct limitation. It is claimed that ties are phallic symbols, that their geometric patterns reveal a longing for order, that their frequent use of small repeated motifs conveys anxiety, etc. Such statements may be true, but in the end they are unimportant. What is essential remains the pleasure deriving from choice and abundance. Since their rebirth in the 1980s, there have been ties to satisfy every taste. Between the modern variant of the four-in-hand design and the bow tie, between classicism and fantasy, sobriety and playfulness, every conceivable whim can be given

life. And while desires change over time, men now have the wherewithal to communicate a wide range of their fluctuating moods through color, fabric, and cut. While dressing in the morning or the evening, standing in front of the multicolored patchwork of all our ties, contemplation of the many possible combinations can induce delight, aversion, and just about every other mood in between. Such moods are influenced by the exterior factors that can shape our decision—context, season, color scheme; yet even more mysteriously, by our inner feelings at that given moment in time. Writing a poem again comes to mind: in choosing a tie we negotiate a framework of rules, devising an image that is both socially viable and responsive to our personal needs at a particular moment. And as with a poem, once this exercise has been brought to a satisfactory conclusion, our pleasure is increased by the number of constraints we have managed to overcome.

This is the greatest pleasure associated with ties: the possiblity for daily self-expression. Like the most gratuitous work of art, ties are offerings to oneself and others. Only the churlish would deprive themselves of the additional delights they afford: the pleasure taken in their beautiful fabrics and designs, subtly transforming an entire outfit, giving it a new elegance. The tie designer simply alters the normative image of masculinity by giving his talent free rein. This makes it possible for ties to play an aesthetic role by providing a graceful counterpoint—sometimes quite discreet—to the austerity that otherwise prevails in male dress. Contained in this way, such grace cannot compromise prevailing notions of virility. On the contrary, it tends to exalt them, playing *ying* to their *yang*. And then any tie salesperson will tell you that when choosing ties, most women opt for cheerful or soft-hued designs—not because they like to wear these themselves, but

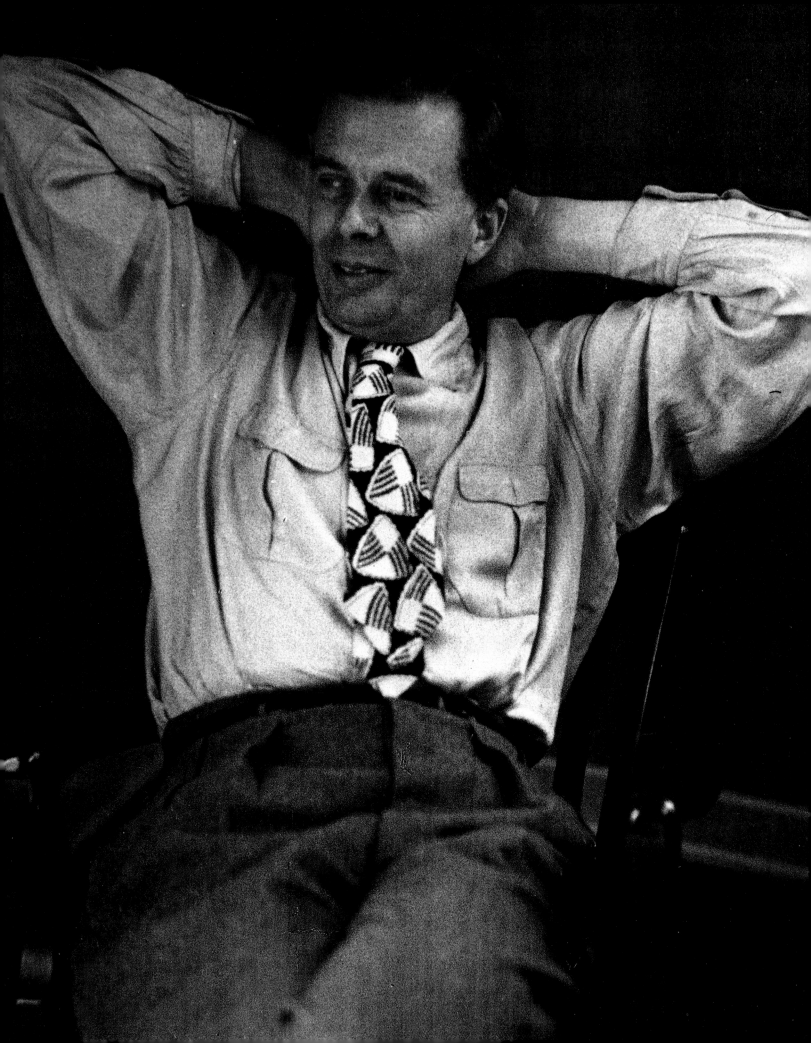

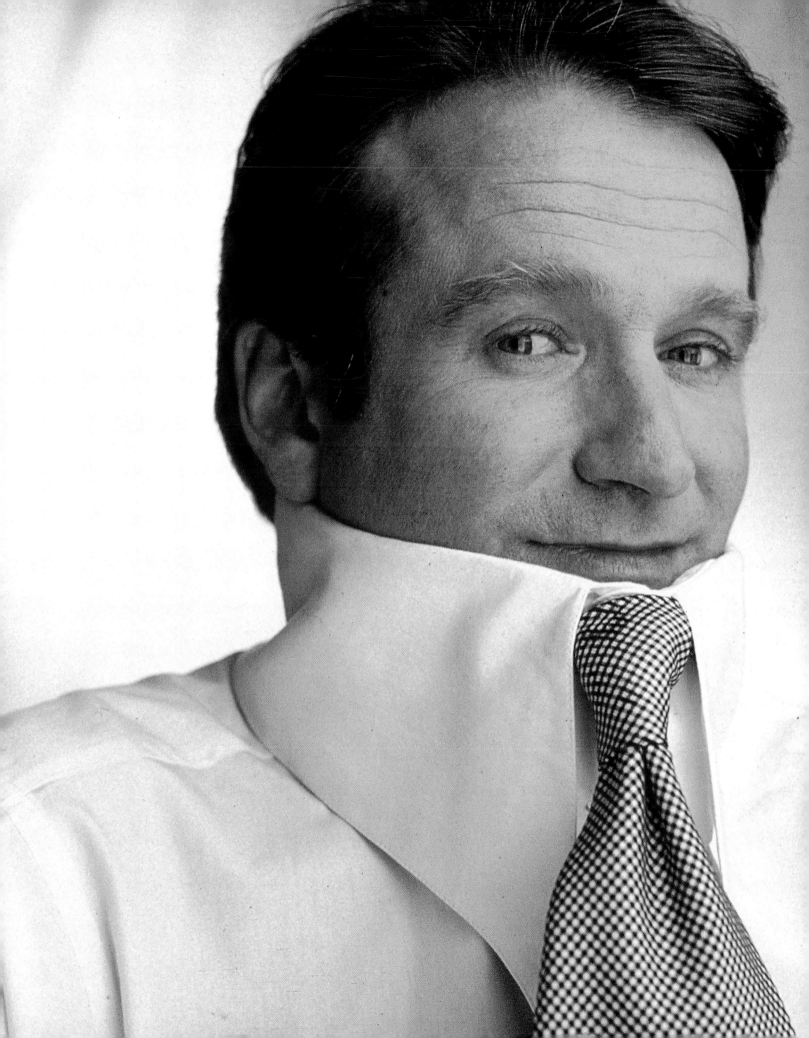

because they find them seductive when worn by men. (Statistics indicate that 60% of ties sold are purchased by women, which helps to explain the growing market over the last decade for colorful ties decorated with small animals, flowers, etc.) A female specialist in this area, Tatiana Tolstoï, recently wrote in her *De l'élégance masculine:* "From whatever perspective I examine it, this little rectangle of silk strangling men's necks induces a variety of emotions in me. How can a tie induce emotions, you ask. . . . To say that eyes derive their allure from the note of color they introduce into the face is inadequate. Something similar could be said of neckties, which provide the sole note of color in the somber universe of men's clothing. When I claim that ties move me, it's not just hyperbole. In a way, a suit without a tie is like the face of a blind person: it has no chance of insinuating its way into my affections the way certain glances can."

Finally, neckties can occasion an especially sensual pleasure: that of touch. A mere list of the fabrics most frequently used in their production—silk, soft wool, and blends of the two—is enough to suggest why this should be so. I'll have more to say later about tactile sensations,

which can sometimes equal sensations produced by touching the skin of a person one loves. But, in addition to the stimulus itself, this pleasure is also shaped by feelings whose roots run deep; it is as though these objects answered a desire—part and parcel of the human condition—to return to Paradise Lost, if only for a fraction of a second. I invite skeptical readers to consider for a moment the pervasive masculine tic of stroking or simply touching one's tie. Reminiscing about his friend the Duke of Windsor, the Italian novelist Giovanni Nuvoletti came up with the following account of this comforting gesture: "I can still remember him, at our last meeting, saying goodbye to the mistress of the house in his divinely simple yet supremely sophisticated way, with his soft pants, his slightly inclined head, and his sad smile creating a dignified but melancholy impression. In a characteristic gesture his left hand played delicately with his tie, automatically and unconsciously, almost making its perfect knot seem like the symbol of a lost era."

Whether considered as a vehicle of self-expression, as a means of accentuating one's charm, or as an object whose touch can calm the spirit, neckties offer decisive advantages. Nowadays, since ties are no longer compulsory to the degree that they were in the past, a man would have to be almost crazy not to wear one.

In *What's Up Doc?*, a 1972 Peter Bogdanovitch film, the American film star Ryan O'Neal plays an absent-minded musicologist (above).

A long-standing cliché has it that the wearing of a tie is a sign of seriousness and conformism. Thus it sometimes becomes an object of derision. The photographer Mark Seliger depicts the film actor Robin Williams—star of the 1989 film, *Dead Poets Society*—as a contemporary version of the Directory period *Incroyables,* who wrapped their cravats right up to their chins. Cover of *Rolling Stone* magazine, February 1991 (left).

Women play a crucial role in the world of men's ties. Because they advise their husbands, and often offer them ties as gifts, wives have a powerful influence on tie fashions. It is largely thanks to women that today we are seeing a certain feminization of tie designs: gentler colors and less serious motifs. A woman with gift ties, drawing published in the American magazine *Liberty* in the 1940s (left).

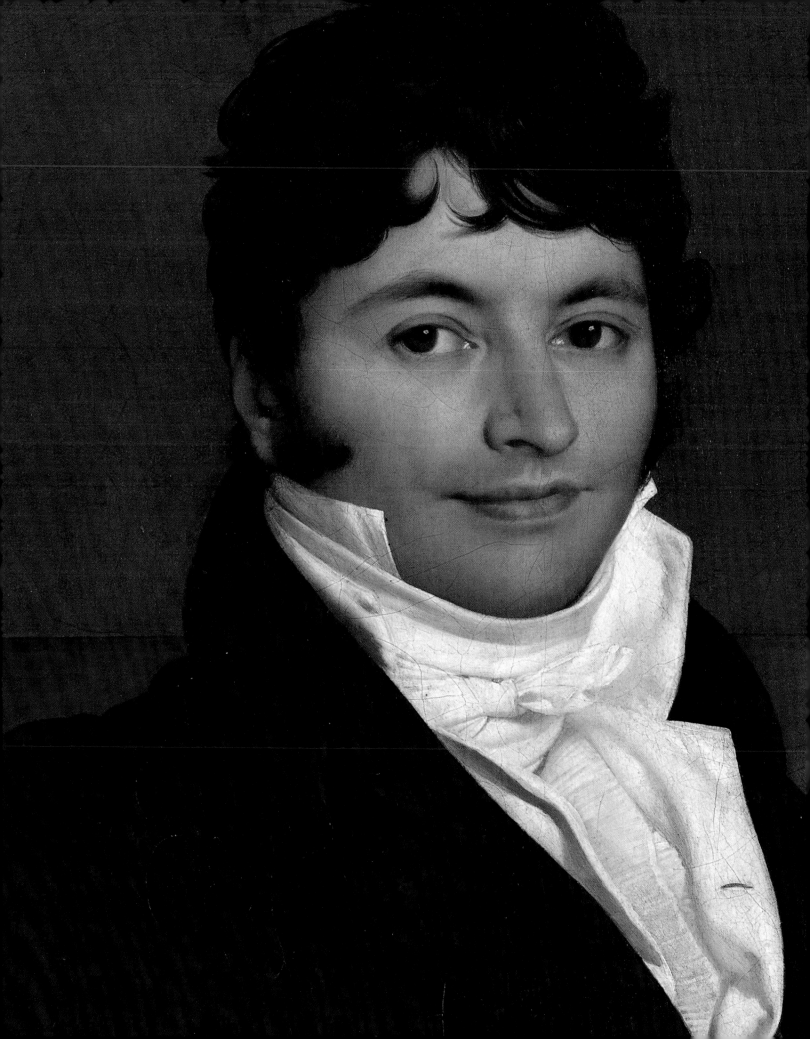

HISTORY

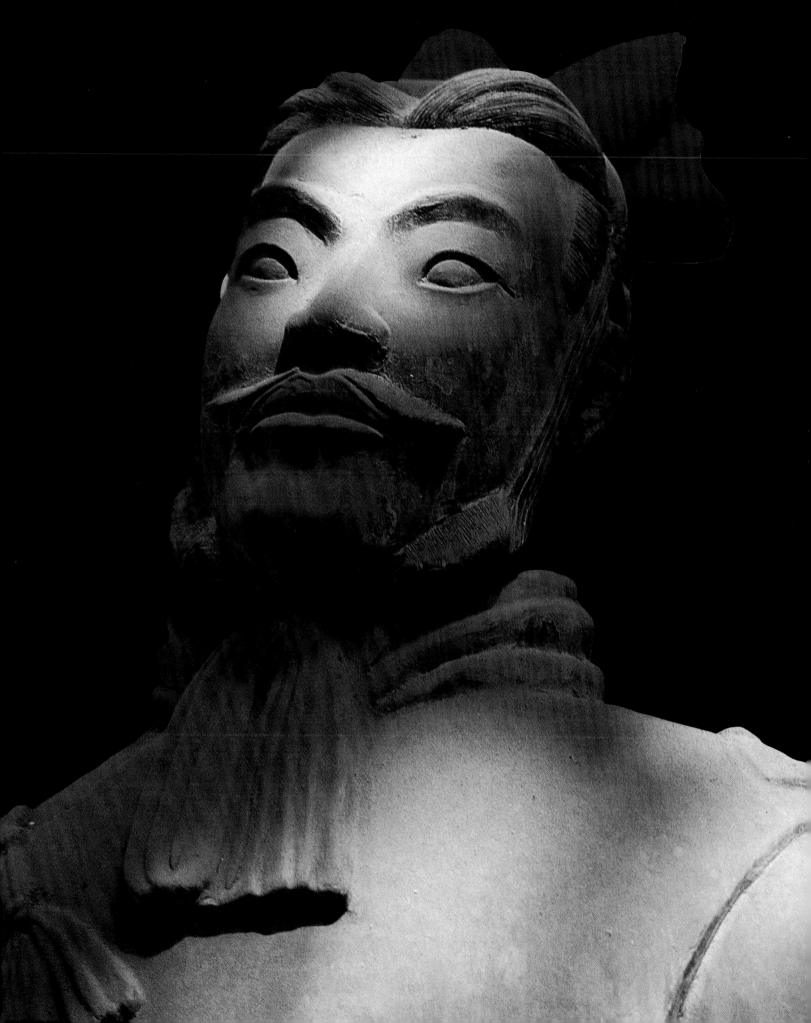

War and military life have always played an important, perhaps determining, role in the history of the tie. The first known portrayal of the necktie or knotted scarf is to be found around the neck of this Chinese terra-cotta warrior. He was found, in the company of 7,500 others, dating from the third century B.C. and all wearing identical scarves, in the tomb of the first emperor of China Ch'in Shih Huang-ti (left).

War sometimes has unexpected consequences never mentioned in history books. These repercussions are less obvious but just as durable and important as the drawing of new national boundaries. The Thirty Years' War, which devastated Europe from 1618 to 1648, still exercises a direct influence over the daily lives of 600 million men all over the globe: those who don neckties every morning. This religious conflict, in which the Protestant Bohemian aristocracy challenged the authority of the Catholic Holy Roman Empire, quickly spread across all Europe, pitting imperial troops against French and Swedish forces. It was a vicious war waged by Central European mercenaries who systematically pillaged the countryside as they moved through it. Around 1635, almost all of the 160,000 infantry and cavalry fighting for the king of France were foreign recruits. Among them were many Croatian horsemen, who wore an unusual article of clothing which made them easily identifiable: small knotted neckerchiefs. Those worn by simple soldiers were of coarse material, but many officers had examples made of silk or fine muslin.

CROATIAN NECKERCHIEFS

To understand the admiration—and the initial amazement—produced by these neckerchiefs we must keep in mind that in the Europe of this era such accesssories were a complete novelty. From antiquity to the second half of the sixteenth century men had left their necks exposed. In the Renaissance they adopted round collars, which in the course of the seventeenth century became ruffs and lace collars. There is, however, evidence of neckerchiefs having been worn in earlier eras. In 1974, 7,500 terra-cotta warriors dating from the third century B.C. and buried with the first Chinese emperor, Ch'in Shih Huang-ti, were unearthed, and they all sported neckerchiefs. At roughly the same time Roman warriors on campaign were equipped in winter with *focale*, knotted scarves serving several purposes, not the least of which was to keep them warm. These same *focale* are worn by the legionaires winding around Trajan's column in Rome, which commemorates the victory over the Dacians in the second century A.D.

These examples have one thing in common: soldiers who were active in cold climates. In other words, the function of history's earliest neckties was to provide protection from a harsh environment. It is thought that the Chinese neckwear was also intended to protect the soldiers' Adam's apples, which their culture believed to be the center of bodily strength and vitality. But dandyish French officers of the Thirty Years' War

Throughout its history, the necktie has been the subject of passing fashions, but it has always provided a good indication of the spirit of its times. The bourgeois rigidities of the nineteenth century were matched by its stocks, which were veritable iron clamps around the neck. A portrait of the Conseiller d'État Philibert Rivière, by Ingres, in 1805 (preceding double page).

These first neckties of history in fact belong to the prehistory of the tie: this first developed in the seventeenth century as a pure ornament. Fifteen centuries earlier, the Roman *focale*, which we see depicted on the base of Trajan's column in Rome, probably contributed to the soldiers' health, and provided a means of protecting them from sun and cold weather (left).

23

This painting by the Flemish artist Michael Sweerts (1624–64) is contemporary with the early days of the cravat in Europe. It gives an idea of the kind of neckerchief that would have been worn by Croatian mercenary officers in the Thirty Years' War (1618–48) before it then went on to be elaborated by the various court aristocracies (right).

Nicolas de Largillière was born in 1656, during the same period as the cravat, and died ninety years later. He provides a good testimony to the spread of the cravat, and its early fashions. In this detail from a portrait of *James Stuart and his Sister* (1695), the little seven-year-old Prince of Wales (who was never to succeed to the throne, and who died in exile in Rome) wears the traditional court-dress cravat characteristic of royal courts throughout the second half of the seventeenth century: a large knot of batiste or muslin, with flaps of fine lace (top, right). But already for the past three years the Steinkirk had become all the rage in France: created on the morning of the battle of the same name, it was easier to knot, less cumbersome, and less liable to fly about in a breeze. The ends of its flaps were passed through a buttonhole in the jacket. This fashion is portrayed here in Largillière's portrait of a young boy of the d'Ormesson family (bottom, right).

were attracted by another advantage of the Croatian kerchiefs: unlike ruff collars, they didn't need to be bleached, ironed, and starched—procedures that were awkward in the field. They could be casually wound around one's neck, tied in large bows, and left to fall as they might. And practical considerations aside, weren't those decorated with fringes and lace just as elegant as the cumbersome collars? For these reasons many French officers adopted Croatian neckerchiefs. After returning home a few continued to wear them, even at court, and around 1650 they became fashionable, especially among the French aristocracy who were always on the lookout for ways to stress their association with things military. The new style was given a boost by the craze for large shoulder-length perukes, which obscured ruff collars and made them seem awkward. Charles II introduced the new style to England when he returned from exile and less than a decade later it was already widespread in the American colonies.

It may well be that another climatic factor also encouraged the adoption of such wear in Europe and America. The rise of cravats and neckerchiefs coincided with an anomaly dubbed the "Maunder minimum" by astrophysicists (after the name of the nineteenth-century astronomer who first studied the phenomenon): probably caused by a decline in solar activity, this phenomenon was marked by a decrease in temperatures over a considerable portion of the globe.

This 150-year "little ice age" was at its most intense between 1645 and 1705, precisely the years which saw the rise of the new neck fashion. It is not impossible that the unusually cold weather made this warmer neckwear seem even more attractive.

This short history has left many questions unanswered. What, for example, is the etymology of the words "necktie" and "cravat?" The first is self-explanatory: it derives from the words "neck" and "tie," for the knot which holds the article in place. But what of "cravat," from the French *cravate*, which designates both modern neckties and men's scarves and neck-bows: is it indeed of Croatian derivation? Modern dictionaries maintain that *cravate* derives from *croate*, the French word for "Croatian," and that it became current about the same time as the article itself—around 1650. Unfortunately, this explanation is too simple to be true. It was disproved about thirty years ago by a researcher who discovered that the word had been used in both France and Italy well before the Thirty Years' War: in France it was used as early as the fourteenth century to designate a strip of parchment and perhaps also a piece of clothing; and in Italy in 1590 the word *cravata*

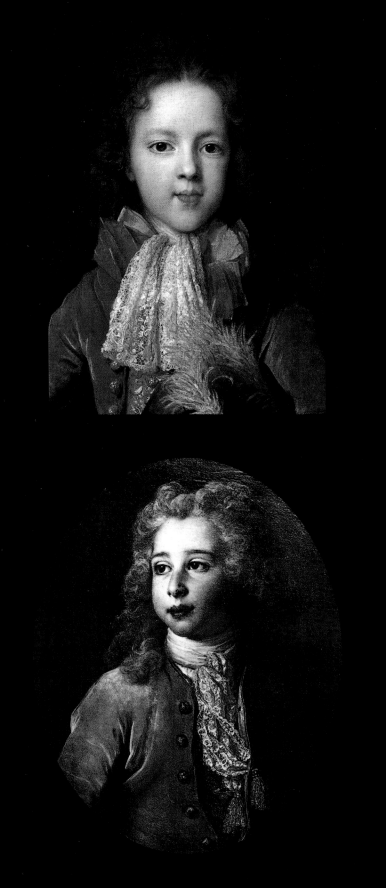

was used to designate the Roman *focale*.

Although the Croatians did not give their name to the mysteriously obscure word cravat, it cannot be denied that their use of this accessory lies at the historical root of modern male neckwear. While there are no known depictions of cravats dating before 1650, many survive from the years immediately following the mid-century point.

The earliest seventeenth-century cravats usually consisted of a thin strip of muslin or cambric, often with lace borders at either end, and in rare instances were made entirely of lace. They were wound twice around the neck and knotted at the front, with the two ends left hanging freely. This procedure is easy to describe but not so easy to execute: a certain dexterity was required to achieve a satisfactory result. And to further refine the effect, many, like Louis XIV, incorporated silk bands of different colors into their knots. Every morning the royal *cravatier* would present the king with a basket full of lace cravats decorated with crimson, sky blue, or orange ribbons. The king made his choice and began his knot, leaving the finishing touches to his attendant. Dress-conscious men who were maladroit, short on time, or without access to such expert assistance could obtain pre-knotted cravats that were attached at the back of the neck. These articles were an early version of ready-tied neckwear which, much to the distress of purists, is still in use today.

THE STEINKIRK AND THE STOCK

At the end of the seventeenth century another military event—the Battle of Steinkirk in 1692, during Louis XIV's campaign in the Low Countries—prompted further changes in male neckwear. In *The Century of Louis XIV*, Voltaire recounts this episode, which despite its anodyne appearance was to have unanticipated consequences: "Men then wore lace cravats and spent much time and effort arranging them. The princes, hurriedly dressing for combat, negligently wound these cravats around their necks; women began to wear ornaments modeled on them.

These cravats were called Steinkirks." The style remained fashionable in France for only some twenty years, while in England and America—where naval officers fancied them—it lasted almost a century. But Voltaire fails to mention the essential point concerning these new cravats: the ends of Steinkirks were twisted around one another and passed through a buttonhole in one's jacket, usually the sixth. Steinkirks appealed to feminine tastes, and many women had buttonholes sewn into their gowns to accommodate them. Others simply tucked the ends of the cravats into their corset laces.

In France, Louis XIV's death in 1715 coincided with the end of Steinkirks and the appearance of another kind of neckwear which was to remain current in various forms until 1850. Initially this was a simple rectangle of white muslin folded into a narrow band, wound two or three times around a raised shirt collar, and secured at the back with a pin. It was not long before fitted versions became available: high collar-like muslin neckbands equipped with easily fastened hooks and often reinforced with cardboard. These articles were called "stocks" or "neck stocks" in England. One notable characteristic of these white cravats was the absence of loose ends falling over the chest and hiding the opening of the shirt. This prompted the simultaneous development of the jabot, which was attached to the shirt front. Another feature was their considerable discomfort, for they held the neck rigidly upright and cut into the lower surface of the jaw. But a third characteristic made this discomfort worthwhile: this style imparted to its wearers a beautifully virile presence; it forced them to remain erect and keep their head and chin forthrightly forward. Black stocks eventually became a standard feature of European military uniforms—presumably because of their martial allure, for they were otherwise ill-suited to equestrian and combat wear.

Several refinements were eventually introduced into the stock which somewhat softened its martial air. Once long perukes had given way around 1740 to periwigs and back-tied natural

The Steinkirk—worn here (below) in about 1700 by the Grand Prior of France, Philippe de Vendôme—went out of fashion after the death of Louis XIV. While the king exiled the Grand Prior for his culpable inaction at the battle of Cassano d'Adda (1705), he recognized the gallantry of Duke Louis-François de Boufflers, Marshal of France, who played an important role in the victory at Steinkirk. His son, Joseph-Marie, peer of the realm, brigadier of the king, and colonel of the Bourbonnais regiment, was born too late (in 1700) to wear the Steinkirk. Here, in a portrait by Jean-Marc Nattier, we see him in armour, wearing a large black velvet bow on a band of white batiste (above).

One of the most refined neckwear accessories of the eighteenth century, the *solitaire*, probably invented in England but very fashionable at the court of Louis XV, owed its rise to the fashion for tying the hair back. Elegant, delicate and refined, it fitted perfectly with the libertine ways of the times. In *Dangerous Liasons*, adapted for film by Stephen Frears, John Malkovitch as Valmont wears one as an element of charm and an essential adjunct to his outfit. Here the *solitaire* is seen in a portrait by Jean-Baptiste Perronneau (1715–83), worn on a band of muslin by Jacques Cazotte, the author of *Diable amoureux* (right).

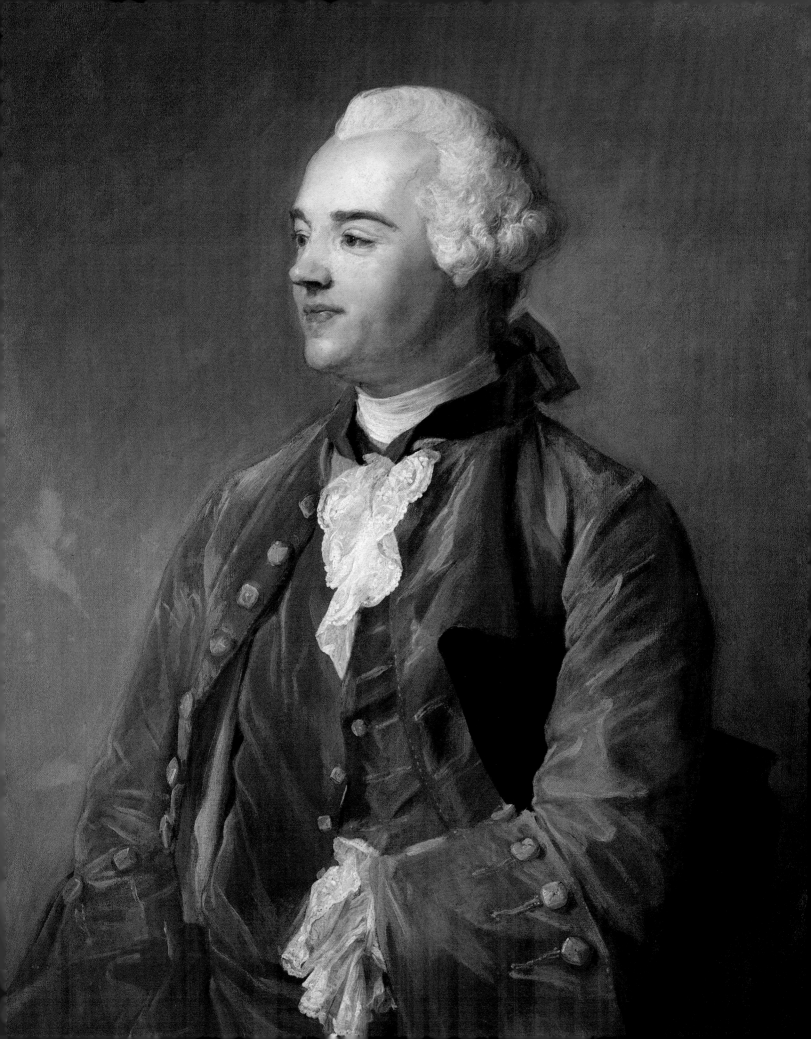

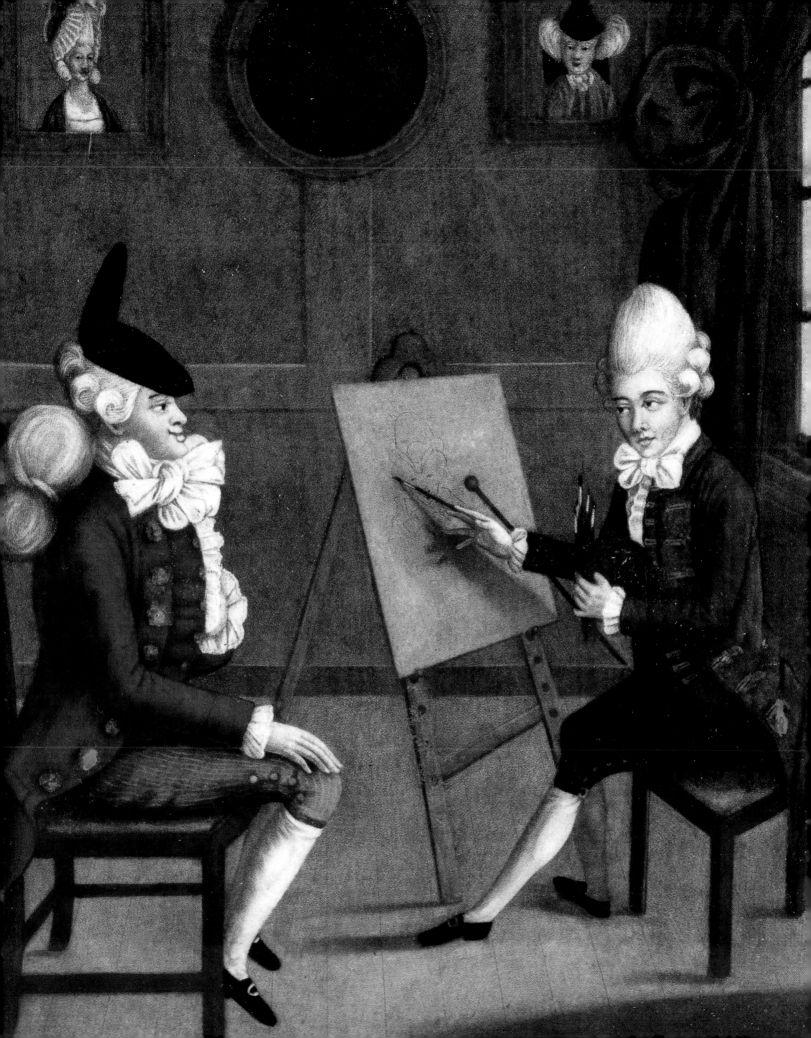

Although the revolutionary upheavals of the late eighteenth century led a number of harebrained individuals to ban the cravat, Robespierre, for his part, never left his house without an immaculately white one, prolonged by an artfully pleated jabot. Anonymous portrait (above).

In the early 1770s, young Londoners from well-to-do families made a fashion of eccentricity and excess. They were called "Macaronis"—this was also the period when Italian pasta first began to appear in London. The extravagance of Macaroni fashion extended to their cravats, which were often of silk, sporting a gigantic lace bow. *The Macaroni Painter*, mezzotint on glass, anonymous, *circa* 1800 (left).

hair, men began to bring the ends of the black silk ribbons, which secured their hair, around to the front, knotting them on top of their white cravats. These ribbons were known as *solitaires*, a name inspired by the lonely effect which was created by the black filigree against the surrounding mass of white muslin. Fashionable all over Europe, they were especially popular in England, where they were first devised, and in France, where they remained a standard item of elegant male dress throughout Louis XV's long reign. The stock, which would torture men's necks for more than a century, was refined around 1770 by the addition of a bow sewn onto the front. This offered a convenient alternative to the bows that some men continued to fashion from strips of muslin wound around their necks.

MACARONIS AND *INCROYABLES*

These simple muslin bands were, along with the stock, emblems of a sobriety traditionally associated with English male attire—as opposed to that of France, which was renowned for its ruffles and lace. The Anglomania that overtook France beginning in the 1760s—rooted in the growing acceptance of liberal political ideas advocated by the *philosophes*—made it easier for this fashion to take hold there. However, it was during these same years that the stock came under attack, sometimes quite viciously. The first to renounce it, beginning around 1770, were young English aristocrats who, in the wake of their Italian grand tours, decided to adopt the delicate extravagance of continental dress. Some of the latter, dubbed "Macaronis," created a sensation by appearing in London with rouged cheeks, enormous perukes, white silk breeches, striped stockings, pumps with diamond-studded buckles, and voluminous bows on white cravats. Such eccentric, effeminate dress remained a part of the London scene for some forty years.

The French Revolution further picked away at the sobriety of English cravats by encouraging many men to dispense with them entirely, for at the height of Revolutionary zeal they were viewed as symbols of a despised aristocracy, like breeches, silk stockings, and the jabot. The *sans-culottes* (literally, "without breeches") were in many cases also *sans-cravates*. Marat, for instance, wore his shirt collars conspicuously open. But this moment of extremism was short-lived. Although some *sans-culottes* revived the Steinkirk (now made of coarse material), many of the principal revolutionary leaders (Mirabeau, Robespierre, Danton etc.), born into wealthy bourgeois or aristocratic families, never gave up their impeccable white cravats. Shortly after Thermidor, which marked the end of the Terror, Parisians became infatuated with the "Garat," named after a celebrated singer of the day who was obsessed with cravats. He preferred them immense and high. Large, puffy knots like the ones he favored were known as *choux*. One evening, while giving a recital in a fashionable salon, Garat began to feel ill and fainted, falling backwards into a chair. The guests patted his hands and feet, opened the windows, and fanned him, but nothing seemed to help. Then it occured to one of his female admirers to try loosening his cravat. Garat finally opened his eyes and, gathering his strength, whispered to her: "Madame, take care not to muss my *chou*." In the meticulous preoccupation with his appearance, Garat might be described as a precursor of the sartorial madness which, under the Directory, seized some young Parisians anxious to savor life's more extravagant and luxurious pleasures in the wake of the dark days of the Terror. These bizarre male figures were dubbed *incroyables* because of their conspicuously eccentric and improbable attire featuring immense lapels, exaggerated profiles (tiny waists and broad shoulders), long hair combed to either side like "dog-ears," and above all enormous cravats encasing the entire length of their necks—shawl-like accessories in shrill colors and sometimes even striped.

The *incroyables* had much in common with the English macaronis. Both groups were composed of the idle scions of wealthy families determined to convey through bizarre dress a sovereign contempt for the bourgeois and aristocratic conventions of their fathers. In their imaginative transgression of the prevailing aesthetic norms of self-presentation, they illustrate a recurrent phenomenon in male fashion: a younger generation's radical, provocative rejection of "good taste" in dress. In a sense, the macaronis and *incroyables* were ancestors of the zoot suiters, hippies, and punks of more recent vintage.

THE GOLDEN AGE

As definitively exemplified by George Bryan Brummell, and especially at its beginnings in the first half of the nineteenth century, dandyism represented the exact opposite of *incroyable* extravagance. An exaggerated preoccupation

In France, the extravagance of the London Macaronis was soon matched by the *Incroyables*. In his *Tableau de Paris*, Louis-Sébastien Mercier carped at these eccentric young men whose "heads rest on their cravats as if on pillows." Their necks and chins more or less disappeared from sight, in a huge shapeless cravat, wrapped round their necks several times, and sometimes made even more voluminous by the addition of a small cushion—a fertile subject for caricaturists. Drawing from *Modes Parisiennes, Incroyables et Merveilleuses*, after an engraving by Horace Vernet, 1795 (below).

"My first thought is for my cravat / It is our test of good taste / I work for hours in hopes that / It will appear to be knotted in haste." This anonymous ditty, contemporary with George Bryan Brummell (1778–1840) expresses the importance that cravats had for the dandies. Brummell himself put considerable effort into the knotting of his batiste or white muslin cravat, in order that the knot might appear casually done. King George IV, his protector, often went to "Beau" Brummell's house in order to be present for this magic moment, which was the end point of a dressing routine that might take several hours. Brummell's life—his glory and his fall—were sufficiently peppered with spicy anecdotes to give rise to several films and plays. Stewart Granger in *Beau Brummell*, filmed by Curtis Bernhardt in 1954 (above, right). The actor Richard Mansfield playing Brummell in a London theater in 1906 (below, right).

with personal appearance was crucial to both approaches; but Brummell, who took as long as six hours to get dressed, set out precisely to render himself inconspicuous. To achieve perfect transparency through the exercise of good taste in dress: such was the goal of this favorite of the Prince of Wales (the future George IV), who from his youth was the uncontested sovereign of English, and then of European fashion.

Subtle and delicately varied colors, immaculate linen, and meticulous attention to detail: such were "Beau" Brummell's principles, which can be seen as guidelines for dressing richly but without ostentation. Despite such rules, however, his achievement remained mysterious and inaccessible to most mortals, for there was something indefinable about his allure. The cravat was a key component of his ensembles, and its preparation occasioned an implacable ritual, described as follows by William Jesse, Brummell's first biographer: "The collar, which was always fixed to his shirt, was so large that, before being folded down, it completely hid his head and face, and the white neckcloth was at least a foot in height. The first *coup d'archet* was made with the shirt collar, which he folded down to its proper size; and Brummell, then standing before the glass, with his chin poked up to the ceiling,

by the gentle and gradual detention of his lower jaw creased the cravat to reasonable dimensions, the form of each successive crease being perfected with the shirt which he had just discarded." The dandy was intractable, pursuing a perfection whose secret was known only to him. One fine morning a visitor encountered Robinson, Brummell's faithful valet, in the stairwell of his house in Chesterfield Street, carrying a great quantity of rumpled cravats under his arm. Asked about them, the valet responded: "Sir, these are our failures." Brummell wore only immaculate white cravats of muslin or cambric, made to retain the desired shape by the discreet use of starch—a technique he himself devised. As is well known, he ended badly: ruined by gambling and exiled to France, he fell into complete destitution. As a crowning insult he was obliged to wear black cravats; he could no longer afford to have white ones laundered.

When Brummell died in 1840, a heated controversy was raging that pitted partisans of white cravats, affiliated with traditionalism, against those of black cravats, associated with liberal politics. With rather heavy-handed irony, the newspaper *L'Illustration* described this new battle between the ancients and the moderns as follows: "One of the great affairs of the moment is the combat between black cravats and white cravats. It has all the features of a proper duel. Can one now wear a black silk cravat in society? Established custom squarely precludes it, but the new fashion gives us leave to do so. . . . What is most surprising about this conflict is that the young have adopted the black cravat while the old defend the white. Where will all this lead us? What position will the government take? Our sources tell us the ambassadors of the great powers are divided on the question. And we have heard reports about remarks made by a woman deeply opposed to the innovation, who even issued the following threat: 'If the men should be so indecent as to hoist the black cravat, we will cease to appear in public with our bosoms exposed.'" This terrifying prospect did not prevent the spread of the black cravat, which effectively triumphed from about 1850. Traditionalists were not happy about this development, but recent events

Count Alfred D'Orsay (1801–52), an art lover, a painter, and sculptor, was one of the great dandies of the nineteenth century. By the age of twenty he had become the lover of the beautiful Lady Blessington, and the protégé of her rich and aged husband. He then became the latter's son-in-law. The very elegant D'Orsay, an irresistible charmer, seduced all London. Moving to England in the company of his mistress, he became a friend of Dickens, Thomas Moore and Thackeray. In this portrait by George Hayter dated 1839, he can be seen as a pioneer of the black cravat. This had just recently made its appearance and was soon to take over from the white cravat (right).

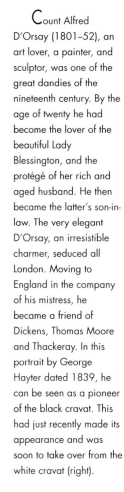

THE THEATRE
ILLUSTRATED MAGAZINE
OF DRAMATIC AND MUSICAL ART.

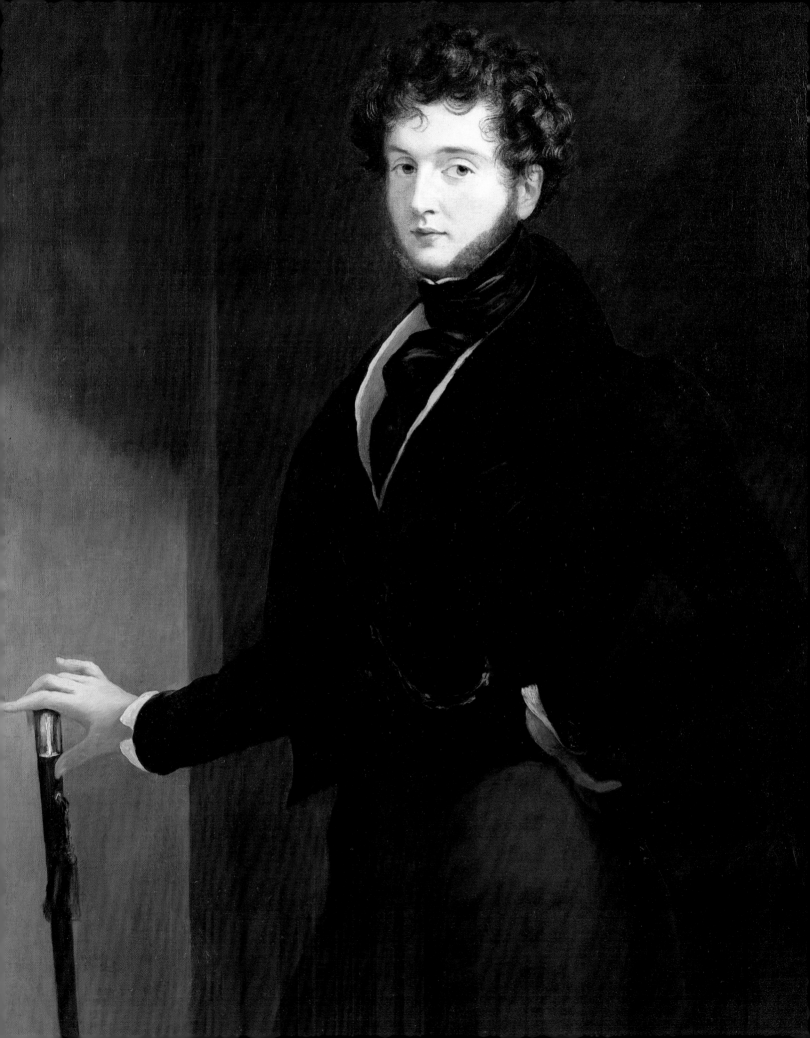

had made them more accepting of it: at least black cravats were preferable to the red ones, horrific in their eyes, which had enjoyed a brief vogue among French and German revolutionaries in 1848.

This episode should not be allowed to obscure the great diversity of forms invented during the first half of the nineteenth century, a true golden age of the cravat. One reflection of this phenomenon is the extraordinary success enjoyed by books on male neckwear which in the 1820s were intended to instruct and edify aspiring men of taste. In 1827 there appeared in Paris a small volume entitled *L'Art de mettre sa cravate de toutes les manières connues et usitées, enseigné et démontré en seize leçons*. This treatise—whose instructions for

knotting fourteen different cravats and eighteen variants were complemented by wryly humorous moral and psychological observations—was attributed on the title page to one "*baron Émile de l'Empesé*," an obvious pseudonym (in French *empeser* means "to starch"). At its head was the following quip: "The art of tying the cravat is to men of the world what the art of dining is to politicians." The work was immensely successful and was published in eleven editions. As it was issued by Honoré de Balzac's printer, there were suspicions that the novelist was its true author, and a telling detail lent support to this theory: the text is followed by a list of the finest Parisian manufacturers and sellers of cravats, and such favorable publicity

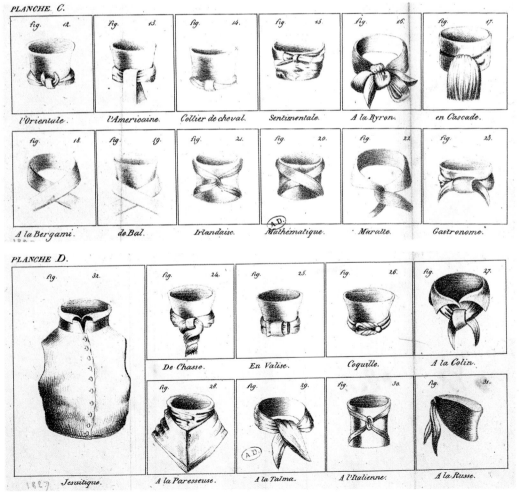

PLANCHE C.

fig. 12. l'Orientale. — fig. 13. l'Américaine. — fig. 14. Collier de cheval. — fig. 15. Sentimentale. — fig. 16. A la Byron. — fig. 17. en Cascade.

fig. 18. A la Bergami. — fig. 19. de Bal. — fig. 21. Irlandaise. — fig. 20. Mathématique. — fig. 22. Maralle. — fig. 23. Gastronome.

PLANCHE D.

fig. 32. Jésuitique. — fig. 24. De Chasse. — fig. 25. En Valise. — fig. 26. Coquille. — fig. 27. A la Colin.

fig. 28. A la Paresseuse. — fig. 29. A la Talma. — fig. 30. A l'Italienne. — fig. 31. A la Russe.

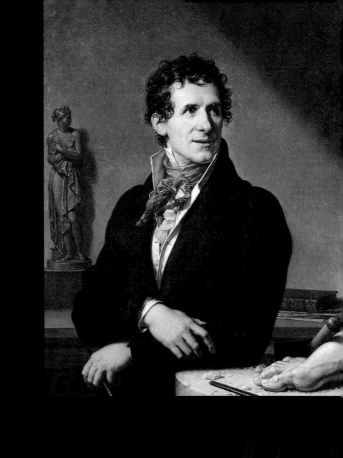

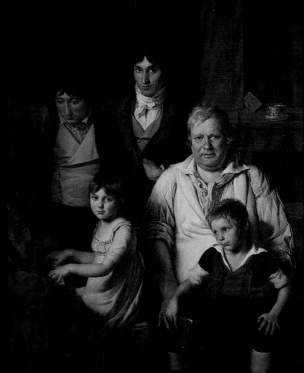

Lord Byron (1788–1824) will forever embody the figure of the Romantic poet and hero. He rarely wore a cravat, and the one that he preferred was more like a long scarf knotted fairly loosely about a soft collar, which fitted his temperament perfectly. When he died, treatises on cravats conjured up a necktie *à la Byron*. The only relationship between this large bow and the poet's scarf was in its looseness and in its romantic appearance. Lord Byron at the age of nineteen, an engraving by Blanchard after a portrait by George Saunders (above). Byron's style of scarf, which one can see as the direct ancestor of our modern tie, was not rare in Britain during that period. We also find it around the neck of the painter William Hilton (1786–1839), in a portrait by John Clare dating from 1820 (below).

might well have served to settle outstanding debts to these same establishments. In fact the treatise was written by Émile-Marc de Saint-Hilaire, a friend of Balzac's, but the great novelist was indeed responsible for the preface. It was eventually discovered that Saint Hilaire's text had been based in part on a similar work which appeared in 1823, *Cravatiana ou Traité général des cravates* a free adaptation of a volume published anonymously in London in 1818, *Neckclothitania or Tietania*. Of English origin, *L'Art de mettre sa cravate* was itself translated in 1828 with some changes into Italian (in which version its author was said to be one "conte della Salda," or "Count Starch") and into English as *The Art of Tying the Cravat* by "H. Le Blanc." The circle was closed, making this work one of the first international best-sellers.

"The cravat of a man of genius is quite different from that of a man of mediocrity," wrote Balzac in his preface. "If, as Buffon said, 'style makes the man,' we might say in turn that *the cravat is the man.*" Every man should come to know which cravat was best-suited to his temperament, and learn to knot it in accordance with the rules of the art. Such was the goal of this work, which after a few historical observations and some indispensable tips about laundering, starching, knotting, and ironing, arrived at its principal subject matter: descriptions of the various knots. There was a knot to suit everyone's needs: "For precise minds, the *cravate mathématique*; the *cravate Byron* can only be worn by a very few of our poets. Do you aspire to make a career as a wooer? Then adopt the *cravate à la Bergami* (taking care to wear the matching side-whiskers and stockings)." Some cravats described in these pages are what would later be called bow ties (the cravat *en valise*, the Byron, the *sentimentale*),

while others were plastrons (the Gordian knot, the hunting cravat), and others still were more like neckerchiefs or scarves (*à la Talma, à la Colin, en cascade*).

The Art of Tying the Cravat and its various translations occasioned some humorous exchanges which convey the subject's importance to contemporaries. In the *Physiologie de la toilette*, generally attributed to Balzac, the cravat was "considered in itself and in relation to society and the individual." The author poked fun at the baron de l'Empesé: "And his book! It can only occasion uncontrollable laughter. With its divisions, categories, classifications, and prohibitions it amounts to an Aristotelian lawbook, a veritable code *à la Boileau.* . . . Thus will genius be clapped in irons, routine coddled, and public taste perverted, unless a few strong spirits can be found to defy these ridiculous constraints and march resolutely forward, safeguarding the cravat's natural freedom and *élan.*" Targeting with a delicious wit the rigidity of the social and artistic rules prevalent in his day, the author defended a romantic approach to the cravat, maintaining that one should ignore all attempts to set limits to the imagination and allow instinct, inspiration, and spontaneity free rein in the matter of neckwear. But this was a romanticism that allowed for praise of a "well-tied" cravat, which, the author asserts, "suffuses the entire toilette like a perfume: it is to the toilette as truffles are to a meal."

This age of unparalleled variety and fantasy in the domain of cravats—which also left such charming literary traces—continued for almost half a century. But by 1865, E. Kerckhoff could say of the cravat in his *Le Costume à la cour et à la ville:* "It is easy to convince oneself that the fashion has reached its peak, and that reaction is beginning to set in." A reaction facilitated by changing mores and the rise

For a nineteenth-century artist, when it came to dress the crucial thing was to free oneself from the constraints of the bourgeoisie. Cravats lost their stocks, often became enlarged into *lavalières*, and sometimes even disappeared. The poet and theatre writer Édouard Pailleron, whose Bohemian appearance did not stand in the way of his becoming an Academician, illustrated this tendency in a particularly original way. In this portrait by the American artist John Singer Sargent, dated 1879, he wears a string tie with tassels, casually knotted over a red scarf, at once refined and unconventional (right).

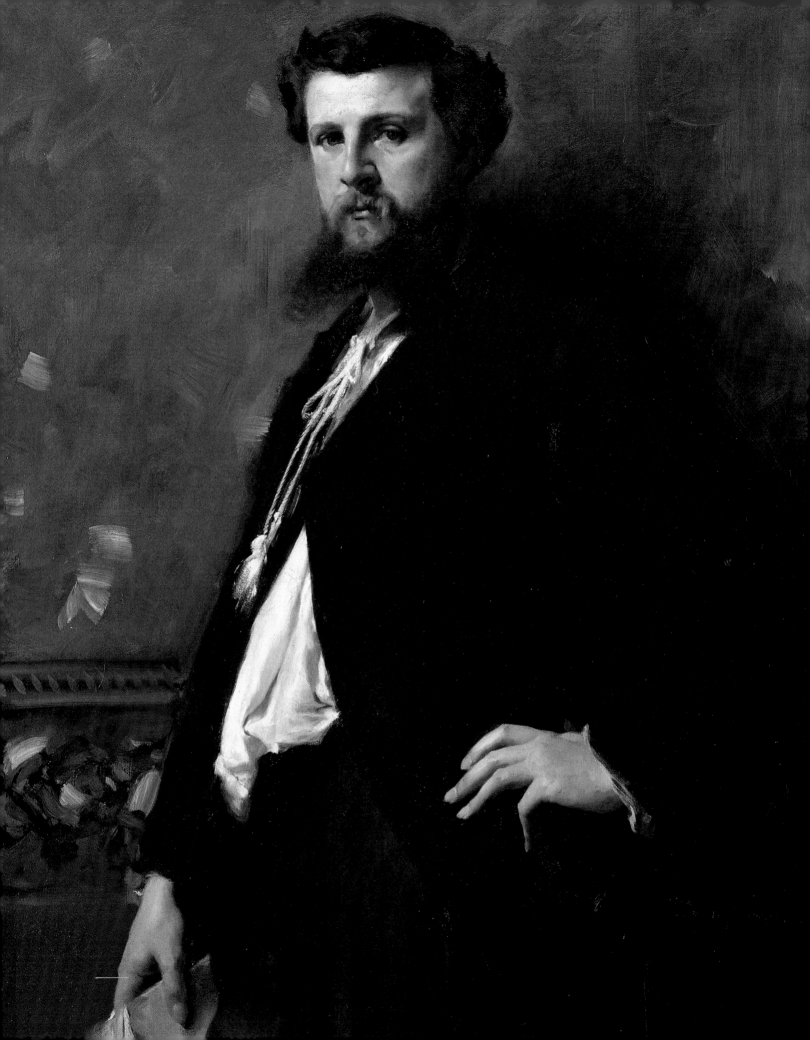

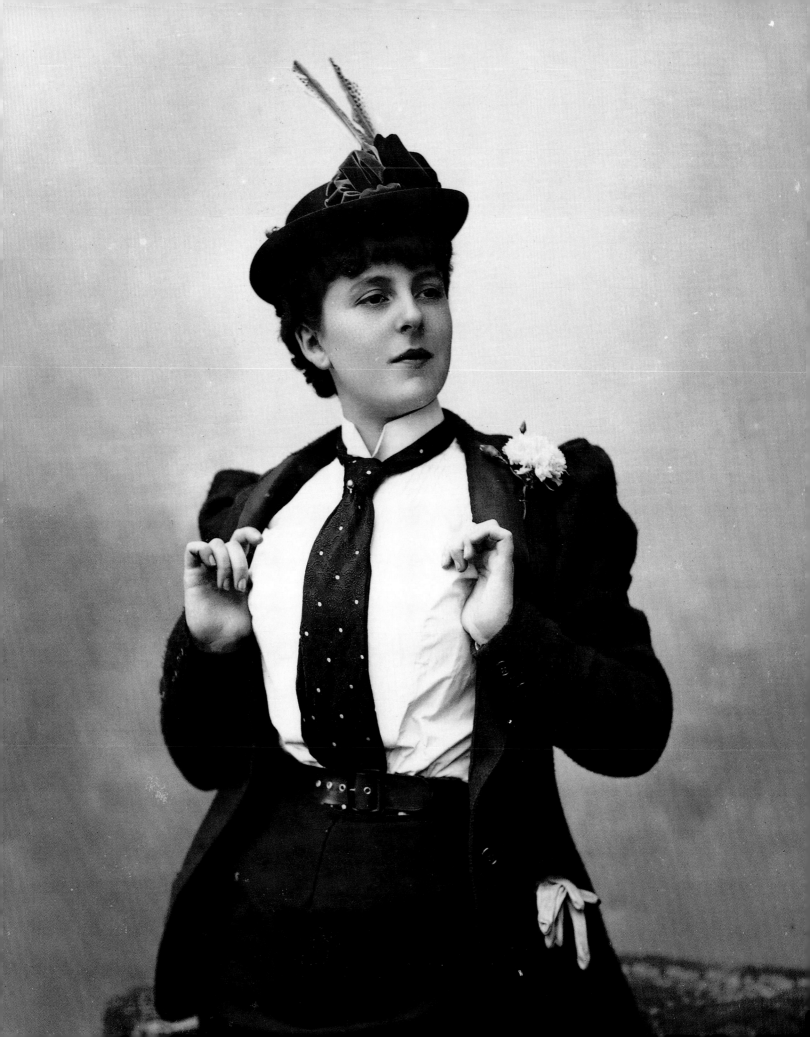

For women, wearing a man's tie has long been indicative of a desire to free themselves from the conventional roles assigned by society. There is more than a hint of provocation in the way that the actress Émilienne d'Alençon, a great courtesan and one of the queens of the demimonde in Belle-Époque Paris, sports this polka-dot four-in-hand. Photograph by Nadar, *circa* 1891–2 (left).

The American feminist Amelia Jenks Bloomer (1818–94) was politically active in the cause of freeing women from their corsets and crinolines. The functional style of dress which she imagined for them included a tie (above).

of a new social class obliged to wear cravats: that of the office worker. A reaction that would result in the birth of the modern necktie.

WOMEN IN CRAVATS

The constant presence of women in the masculine universe of the cravat is perfectly illustrated by the *lavalière*. Usually black, loosely wound around a soft collar, and tied in a large floppy bow, this cravat became the style of neckwear preferred by nineteenth-century liberals and bohemians. Its softness and great volume—considered as feminine qualities—were in marked contrast with the bourgeois, military stiffness of the stock. Doubtless this is why it was named after a woman who two centuries earlier had worn similar though brightly colored cravats with much grace: the duchesse de La Vallière. A favorite of Louis XIV, she was in fact imitating her sovereign's penchant for artfully knotting a strip of precious material around his neck. Nonetheless, she was one of the first women in history to adopt "male" neckwear. Like her contemporaries she was drawn to the style by its vivid colors and delicate laces, while also savoring the gracious, feminine air it imparted to its wearers.

For a long time women wore cravats only to please—out of pure coquetry. In the nineteenth century, when feminist ideas began to be voiced and the cause of equal rights for women gained credibility, men's ties began to be worn as an emblem of feminine emancipation. George Sand and Flora Tristan, who wore male clothing and, of course, ties, were among the first to fly in the face of convention. Early feminist movements were particularly outspoken about the need to liberate women from the burden of their elaborate dress—with its corsets and crinolines—advocating instead a wardrobe more conducive to an active, free, and even athletic style of life. In the 1850s the American feminist Amelia Jenks Bloomer was the inspiration for a so-called functional feminine outfit whose most

curious feature was not a necktie, but rather its broad pants tied at the ankles and worn underneath a skirt with its hemline extending just below the knee. These "bloomers" were indeed revolutionary, and they occasioned much hilarity in fashionable salons. Their only real problem was that they arrived on the scene too soon. Less than a century later, short skirts and pants had become perfectly acceptable articles of feminine dress. In the meantime, suffragettes had mounted a concerted campaign advocating voting rights, equal employment opportunities, and the advantages of sports for women. The First World War aided their cause, demonstrating that women were perfectly capable of replacing men in all economic sectors and social strata.

These changes in the status of women were at the origin of an unmistakeable tendency in the years just after the war and the "roaring twenties" to masculinize feminine dress. In its most extreme manifestations, there was little or nothing to differentiate the appearance of *garçonnes*—the feminine variant, coined in these same years, of the French word *garçons* ("young men")—from that of their male counterparts: women too wore short hair, jackets, pants, shirts,

"If this portrait of George Sand / Leaves your mind a touch perplexed, / That's because genius is abstract / And, of course, it has no sex."
This rhyming caption was appended to the caricature of George Sand, dated 1848 (above). The writer wore a tie in the same way that she smoked a pipe, in order to break with a certain image of femininity.
Half a century later, Colette, the celebrated French novelist, also made a strong personality statement by wearing a tie. The author of *Gigi* poses here for a 1909 advertisement for Waterman pens (below).

In this fashion engraving from the 1870s, the "elegant young man" makes a brash statement by wearing bright colors on both shirt and tie. Such things were not yet considered to be in good taste (right).

and ties. But only a few city-dwellers indulged in this form of gender scrambling. They were attracted by the aura of scandal surrounding a group of fascinating and emancipated women who made no secret of their unconventional ways—among them Rachilde, Nathalie Barney, Colette, and Radclyffe Hall.

The significance of women adopting male neckwear changed radically over the years: initially a playful appropriation of lace cravats or colorful ties intended to seduce the opposite sex, it gradually evolved into a means of affirming women's entitlement to equal rights by imitating men, and it finally became a way of broadcasting their indifference to men by effectively excluding them. This evolution parallels that of the tie itself, which, becoming more sober and subdued, came increasingly to seem like an exclusively male accessory. Thus in the course of the nineteenth century, and even as recently as the 1960s, when traditional gender distinctions became blurred, a woman wore a cravat or a tie to communicate her independence and signal her feminist convictions.

MODERN TIMES: THE FOUR-IN-HAND TIE

Although we do not know precisely where, when, or by whom the modern necktie was invented, the reasons for its advent are self-evident. In the middle of the nineteenth century, at the height of the industrial revolution, more and more men obliged to wear cravats found that, unlike dandies and followers of the baron de l'Empesé, they could not afford to spend considerable amounts of time knotting them every morning. Members of the new work force required neckwear which was easy to put on, comfortable, and sturdy enough to survive an exhausting work day. The need for a practical tie—one that neither impeded movement nor came undone—was also felt by men in the leisure class who were beginning to lead more active lives, often hunting, playing tennis, golfing or participating in other sports.

These circumstances prompted two changes in male attire: a tendency to wear jackets and vests with larger openings in the front; and the arrival of soft, turned-down collars. The first of

This portrait of Johannes Brahms by the Austrian artist Wilhelm August Rieder (1796–1880), dating from *circa* 1860, is suggestive of an epoch in which everything seemed possible: this complex and asymmetrical knot is perfectly executed, despite appearances to the contrary. The spread of ready-tied knots would soon make inroads on men's aspirations to originality or improvisation (right).

The appearance of the four-in-hand in the 1860s marked a revolution in the history of neckties: it gradually came to replace the cravat that resembled a bow tie. This advertisement for the Maison du Phénix dates from 1863. It shows the three neckties which, for a few decades to come, would feature almost equally in men's wardrobes around the world: the bow tie (although it was not yet called this), the ascot, and the four-in-hand. Note the dots, stripes and other small geometrical patterns, classic motifs that are still in common use today (right).

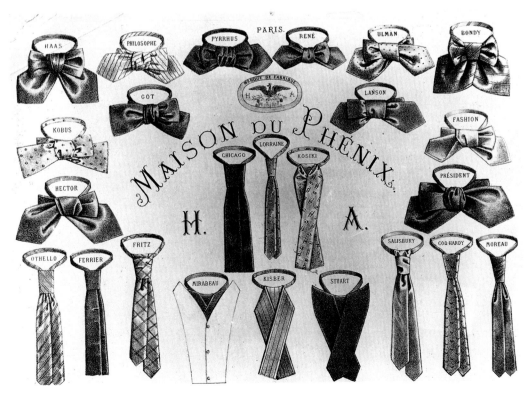

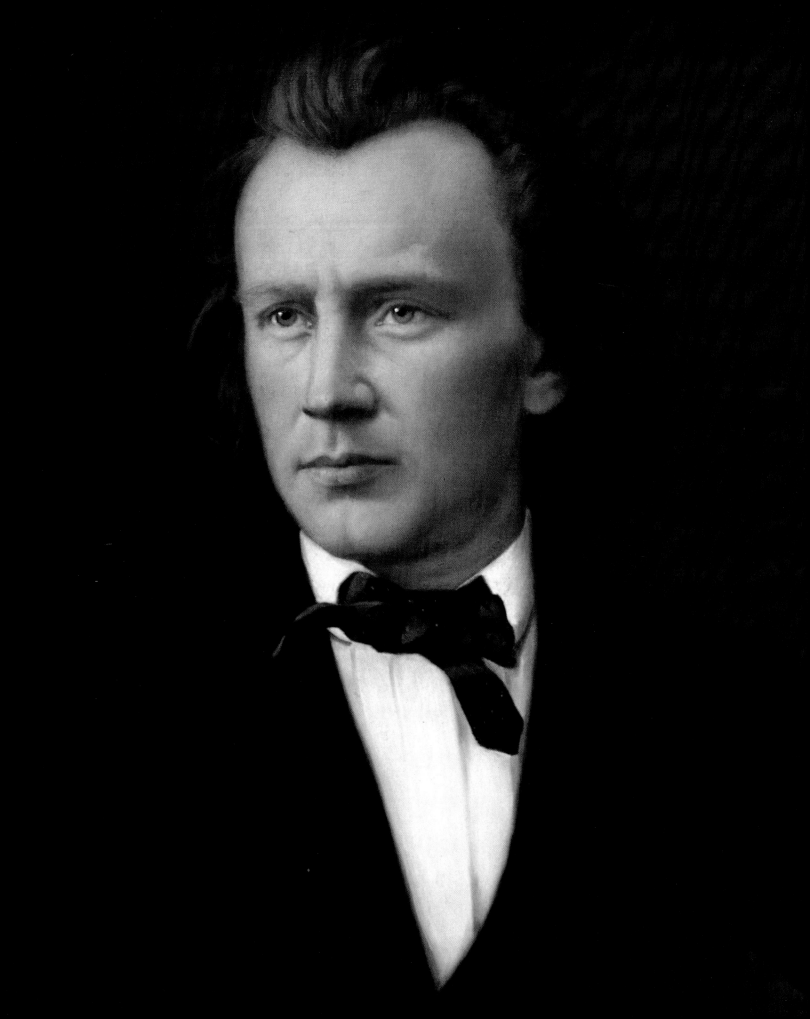

At the end of the eighteenth century, the famous American boxer James Belcher initiated the fashion for the bandanna in the United States. Until that point bandannas had been restricted to the working class. This highly colorful neckerchief could be worn in many ways. It had what resembled a four-in-hand knot, wrapped round the neck only once, and its ends were left to fall free—all characteristics of the modern necktie. Anonymous portrait (right).

these changes entailed the development of a longer accessory to fill the new shirt front void; the second led to the production of narrower and suppler neckwear than the conventional cravat, one which required only a single circuit of the neck. The modern necktie, which is still worn today, was born. It was long and thin, stable and easy to knot. The English baptized it the "four-in-hand" because its knot with two long, trailing ends resembled the reins of the four-horse carriages cherished by the English aristocracy. The design was not entirely novel. It owed much to the bandanna, a small brightly colored kerchief originally made of silk, imported from India from the early eighteenth century on, and worn around the neck. Imitated in cotton and linen by English manufacturers, bandannas were quickly taken up by members of the European working classes and enjoyed a considerable vogue in America where they were launched by the famous boxer James Belcher. Four-in-hands, sometimes called sailor-

knot ties, also owed much to the simply knotted scarfs worn in the early nineteenth century by the Romantics, as seen in many portraits of Lord Byron.

The fashion for detachable stiff collars in the late nineteenth century slowed the spread of four-in-hand ties but did not prevent it. By this time the multiplicity of knots and styles available in the century's early decades was but a dim memory, all but obliterated by the comfortable sobriety of the four-in-hand and bow ties, the latter a smaller, more convenient version of the earlier cravat with its loosely tied bow. Initially these were almost always either white or black (for afternoon and evening wear respectively). Only at the most fashionable evening parties and the race course was yet another type of neckwear considered *de rigueur*. This was the ascot, whose wide flaps were crossed and pinned together to from a plastron on the chest.

The stiff collar's demise, aided by a crusade against its supposed negative effects on the health—migraine headaches, nasal congestion, and deafness among them—was sparked in the 1920s by the triumph of the four-in-hand tie and the parallel victory of the soft collar. But despite its undeniable comfort and convenience, the four-in-hand tie was far from perfect. Nothing more than a strip of silk or cotton fabric, it remained in place only when securely knotted. And this tight knot inevitably wrinkled and damaged the delicate material of the tie beyond repair.

The *lavalière* was the preferred neckwear of intellectuals and artists at the end of the nineteenth and the start of the twentieth century. It was comfortable and easy to tie, but it required a silk that was sufficiently stiff so that the bow would keep its shape. The one depicted here was woven at the turn of the century in Como, a major Italian silk-weaving center (right).

Another cravat woven in Como *circa* 1900, this ready-tied ascot could be worn under a vest in town on elegant occasions. Here we see the highly refined weave—stripes on

a paisley background—which was already being achieved in top-of-the-line ties. Since the First World War, the ascot has tended to be worn only at hunting or hippic events, or occasionally at marriages (above).

The yachting knot tie marked the penultimate stage in the evolution of neckwear: it lies directly at the origins of our modern four-in-hand necktie. Sportive and easy to knot, it was ideally suited for soft, turned down collars. It consisted of a simple band of woven material (usually silk), sometimes folded over onto itself and sewn. It continued to be worn up until the 1920s. Photograph by Jean-Henri Lartigue, dated 30 November 1914: the Brazilian aviator Santos-Dumont is being taken for a boat ride at Arcachon, France by the photographer's elder brother Maurice, aka "Zissou" (right).

It took the ingenuity of a New York tie maker, Jesse Langsdorf, to solve this problem. He came up with the idea of cutting the fabric on the bias and sewing it in three segments, a technique which improves elasticity and facilitates a fabric's return to something very like its initial state after each use. Langsdorf patented his design in 1924 and made his fortune a few years later by franchising it to several other manufacturers. Since then most men have worn "Langsdorf" ties and the accessory's formal evolution has been at a standstill.

True, the tie assumed a narrower, more rectangular shape in the 1950s and then a broader one in the 1960s, but these were mere passing fancies. The basic format has remained unchanged: a long piece of fabric tied

with a simple knot, making for neckwear that is practical, comfortable, and durable. On the other hand, this neckwear is often sober, not to say austere, as its style precludes the poetry of elaborate knots, the grace and plastic interest of puffs, and above all the rich possibilities for self-expression previously afforded by the cravat. By way of compensation, a theater of invention emerged in the realm of fabrics and ornamental motifs, a development pioneered by a few Parisian designers with the cooperation of Lyons silk manufacturers. Since the 1930s the history of ties has become that of their materials, color schemes, and decorative patterns. Enormously varied, the fabrics and designs of the twentieth-century tie merit a separate chapter of their own.

In the early 1900s detachable stiff collars and four-in-hands were often seen together. Two spectators at the Harvard Stadium, featured in an advertisement in a 1914 issue of the American magazine *The Printing Art* (left).

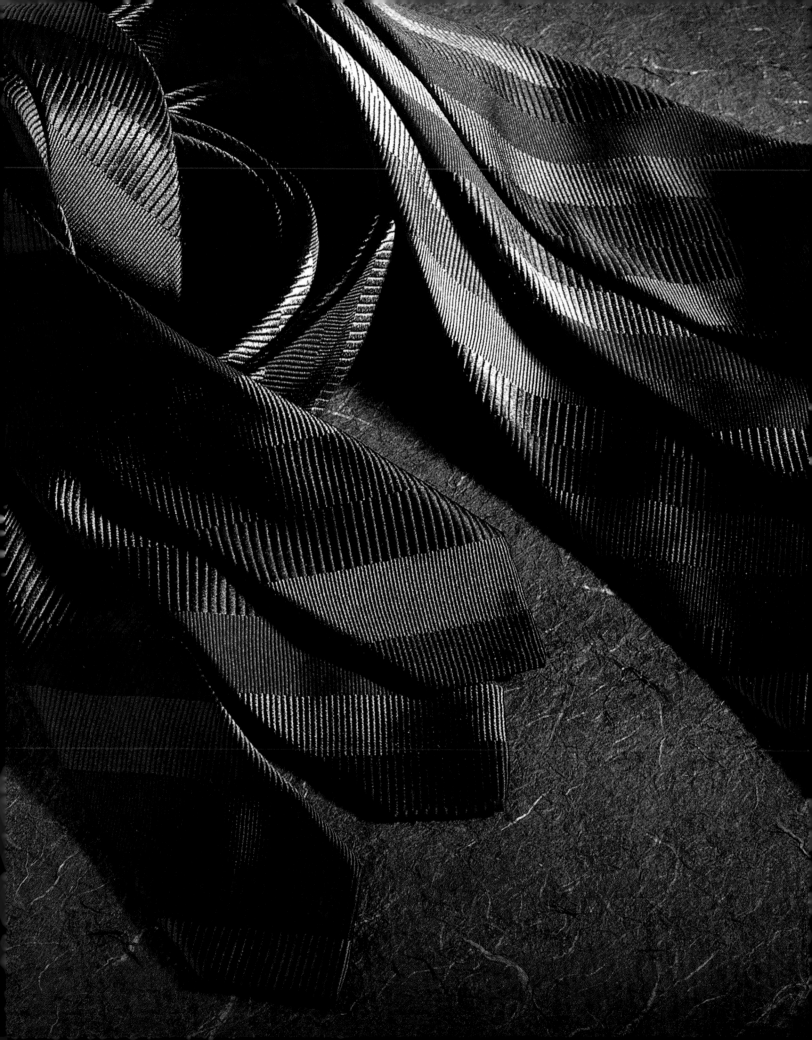

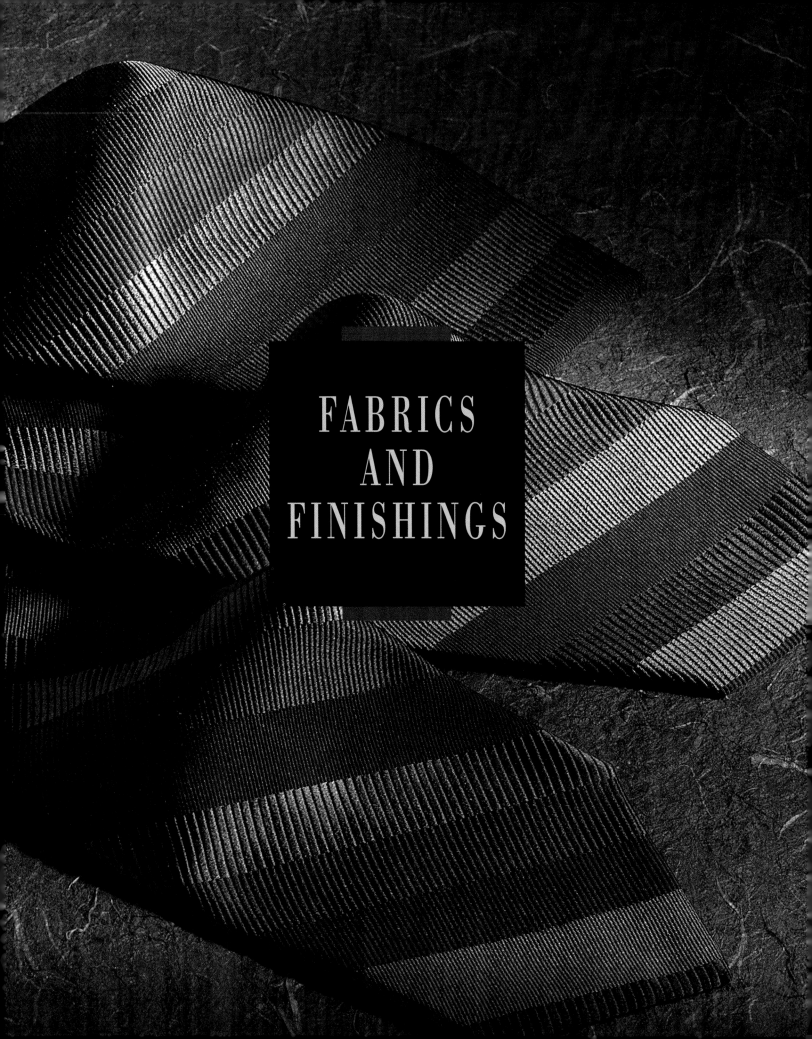

FABRICS
AND
FINISHINGS

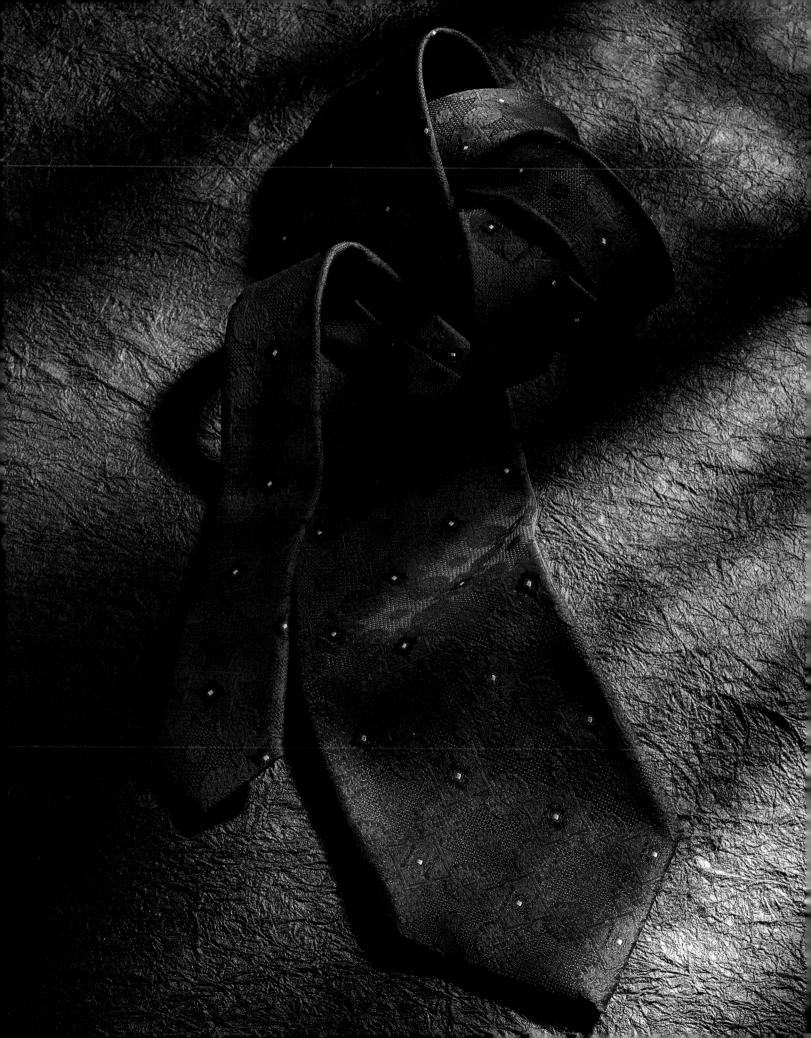

The finest traditions of the Italian silk-weavers of Como are revealed in the exquisite geometric weave of this Sulka tie (left).

A truly evocative expression for the most tangible of pleasures associated with the necktie is the "hand," a term used to designate the feel of a tie—its fabric, fall, weight, and texture. In addition to various shapes, colors, and design motifs, the materials that go into making ties are either thick or thin, polished or rough, more or less able to retain their shape. . . . All of these factors influence the sensation ties produce when stroked. Connoisseurs appreciate a beautiful hand. It is a function of ties to be agreeable to the touch. Ideally, the tactile qualities of a tie should produce a sensation not unlike that of living skin. Only through the work of many skilled, dedicated craftsmen and technicians can one hope to experience this unique and subtle satisfaction.

A THOUSAND AND ONE SILKS

Silk is undeniably the fabric of preference where ties are concerned. Smoothness, softness, brilliance, tensility (a silk thread is almost as strong as a steel one of equal diameter), and resilience (a three-foot thread stretched to three and half feet will subsequently revert to its original length)—as well as the ease with which it can be dyed—are its principal qualities. In addition, the variety of different silks is considerable: from solid-color silk sateens to multi-hued silk fabrics combining different weaves (juxtaposing different configurations of weft and warp in a single piece of fabric)—nothing that the eye or hand might desire should ever be considered as impossible.

The tie needs to be as pleasing to the hand as it is to the eye. Thus its production involves the talents of designers, as well as weavers and printers. Charvet ties woven in three different reps (preceding double page).

Two great necktie families divide the kingdom of a thousand and one silks: Jacquard, or yarn-dyed, ties and piece-dyed ties. In the first case, designs are woven directly into the fabric with differently colored threads on Jacquard looms. In the second case, colored patterns are printed directly onto the raw, dyed, or figured silk.

Woven silk. Because it allows for highly detailed motifs and enjoys an incomparable richness of texture and luster, woven silk is regarded as the *nec plus ultra* of necktie fabrics.

Often sumptuous in appearance, woven silk ties are considered the "dressiest" and perhaps the most elegant of neckwear. *Le Chic Anglais*, a guide to dressing like a British gentleman, which was written for a French audience by the British journalist James Darwen, states in no uncertain terms that "a gentleman's ties be made of woven silk." More costly to produce than ties made of piece-dyed silk, they represent only about 5% of the total production of silk ties. But woven silk ties are returning to favor as a result of the growing taste for glossy, though not flashy, ties. This process alone can temper a color's innate brilliance by incorporating it into a complex surface texture. One must visit the Charvet shop in Paris—the reigning specialist in the field—to fully grasp the talent, imagination, attention to detail, and above all the passion reflected in beautifully woven silk. The silver reflections of a blue tie will turn pink at the slightest movement, while paisley patterns metamorphose as the light changes. Fine weavers of necktie silk—most of them now either Italian, Swiss, English, or German—are true magicians.

Once a tie's texture and design have been determined, things are turned over to a weaver or a professional specialist who begins work on the pattern drafting process devised by Lyons silkmakers. This begins by depicting on graph paper the precise warp and weft configuration needed to produce the requisite texture and design. It is a slow process demanding meticulous care—its difficulty being proportionate to the design's complexity. Until recently these drafts were drawn exclusively by hand; now computers often do the job. At the beautiful modern site of the Campi weaving mill in Como, for example, in 1993 half of these drafts were drawn by computer—whereas four years earlier they had all been done by hand. The new technology results in a more competitive industry but places limits on variety: for the time being, certain, more refined effects elude the reach of artificial intelligence.

The pattern draft is then used to produce a perforated

The silk used in high-quality ties requires particularly careful attention: throughout the process of production, silk processors, weavers and printers maintain the closest quality controls. The control label of a bale of Chinese silk, which will be processed in Como (above).

The motif is broken down into warp and weft on a sheet of graph paper, which enables the weaving loom to be set up. Nowadays this work is increasingly carried out by computer. These pattern drafts, accompanied by their corresponding fabric samples, date from between 1925 and 1940. They are preserved by the Ratti company in Como. The most recent—the large leaf motif—was handmade, when he was an apprentice, by Antonio Ratti himself (left).

The Jacquard loom was invented in the nineteenth century by Joseph-Marie Jacquard. It enabled fabrics to be woven with highly complex designs and large motifs. The woven silk used for modern ties still comes from looms of this type, although they have been modernized and often operate in conjunction with computers. Jacquard loom dating from 1898, from a private collection in Jonzieux, France (right).

card. This is done by hand—with the help of a puncher—or, more recently, by computer, which is linked to a scanner and mechanical punching device. The punched card is then placed on the loom. In the case of electronic looms—which are becoming increasingly widespread—the card stage is rendered unnecessary by the use of digitized information to program the weave.

Having been de-gummed and having lost some of their weight during the hot dying process, dyed threads on the loom are subsequently immersed in a vegetal bath or a solution rich in metallic salts to restore their initial density. This procedure is largely responsible for the seductive texture of Jacquard silk ties. The most beautiful are woven of continuous threads without the use of spun silk (discontinuous filaments spun from silk waste). Spun silk is often used in piece-dyed ties, which are generally less glossy than those made of woven silk.

Woven silk ties are the only accessories with such refined weaves that most American and European men are given the opportunity to wear, and can feature a remarkable variety of textures. Plain weave—the most widely employed—can be varied to produce rep (with longitudinal ribs), ottoman (with crosswise ribs), crêpe (whose rough surface is created by weaving with various tensions), and faille (with a more conspicuous grain and crosswise ribs). Twill—more frequently used in printed ties—has diagonal ribs. Satin weave produces the smoothest, softest, and glossiest of all woven silks. The weaving process eliminates roughness in satin by covering each weft thread with at least four warp threads (or vice versa); such overlaying of several threads is called a float and is often a design feature of richly woven ties.

A tie offers a man an almost infinite variety of woven silks, a variety which he will not find in any of his other garments. (Right-hand page, from left to right): two satin weave ties with float motifs; a tie in grenadine; a tie with rep background decorated with ottoman dots; a solid color rep tie; a tie with flecked motifs.

At the premises of the Richard Atkinson company—which specializes in ties made of a wool and silk poplin—traditional tools are still in use, among the spools of silk: a shoemaker's knife, used to cut the fabric; a weaver's hook; two shuttles to guide the weft thread during the weaving process; and a pair of tweezers designed to remove imperfections from the fabric (right).

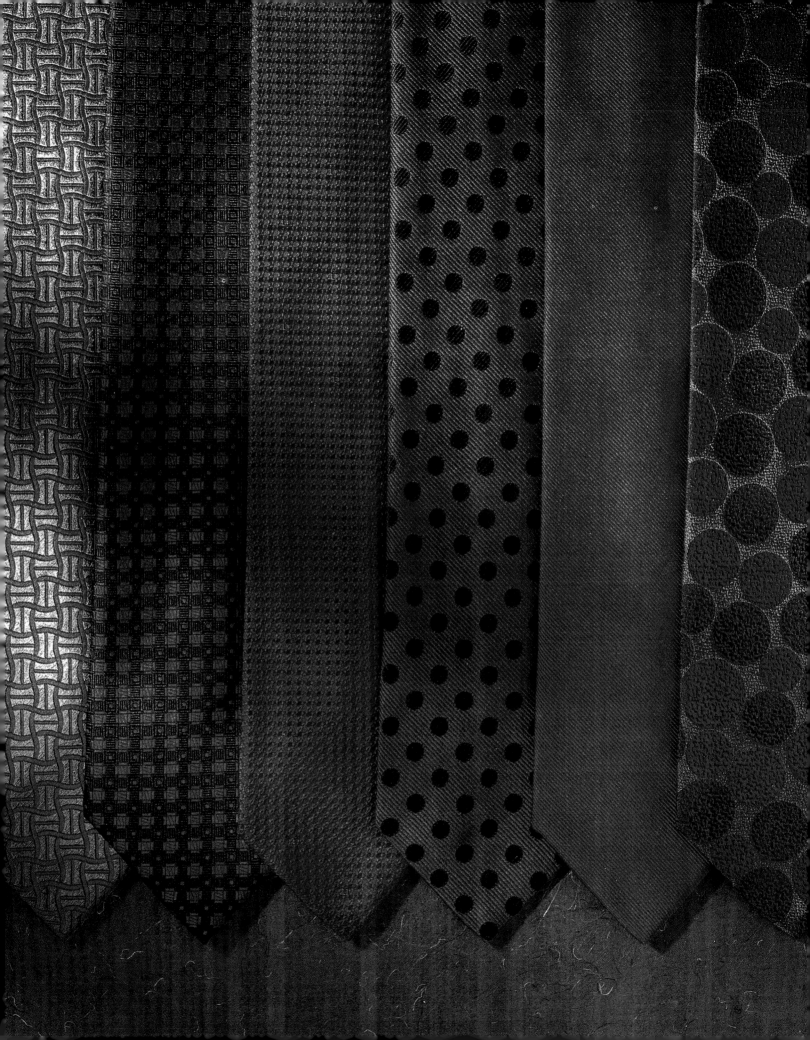

Switzerland today boasts several major silk-weaving mills. Most of them work for tie manufacturers. One of the most prestigious, the Gessner company at Wädenswil on Lake Zurich, is known for the fine detail of its patterns. The Gessner factory in 1896 (right).

Each of the weaves used for ties produces a different sensation to the touch. Combined with the quality of the silk and certain characteristics of manufacture, it gives the finished product a particular "hand." (Right-hand page, from left to right): a tie with fancy reps; a tie with four different reps; a tie in sackcloth plain weave; a tie in basket weave; a tie in various twills; a tie with a satin background and woven paisley motifs.

Silk weavers and printers are careful to preserve their archives of what they have produced in the past. These albums are extraordinary source documents for the history of textiles, and are also working tools, since present-day designers often draw inspiration from them. An album of fabric samples, 1910–30, preserved by the Ratti company in Como (below).

But the best professionals do not content themselves with these three elementary weaves. The most beautiful ties are often manufactured in derivative weaves whose names give some idea of the result: basket weave, flecked crêpe, or finely ribbed rep. Highly refined woven ties tend to feature a combination of these, or variations on them: paisley designs in rep and twill weave; checks in alternating rep, twill weave, and flecked weaves; or striped and dotted patterns executed in several different sizes of rep. Charvet's marvels include ties made of small, satin rectangles with basket-weave borders, set against a rep background.

Finally, some ties are made with thin silk gauze or with grenadine (silk derived from the latter and venerated by a few especially demanding individuals). This very sheer silk—in fact an imitation gauze—is a bit like knit fabric because

of its loose weave. The particular feel and exceptionally smooth surface result from the winding circuit of its weft threads. Grenadine ties are also much appreciated for the elegant way they knot. They are favored by the designers Sulka and Gianfranco Ferre.

Rather modest woven silk ties that feature only a single texture also exist. But it through the manipulation and juxtaposition of different weaves, by emphasizing either the warp or the weft to make a color appear or disappear, by alternating motifs, and by multiplying subtle effects that weavers, inspired both by demanding clients and designers, effectively bestow on ties their rank of nobility.

Printed silk. Because they are often less expensive, simpler in appearance, and can accomodate decorative motifs of every conceivable variety, printed silk ties are the most widespread variety available. But in addition to reasonably priced models (around $30.00), one can find printed-silk ties featuring subtle patterns and refined color schemes. These require considerable expertise and skill to produce and as a result are rather expensive. Two aspects of their manufacture are especially crucial: the printing process and the dosing of their dye ingredients.

A visit to the main factory of the fabric printer Ratti, in Guanzate near Como, makes it easier

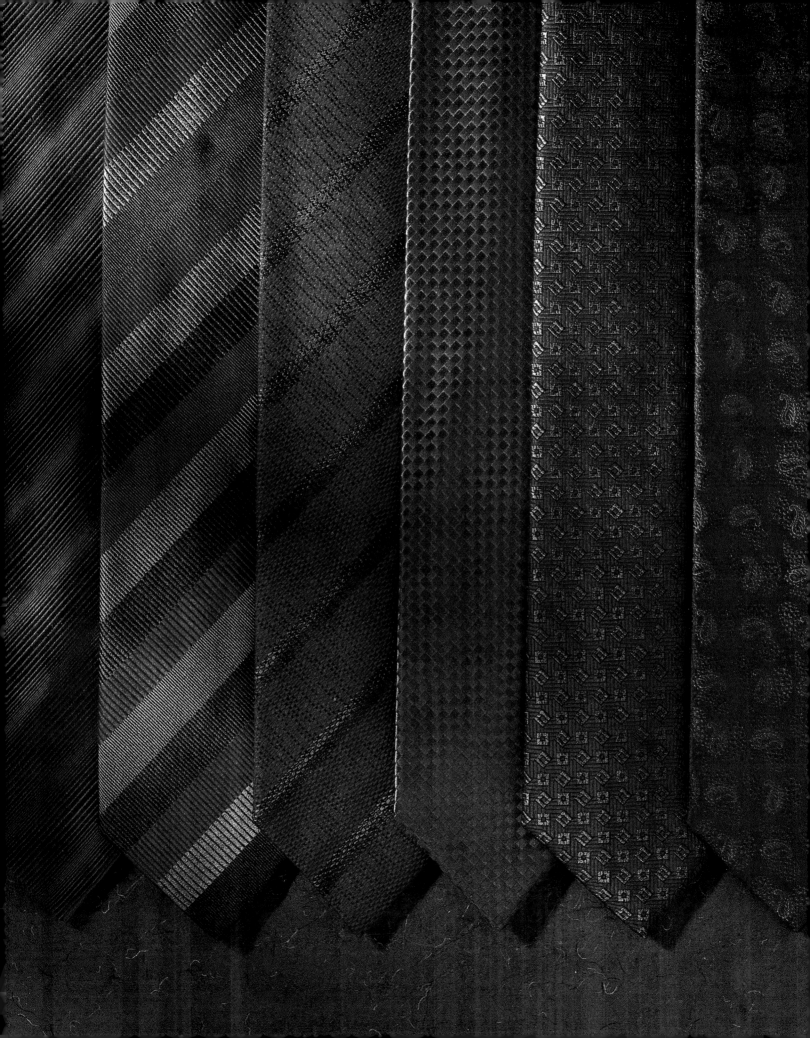

Como is the world center for the weaving of high-quality silks for ties: some twenty-five companies, many the size of full-scale industries, make up the Comocravatta consortium, which supplies the world's most renowned tie designers and labels. Headquarters of the Ratti Group, a prestige silk producer (right).

to grasp the degree to which certain Italian silk manufacturers manage to reconcile quality considerations and market competitiveness.

This enormous, technologically advanced facility is capable of producing thirty kilometers of silk per day. But the factory's impressive level of efficiency does not prevent Ratti from turning out some of the world's most beautiful silks—used in ties designed by Versace, Valentino, Armani, Gucci, Ferragamo, Sulka, Givenchy, Ralph Lauren, and Robert Talbott, to name just a few.

Pre-woven raw silk arrives in Guanzate in immense rolls containing as much as several hundred meters of fabric. Ratti uses Chinese silk, but most of the world's supply comes from Brazil and Thailand. In the great majority of cases, printed silk ties are made of a twill weave featuring diagonal ribs that are especially thin.

Complex and richly colored patterns are usually obtained by the additive process, which involves applying each color in successive stages to the raw silk.

Another procedure, called discharge printing, functions by subtraction: this involves dyeing the fabric a solid color and then selectively removing or discharging this first shade by screening, using a corrosive substance which acts like a bleach, thereby creating "negative" design motifs. Whether dyed or raw, the piece of fabric—often as large as 40 by 200 meters—is placed on a table to receive its colors. Each pattern is printed on about a square meter of material by means of a polyester monofilament screen. Certain carefully delineated portions of this screen remain permeable so that the applied ink only reaches the desired areas. For a pattern using five colors, five different screens must be successively printed on the same surface. On certain printing tables each of these screens is moved in sequence across the fabric, while on others it is the fabric that is moved beneath each successive screen. The Ratti factory in Guanzate is equipped with a dozen such enormous tables which operate according to one or the other of

the two printing processes. They are completely automated: the design screens move or the fabric slides through, receiving the colored imprint while being observed by only one or two skilled workers.

What most determines the quality of an impression is the manner in which the image is applied on these screens. Here too computers have been introduced, but this technological advance is still in its infancy. Traditional color separating is a process executed entirely by hand, and is an art reserved to specialists, some of whom have acquired considerable prestige—such as Gandit, whose distinguished clientele includes Hermès. In the case of printed silks with delicate motifs and subtle color schemes, color separators are required to work with extraordinary precision. Their point of departure is a colored rendering of the motif to be printed. They must identify all of the colors and then block out each surface to be printed in a given hue on a separate transparency. If a design uses five different colors, the color separator must superimpose five different films in order to produce the entire printed design. Each film is then placed on a sheet of glass above ultraviolet lights and below a screen coated with a photosensitive varnish which hardens when it comes into contact with ultraviolet rays. All areas on the screen except those protected by the ink transparencies are rendered impermeable when the lamps are turned on. The screen is then sprayed with water and the unhardened varnish washes out, leaving open areas of mesh for dyeing.

It is easier to comprehend the degree of precision involved if one knows that tie designs can feature almost imperceptible points of color which must register perfectly —with no room for gaps or overprinting. Thus the

Printers acquire their woven raw silk—most often twills—mainly from China. It undergoes a number of processes (washing, softening, etc.) before being printed. Rolls of silk in the Ratti factory at Guanzate (above).

Founded in 1942 at Bourgoin-Jallieu in France, the Marcel Gandit company specializes in producing the frames which are used for printing on silk. They are responsible for the printing of all Hermès ties. Gandit color separators at work (below). Each of the colors of the pattern will require a separate film, which is transferred onto the fabric of the printing frames by a photosensitive process.

Since each color of a pattern needs a separate printing screen, the cost of a printed silk tie depends on the number of colors in it. They are usually restricted to four or six, but some companies have no hesitation in offering many more. Flammarion 4 tie reproducing a detail from a Monet painting. It is made up of fifteen separate colors (above).

preparation of a screen is a lengthy operation that can only be carried out by highly skilled craftspeople—these factors increase the price of such screens, which can sometimes reach as high as several thousand dollars. This explains why printers store most of their screens as precious archival materials—in case they should be requested to reprint an old design. Ratti possesses more than 120,000 screens, half of which are kept in Guanzate. The more colors used in a tie, the larger the number of screens needed to print it, and the higher the associated production costs. Most contemporary ties require the use of four or five colors. But printed ties by Hermès and Ferragamo, for instance, often feature six, eight, or even twelve different hues. Flammarion 4, a French company that oversees the production of ties sold in selected bookshops and museums, has marketed a design that reproduces a detail from one of Monet's water lily paintings and that requires the use of 15 screens. The Parisian design house, Léonard has devised a series of *haute-couture* ties with figurative designs employing between twelve and twenty-six different colors, depending on the model. These unusual pieces, manufactured by the Orisini company—which is located between Milan and Como—make for the world's most expensive ties.

Naturally, twenty-six screens, even if superbly crafted, do not in themselves guarantee a beautiful finished product. The color scheme used by the designer must also be duplicated. Color accuracy is a prime indicator of a printer's quality. Techniques of dye composition and manufacture—the French call this phase *la cuisine des couleurs*—are closely guarded secrets. In the case of Ratti, ingredients are now measured—to the gram—by computer. This technology makes subtle nuances in color possible, but also, more important, the perfect retention of formulae: each color formula can be stored in the computer's memory and clients can be absolutely sure of getting the same colors should they decide to reissue a certain design. But other textile manufacturers equal in prestige to Ratti continue to use time-honored methods: David Evans, the oldest British fabric printer, based in Crayford, in Kent, still prepares indigo by having workers wearing tall fishing boots crush the ingredients underfoot in a sandstone tub. This indigo is used to prepare madder which is made from a plant of the same name whose roots have been used since antiquity to make a deep red dye. In today's world of silk production, the term "madder" is used to designate a number of dyes derived—with the addition of metallic salts—from synthetic madder or alizarin, which was discovered by two English chemists at the beginning of the nineteenth century. A final indigo bath makes their tones particularly tempered and deep. Whether blue, red, green, or yellow, madder silks are recognizable by their mellowness, matte surfaces, and somber reflections. They are largely responsible for the allure of David Evans's celebrated, traditional paisley patterns. Real madders must be woven exclusively of raw silk (not spun silk) which has been boiled before weaving to remove its natural gum. After the indigo bath, a new gum is added which produces the velvety texture that is one of the characteristics of madder ties.

For many centuries colored patterns were obtained on silk through block printing. Wood blocks preserved by Gandit (below).
The English company David Evans has specialized for over a century in paisley patterns. Although they have abandoned the old procedures of block printing, the company continues to manufacture madders in traditional ways. The madder process (named after the dye of the same name) gives deep, gentle colors and a sumptuous feel which is much appreciated by connoisseurs. Fabric samples of David Evans madder silk (below).

The dyes are intended to delight the eye, but that is not their sole function: they also play a role in determining a tie's hand. The number and nature of the dyes used, especially dark hues—the heaviest—slightly influence a tie's weight. As a result, the same basic design printed in different colors will feel somewhat different to the touch. To become convinced of this, one need only close one's eyes and make the requisite tactile comparisons.

Printed figured silk. Numerous fashion houses—including Armani, Léonard, and Hugo Boss—now offer ties that have not only a printed design but also a pattern that is woven into the silk fabric. First of all figured silk is created by manipulating the warp and

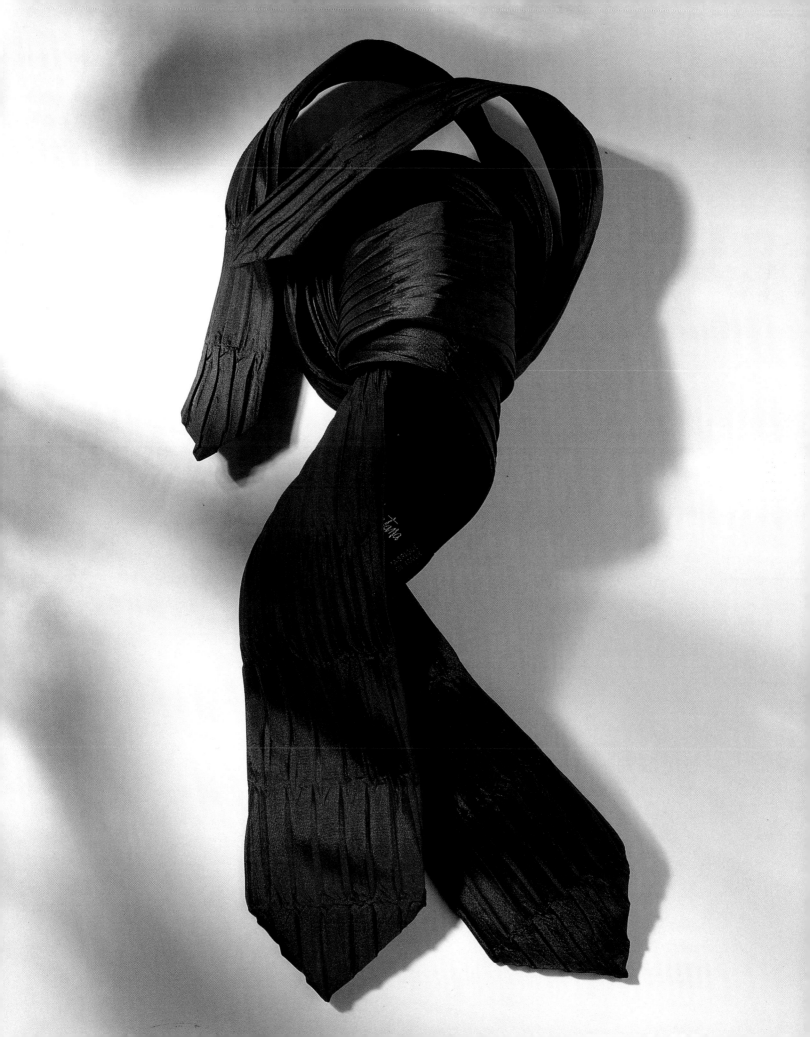

weft threads. This figured fabric is then dyed into a solid color. Finally the beautiful woven arabesques, complex interlaces, or vegetal motifs, are printed with the most diverse designs.

Special effects. Thanks to its qualities of lightness and resilience, which facilitate its being manipulated in countless ways, silk is used to make a remarkable variety of ties. In addition to traditional silk ties, there are other varieties which are more original in appearance. The most widespread current instance is naturally the silk knit tie, whose vogue, which began in the 1970s, has proved longer-lived than the fad for the wool knit tie of about the same vintage. Their silk threads are simply knitted by machine instead of being woven. Ties made of this material have a style and hand all their own, simultaneously sober and informal. In his novel *Oedipus in Stalingrad*, the Austrian writer Gregor von Rezzori describes one such tie perfectly: "He grasped a coil of black knitted material that unrolled beneath his fingers into a long thin ribbon. . . . The tie's silk, which grated slightly at the touch, suggested an athletic character with a streak of puritan austerity." (It is by wearing this tie that the novel's hero, a young dandy and fashion journalist, subsequently attempts to make a favorable impression on a general's widow whose daughter he hopes to marry.) Silk knit ties are usually a single color and always have squared ends. In Paris, their most demanding adepts shop at Hermès, Charvet, or Sulka. However, the German manufacturer Ascot is the uncontested leader in this field.

Rarer still, but exuding a subtle ecology-conscious refinement, are shantung ties, which are often worn in Thailand: these are made of woven wild silk—that is, silk produced by caterpillars in the wild, which is tougher and thicker than the domesticated variety.

For formal occasions there are also moiré, or watered, silk ties, with their beautiful undulating reflections. A true moiré process involves deviating and crushing a fabric's grain to modify its surface in such a manner that it reflects light to produce the desired motif. Unfortunately, only one manufacturer—in Lyons—now produces moiré fabric, and moiré ties have virtually disap-

peared. The designer Sulka once had a special moiré line. Today this firm sells woven imitation-moiré ties. In the same dressy register, but with a more contemporary inflection, are pleated ties, which made a timid appearance in the 1950s and now have been taken up by Armani and Claude Montana. Pleats in the silk—obtained with a hot press—give these ties both a sophisticated air and an attractive swell. Claude Montana, whose tie designers are among today's most inventive, also offers marvelous crinkled silk (the crinkled appearance is obtained with a hot press) and flocked silk, made by attaching cotton fibers to the silk with an adhesive. We should applaud these attempts to rejuvenate the tie through the use of such original approaches, which despite their unconventional appearances, never venture into the realm of bad taste.

More and more design houses such as the German company Ascot and the Italian firm Ermenegildo Zegna have recently marketed ties made of washed silk imitating wool and tweed. This effect is achieved by rubbing away the silk's natural gloss and placing it into extra-large washing machines along with sand or small pebbles.

Finally, there is another preparation which produces the softest fabric of all: gum silk. In this process, the tie silk is bathed in a gum-based preparation to give it a velvety texture like that of suede or brushed denim. It is used, as already

Waffled, creased, pleated, flocked: "special effects" give a particular verve to the collections of the more audacious creators. Claude Montana ties in pleated silk (left).

A classic tie, which numbers among its devotees the Academicians Jean d'Ormesson and Pierre-Jean Rémy: the silk knit tie. Knit ties always have squared ends, and are finished without an interlining. They are the only ties which should not be hung in a wardrobe, because they would lose their shape. Old England tie (left).

Veritable moiré silk ties, which were once the speciality of the Sulka company, are no longer made. Sulka ties from the 1950s, Karen Petrossian collection (below).

noted, to make real madder ties, a British specialty. Italian fabric printers manufacture an imitation madder silk produced by applying special dyes (though without the indigo bath) and then by adding the gum. When this process is used on twill the madder-like result is called gumtwill, while the resulting gum silk is called *seta daino,* or suede silk. Ferragamo, for instance, includes gum silk ties in all of its collections. There is also an especially heavy variety of gumtwill that is known as antilope.

Silk weight. One of the most important factors influencing the quality of a tie's hand is weight. Where ties are concerned, the heavier the silk, the greater the sensation of plenitude and comfort produced by it when touched. But the fabric will be burdensome to precisely the same degree. Silk weight varies depending on the number, nature, and thickness of the warp and weft threads (each one woven from a variable number of cocoon filaments, or baves), as well as with the dyes and treatment process employed. Of Japanese origin, the unit of measure used for printed silk is the *momme* (a French word pronounced "mummy" by professionals throughout the world), which equals 4.33 grams per square meter. The British and Americans prefer to measure in ounces. Today, tie silk tends to be between 10 and 45 mommes. But while 10–14 momme weight silk is most often used, the luxury market begins with the 18–20 mommes range. The thick twill used in Hermès ties—woven from bave silk threads (most are 4 bave)—weigh 18 mommes (and all ties produced by this designer weigh exactly 39 grams). David Evans sells ties made from outrageous, sublime silks weighing 60 ounces (or 45 mommes) and selling for about $100 per meter. Rumor has it that the Duke of Edinburgh is extremely partial to them.

As for woven silk ties, their weight is measured more simply in grams or ounces. While most register between 80 and 100 grams, Charvet's luxury woven ties as weigh as much 120 grams per square meter.

OTHER MATERIALS

Of the almost 800 million ties sold throughout the world each year, how many are made of silk and how many of other materials? No one can say with any degree of accuracy (though we do know that only around 20 million—considered top of the line—cost more than $50.00). But we can be sure that silk is used much less often than synthetic materials: acetate, rayon, nylon, and above all, polyester. Today's polyester ties have interesting qualities, which include elasticity, wrinkle resistance, and low cost. But they never have an attractive hand, especially in comparison with silk. To summarize (an extended dissertation on this subject would be out of place here), polyester differs from silk in that the fingers glide across it like skates over ice: its cold surface has no density, depth, or pith to offer any tactile interest.

At least one can say that cotton ties are natural, practical in warm weather, and sporty in appearance. And while they afford no particular pleasure to the touch, they can seduce the eye with their wide variety of colors—cotton is a fabric that dyes remarkably well. Liberty cotton was often used to make ties in the 1970s and 1980s. In any case, the price, ease of maintenance, and simplicity of these ties make them ideal for little boys, who can drip chocolate or jam all over them without definitive disaster. In the same light and summery register, linen is undeniably a nobler material. Along with cotton muslin (cambric, to be precise), it was the standard material of the earliest neckties. But linen has one significant disadvantage: its tendency to wrinkle. This can be mitigated somewhat by the use of a bit of starch; however, pure linen is almost never used today.

Leather ties also had their moment of glory, from the 1950s to the 1980s. Ties made from this material first appeared in the United States in the form of the western bola or string tie, which is secured by a metal clasp and decorated at its ends with small metal ornaments (sometimes made from silver). It was invented in the 1940s: one day an

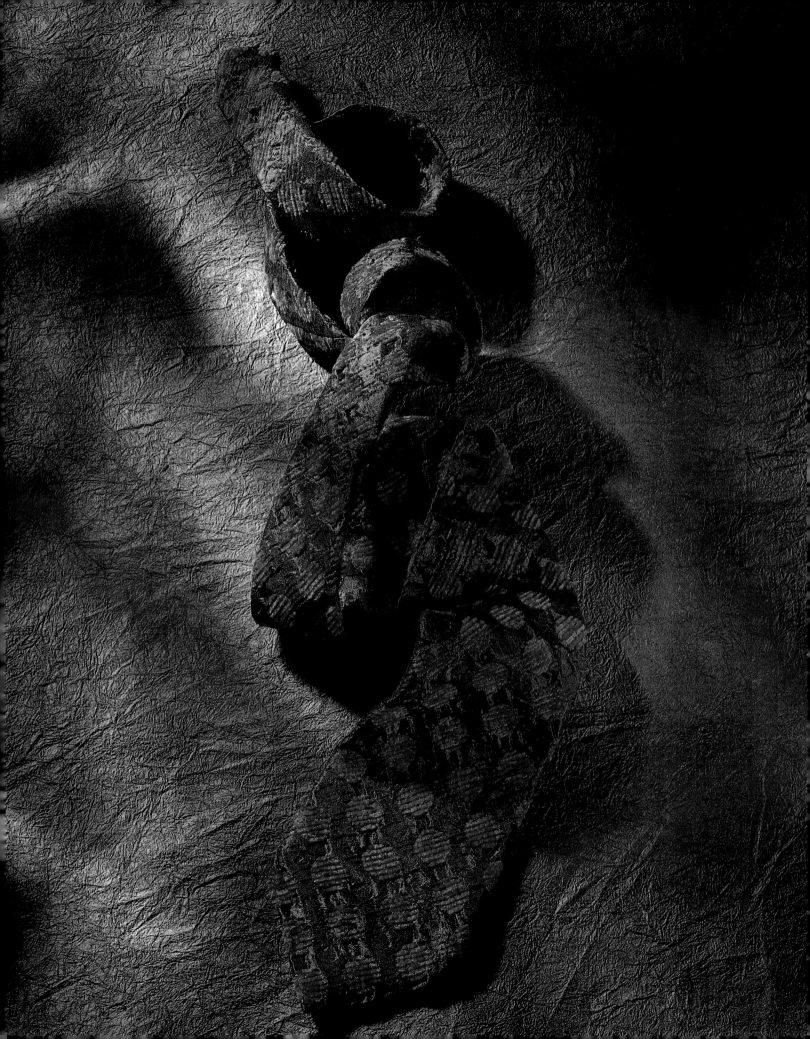

Arizona cowboy by the name of Vic Cerserstaff lost his hat while chasing wild horses. When he eventually found the hat he had the idea of placing its precious leather cord with silver buckle around his neck, to make sure he did not lose *it*. This novel accessory was admired by his companions and before long many American cowboys were wearing bolas—a name derived from the Spanish *bola*, two balled lassos used by Argentine gauchos to trip galloping horses. In 1971 the bola was solemnly proclaimed "the official tie of the State of Arizona," and it has been adopted by lovers of rockabilly and country music throughout the world. Hermès included bola ties in its 1990 spring-summer ready-to-wear collection. A specialist in leather goods, Hermès has also devised classic ties in suede and soft glove leather, including one model decorated with a wave motif designed by Vasarely.

Leather was the object of another vogue at the beginning of the 1970s. Even as the death of the tie was being prophesied—its being an emblem of everything that hippies and young radicals despised about middle-class values—an unknown designer devised narrow, square-

When knit ties were the rage, James Dean, still a figure of adulation among romantic and rebellious youth, passed like a comet through the skies of American cinema. James Dean in his second film, *Rebel Without a Cause*, by Nicholas Ray, 1955 (below).

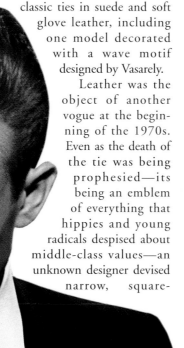

tipped leather ties in an enormous variety of colors. The product met with immediate success and remained fashionable for about fifteen years. Today, aside from the string ties sold by stores specializing in western clothes, leather ties have all but disappeared.

Knitted wool was also rather popular in the 1960s and 1970s, but currently available wool ties have a much less rustic appearance. They are often woven from the noblest materials—Scottish wool or cashmere—and are no longer limited to traditional design motifs such as plaids and heraldic shields. In Paris, Hermès, Sulka, and Madelios sell cashmere ties which have been specially treated for strength and minimal shagginess. Other designers—Michelsons in London and Etro and Ermenegildo in Milan, for example—market a varied line of wool ties, which are especially appropriate for winter wear, above all with tweed suits. For that matter, tweed can be used to make ties. Parisian designer Patrick Hollington has done just that, combining tweed ties with suits inspired by work clothes, one of his specialties. These models are made out of the cuttings from tweed jackets.

But wool is never happier, in a tie, than when combined with silk. Wool and silk blends—especially cashmere and silk—have a superb hand that can only be explained in terms of an exquisite paradox: softness combined with roughness, pliancy with firmness. Although wool and silk blend ties are sold by several designers, the most prestigious creator of this deliciously hybrid material remains the Irish company Richard Atkinson, which weaves (sometimes prints) and manufactures ties bearing the label "Atkinson's Royal Irish Poplin." The most characteristic feature of this Belfast firm (founded in 1820) is indeed that it uses poplin, made of silk warp threads and wool weft threads. The silk lies on the surface, which results in ties that are soft to the touch; the wool lies underneath, which increases resistance and firmness. Atkinson ties feature all of the classic patterns: stripes, hunting motifs, heraldic shields, and small geometric shapes.

Other blends are rarely used, even though the makers of tie fabric have tried just about

The leather tie, which was fashionable in various forms, from the 1950s to the 1980s, underwent a few refinements. For example, this Hermès tie in fine glove leather, designed by Victor Vasarely in the 1960s. The "wave" motif gave the illusion that the fabric was slightly wrinkled. The tie, and the original Vasarely drawing of the motif (left).

In his career in the cinema, Ronald Reagan had many opportunities to wear the bandanna, the cowboy neckerchief, generally made of cotton. Ronald Reagan in the unforgettable *Law and Order*, by Nathan Juran, 1953 (right).

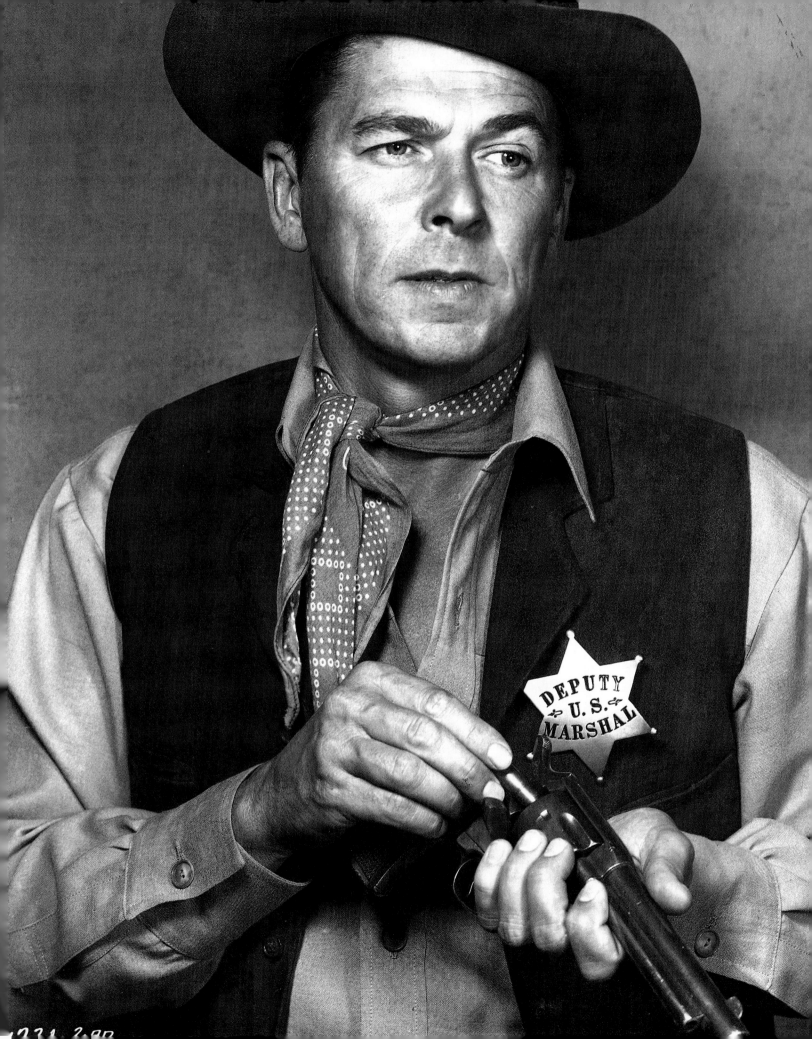

A man wearing tweed in 1967 (right). This carded wool, which is no longer much used by tie-makers, is a wonderful winter adjunct to the outfit of the gentleman farmer. It represents a return to the historical origins of the tie, inasmuch as it has the merit of providing protection from the cold.

every conceivable combination. One can sometimes find ties made of lightweight blends such as wool and cotton, silk and linen, or mogadore, a ribbed fabric of silk warp and cotton or linen weft, which is ideal for warm-weather, striped ties. A few fabric manufacturers also sell tie linen into which a bit of polyester has been introduced, a trick that minimizes wrinkling.

MANUFACTURING

An excellent silk weaver once gave me a tie made from one of his most beautiful weaves: a blue and gold diaper pattern combining three textures: ottoman, rep, and flecked. I thanked him for this sumptuous tie, even though its hand seemed to me a bit limp and fleeting. I wore it for the third time to honor a man I was about to meet: Michel Catris, president of the Barcelona-based Richel firm, one of the world's best tie makers. After an hour's conversation

devoted to the making of ties, I noticed that his bemused glance had settled on the one I was wearing. "Your tie is really very beautiful," he said. "Where did you get it?" I proudly told him my little story. He then nonchalantly asked me to show him the back of its wide end. Horrors! To my great shame the label was half loose, the

The Irish company Richard Atkinson, founded in 1820, has always produced a line of ties in poplin. They are woven and manufactured in its factory in Belfast. Poplin was introduced into Ireland two hundred and fifty years ago. The material has a silky feel (the warp is of silk) and is solid in use (the weft is of combed wool). Its name is said to derive from "papeline," a silk woven in Avignon in the fifteenth century, at the time when that city was the seat of the papacy. Fabric samples of Richard Atkinson's Royal Irish Poplin (right). The company's label (left).

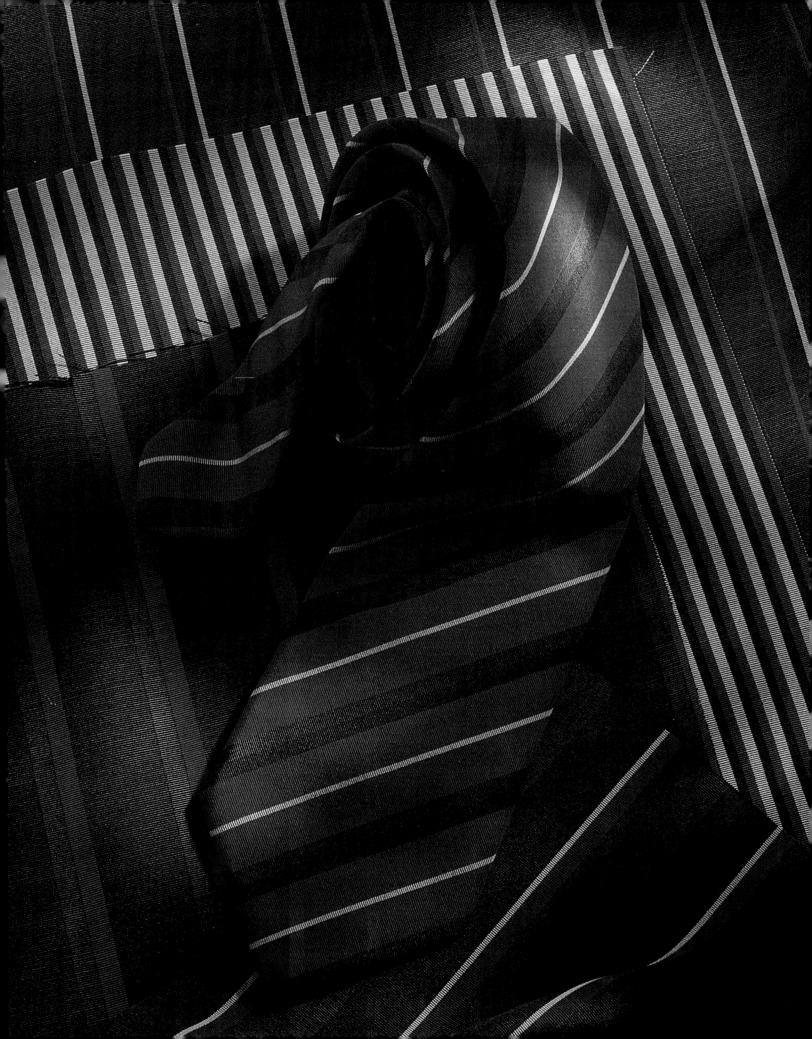

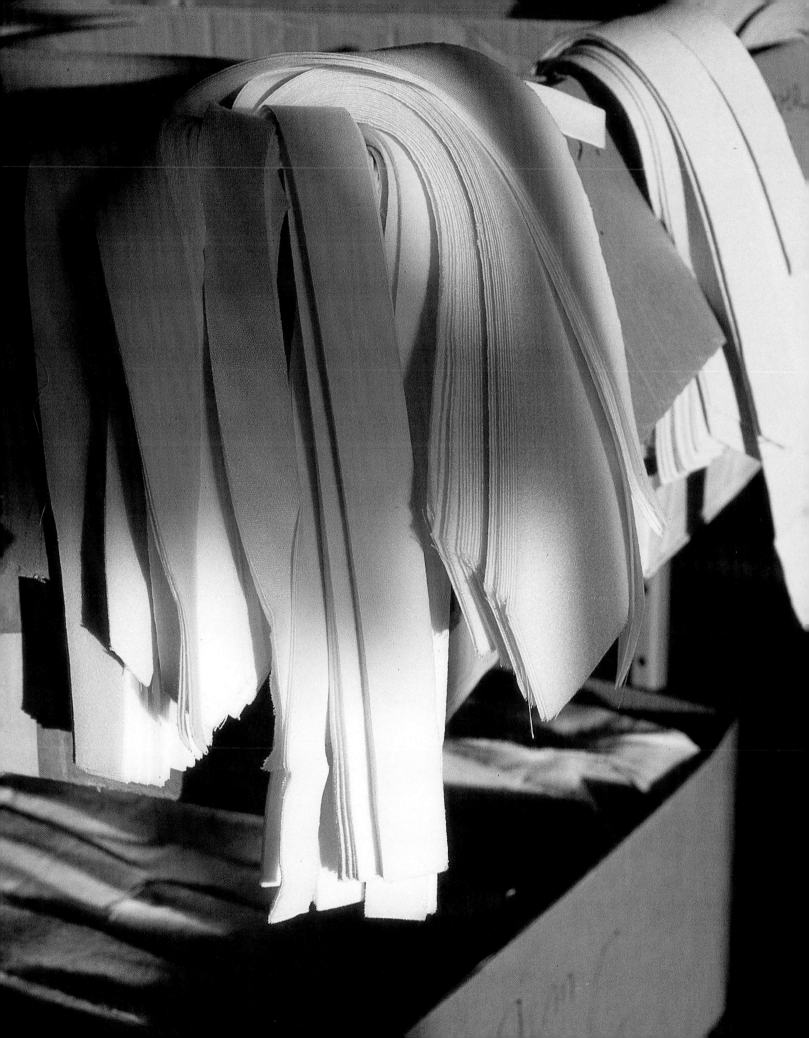

One of the identifying marks of a Hermès tie: the inset printed on the back of the narrow end of the tie, decorated with the company's famous coachman logo. Its color always coordinates with the color of the tie, and suggests to the client a suitable color choice for his shirt or jacket (right).

Totally invisible and always present, the interlining is sewn into the envelope of the tie. The proper fall of the tie and its touch depend on the quality of the interlining. Tie makers are always on the lookout for the ideal interlining material: it might be wool-based, mixed with synthetic fibers and subtle secret recipes, varying according to the nature of the envelope, the total weight of the eventual tie, and even the climate in which the tie is to be worn. Interlinings used by the Thiercelin company in their Bléré factory, near Tours (left).

hem undone, and the lining was beginning to come out. I had no idea how or when this catastrophe had transpired, but Michel Catris' infallible eye had managed to detect it. "If you like, leave it with me a few days, long enough to give it a suitable mounting." It was returned to me less than a week later completely transformed. Not only had the hems been resewn to last for ever, it now had a sumptuous hand worthy of the silk's beauty. It has since become one of my favorite ties.

This anecdote illustrates an implacable law in the matter of ties: even superb material is worth very little if it is not properly fashioned. A tie's hand is largely dependent upon the quality of the fabric around which it is sewn: the interlining.

Classic ties are composed of three main elements: the envelope, or visible fabric, which is sewn from two or three pieces of material (broad end, narrow end, and, most often, a neckband between them); a lining in two pieces, usually made of acetate or silk and woven or embossed with the company's name or initials, which is sewn onto the ends of the envelope; and finally the interlining, a piece of thicker material inside the envelope which serves as the tie's armature. To these three principal elements must be added the label bearing the brand name and the bar tack, through which the small end is slipped so that it stays in place. The bar tack is most often made of the same fabric as the envelope. Then there's the small flap specifying the material used and the place of manufacture which is usually sewn onto the tip of the thin end.

One can easily grasp the importance of the interlining for a tie's hand: when one caresses a tie, the softness and thickness of the envelope are complemented by the greater or lesser firmness of the invisible support concealed within it. The interlining influences the way a tie knot holds as well as the quality of a tie's "fall," which should be free of rumples, warps, and buckles. It should also facilitate a tie's

return to its original form after the knot has been loosened. While the best interlinings are made of pure wool or wool-based fabric, many other materials are used in less expensive ties: polyester, rayon, cotton, and various blends. Orsini, a tie manufacturer for Ermenegildo Zegna, Léonard, and Givenchy, among others, has developed a special interlining for warm, humid climates: it is composed of two thirds polyester blended with an especially elastic wool taken from lambs' necks. Hermès uses a material devised exclusively for its line, a blend of wool and cotton that tends to curve slightly, creating the subtle forward swell that is a distinctive characteristic of Hermès ties. Whatever its material, an interlining should be perfectly fitted to its envelope.

Ties can be made in three ways: entirely by hand, by machine with hand finishing, or (almost) entirely by machine. In the last case mechanization does not necessarily entail a decline in quality. Complete automation is reserved for the mass production of inexpensive ties; some American factories can produce as many as 50,000 a day. The difference between the other two procedures is most apparent in the

While all the major tie makers guarantee a perfection of quality, made-to-measure ties—a privilege accorded only to a few—give that extra "something" much appreciated by demanding tie lovers. Patterns for custom-made ties, preserved by the Charvet company (below).

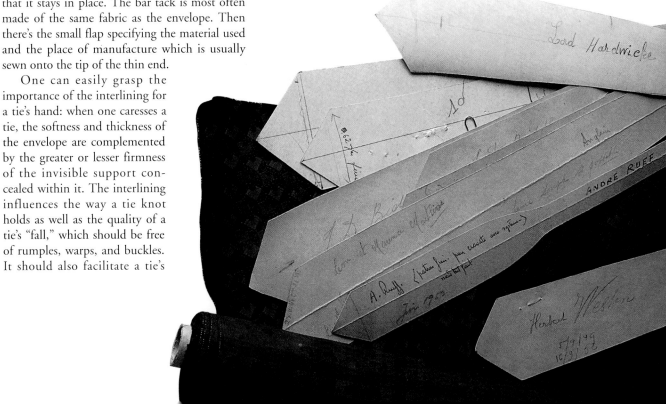

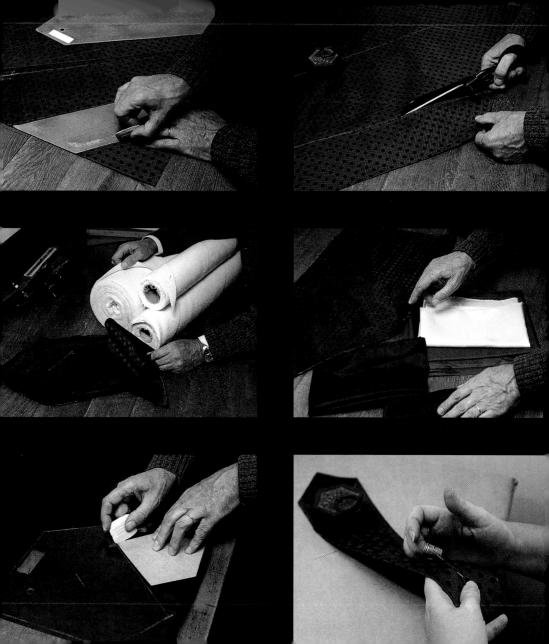

number of ties produced in a given series. Specialists in entirely handmade products—mostly artisans working at home—can scarcely make ten ties an hour. Designers who employ these skilled workers can be certain of the quality of each piece they produce, without exception. The major designers, who sell ties of excellent quality but in larger quantities, opt for companies equipped to perform work in the intermediate category: "finished by hand," an approach allowing for the production of several thousand ties per day.

One such company is Thiercelin, based in Bléré, near Tours, which makes ties for Christian Dior, Sulka, Pierre Balmain, Azzaro, and Façonnable. Its president, Alain Blum, oversees the production of 10,000 ties per day made by some 150 workers. Another hundred home-based workers are responsible for the hand finishing. Thiercelin also manufactures entirely hand-sewn and machine-sewn ties, but both of these endeavors are sidelines. Twenty-four distinct operations are required to produce a hand-finished tie, only the most important of which are described below.

The first step is the cutting of the fabric. Since Jesse Langsdorf devised his ingenious design solution, fine ties have been cut on the bias (at a 45° angle from the selvedge of the fabric). Each part of the envelope is cut with a cardboard pattern whose measurements have been specified by the client. Before the cutting, a substantial number of pieces of printed material are prepared; the pattern is then positioned and cuts are removed from the fabric. On the average, a square meter of material yields four or five ties. The placement of the motifs must be carefully considered, especially when complex as opposed to repeating patterns are to be printed. The two or three exterior pieces are then sewn

together, after which the envelope is smoothed out with by a hot iron, one of the few production stages which cannot be executed by machine. The subsequent operation, by contrast, the sewing of the lining into the two ends, prompted the invention of a remarkably efficient and sophisticated device called a "carrousel": amazingly precise, it sews six linings at a time in cycles lasting only a few seconds. After more ironing comes the crucial moment: placement of the interlining and closure of the envelope. This is done with the help of a long thread sewn lengthwise from one end to the other whose stitches penetrate the interlining. The operation—quite delicate, because care must be taken to keep the needle clear of the visible surface—is effected by a single machine, the "liba," which was invented in the 1970s. "It revolutionized our business," asserts Alan Blum. Run by one or two workers, the liba can sew between 1,300 and 1,800 ties a day, which is thirty times more than a single unassisted worker. The envelope is then flipped over with the help of a rod, and the ends of the interlining are enclosed in their "caps" (the pockets created by the two linings). Finally, the label, the bar tack, and the flap specifying the place of manufacture are machine-sewn onto the back.

Top-of-the-line ties must be finished by hand because of their slip stitch. This is the end of the longitudinal sewing thread, left free for several inches to allow for some play in the stitching. This is indispensable if a tie's fabric is to retain its shape, and all fine ties must have this quality to some degree, for it increases their resistance to the ravages of knotting and unknotting. The slip stitch usually takes the form of a loop which is visible on the back of either one or both of the tie's ends, and inside the envelope, whose edges can be lifted up. This loop,

Some companies offer luxurious subtleties in their ties, as in this lining, made of the same silk as the envelope for two American Modules ties (right).

which is secured by two tacks protecting the seam and fixing the lining, must be executed by hand.

In closing I would like to mention two other particular modes of tie manufacture. First the one practiced by Hermès, which makes only two ties (not including the neckband) from each panel of printed silk. This generous use of fabric allows for the folding of a large amount of the material into the envelope, thereby creating a wonderful effect of fullness, and it means that enough of each silk panel remains for use as the lining. Thus Hermès linings are made of the same silk as the envelope. Having been printed together, these linings are perfectly matched to their envelopes.

The French firms Charvet and Madelios, as well as Robert Talbott of California and Ermenegildo Zegna of Milan, must win the prize for the most luxurious method of production.

All four of these companies have revived a tradition long fallen into disuse: that of the so-called seven-fold tie. Quite fashionable—though already quite expensive—in the 1920s and 1930s, the seven-fold is a tie without an interlining. Its armature is made from the piece of silk itself, which is folded over seven times (three folds on one side, four on the other) before being sewn. The considerable amounts of silk required by this technique explain the high cost of seven-fold ties, the most expensive neckties on the market. Their sole drawback: since the silk is used to create thickness, these ties end up a bit short in length. Yet their shape and fall are perfect; since a seven-fold tie has no interlining they are determined only by the incomparable qualities of silk fabric. As for their hand—light yet deep and rich—it is positively sublime: touching these masses of silk is genuinely thrilling.

An unmistakable sign, the slip stitch, indicates a well-made tie. This "play" of about five inches at the end of the thread closing the envelope is indispensable: it enables the tie's silk to maintain its elasticity, to be stretched without threatening the seam. Often in the form of a loop, it is visible at one or both ends of the tie (right).

Some of the details characterizing a well-made tie: an envelope pattern that matches at the seam and a lining sewn perfectly parallel to the edges. Linings are usually woven with the designer's logo, as on this Richel tie (below).

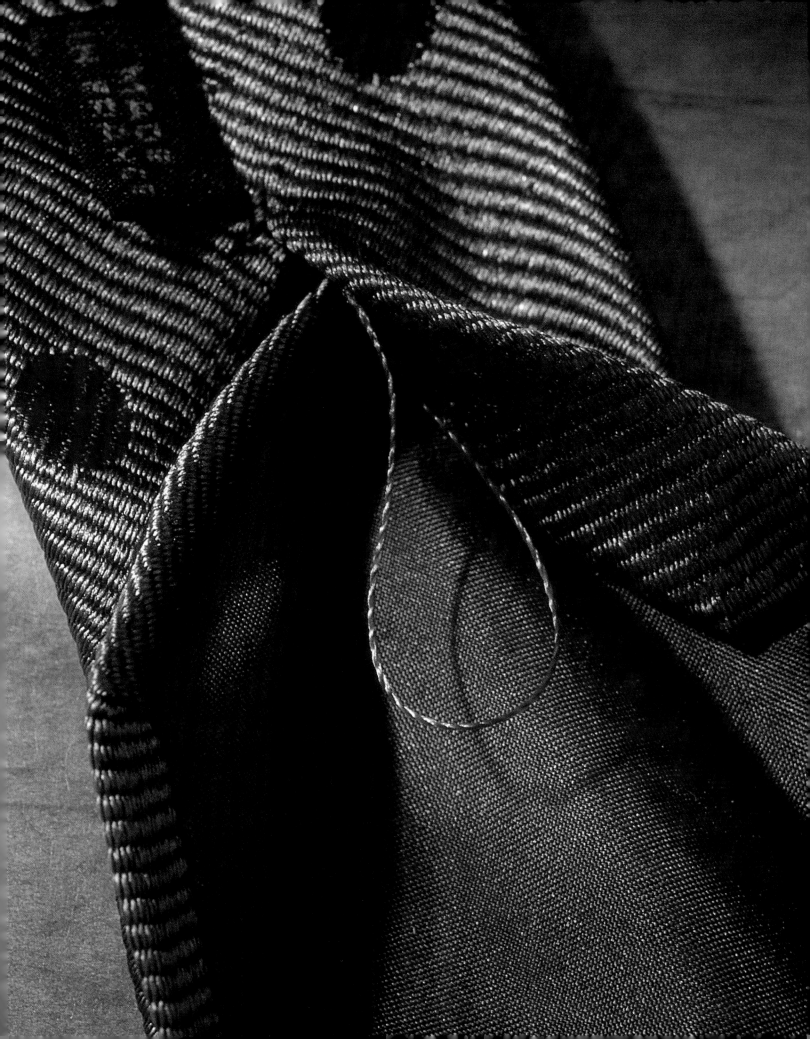

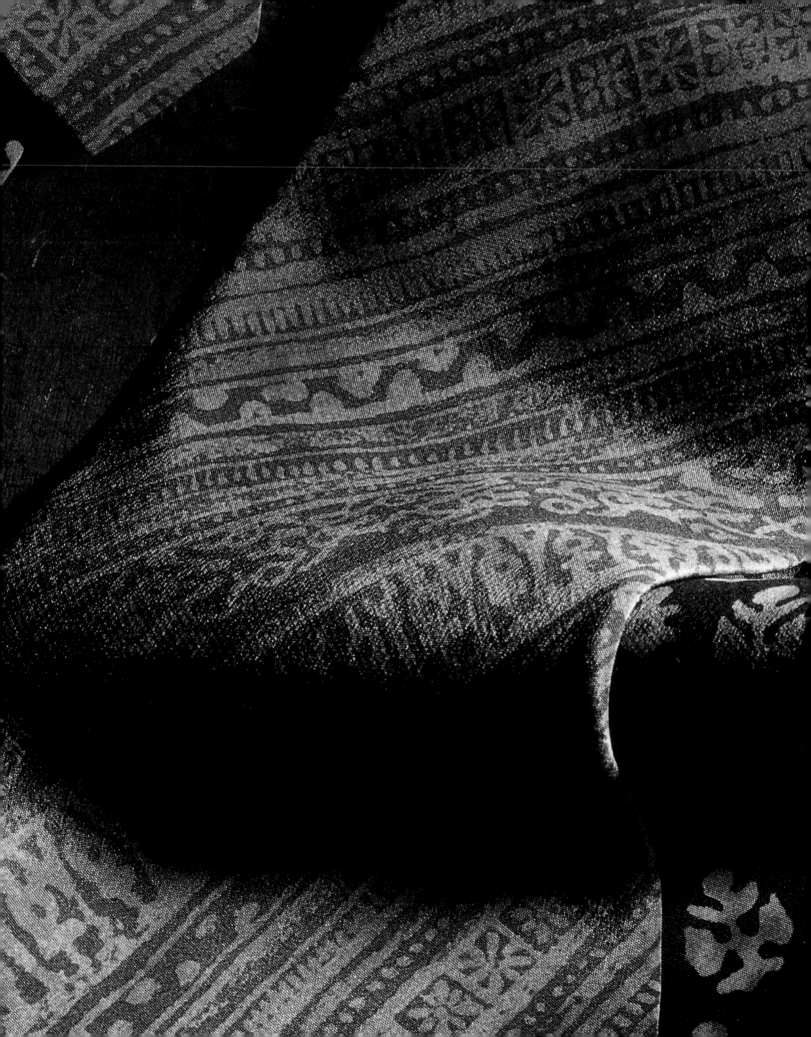

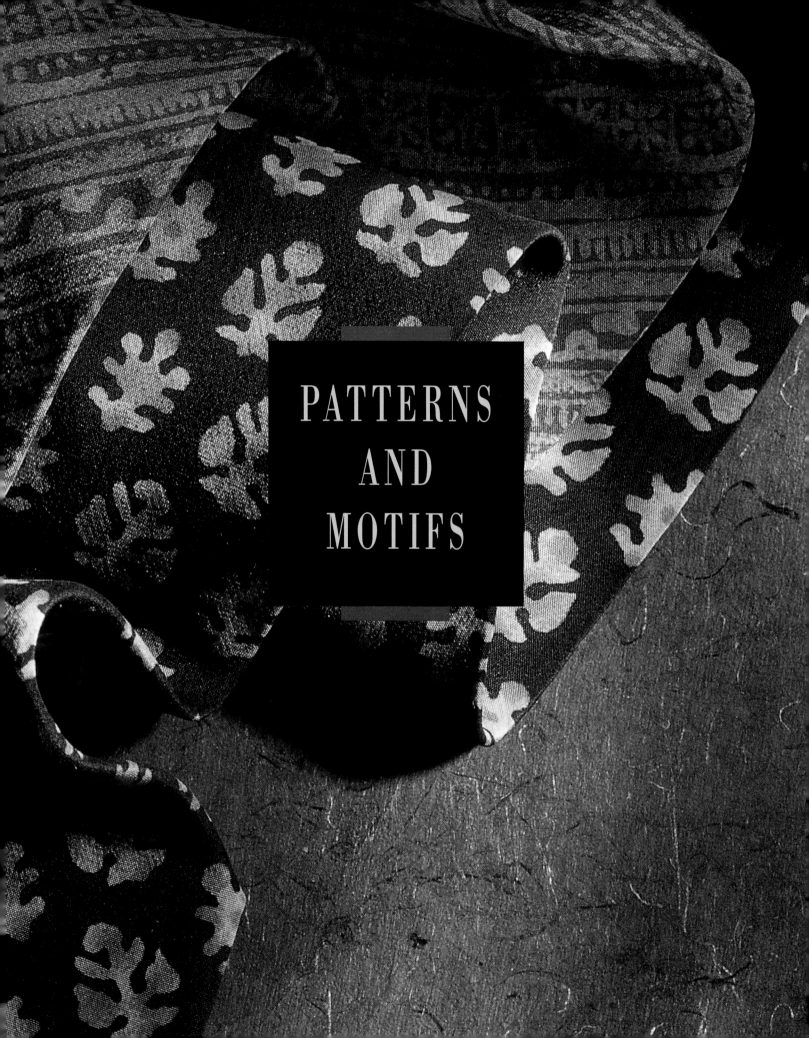

PATTERNS
AND
MOTIFS

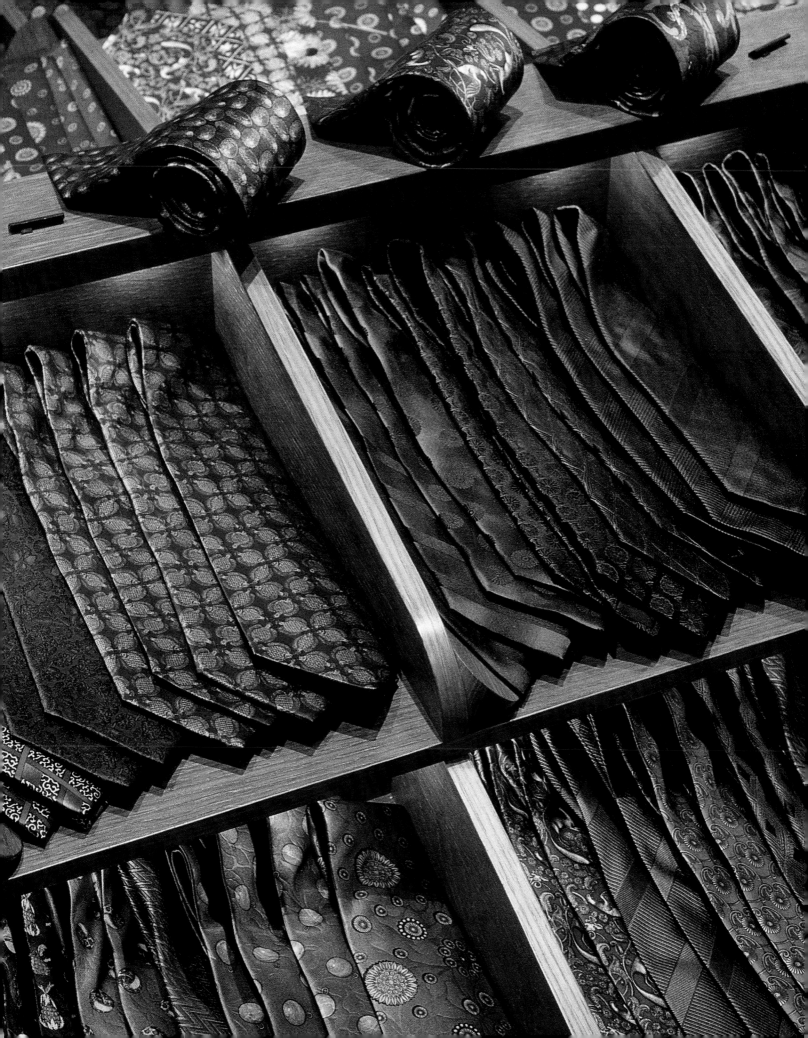

A scattering of multi-colored dots or stirrups, a camel, a fragment of mosaic, alternating stripes, Mickey Mouse, a shield, a field of flowers, a polo player, an Aztec geometric pattern—the only limit to the variety of design motifs currently available on today's neckties is the imagination of the designer. What is more, production techniques, weave possibilities, and color schemes further enrich this already vast array of design choices. Whether tie-lovers want a look that is classic or trendy, discreetly playful or positively outrageous, timid or audacious, decorous or arrogant, sporty or brainy—their alternatives are endless. Since the universal triumph of the austere four-in-hand around 1930, it is the design motif or pattern of a tie that is most used to give expression to the poetry and psychology of the individual wearer. Ancestors of the modern tie were also on occasion decorated with such figures. During the Directory period in France, 1795–1799, the *Incroyables* wore striped cravats, and in the nineteenth century bow ties and the first four-in-hands sometimes featured dots, chevrons, and small geometric motifs. But in general solid colors prevailed, preferably black or white. In 1916 Paul Morand wrote of Boni de Castellane, the famous Parisian dandy of the Belle Époque who dared to wear cravats, which were decorated with dots and stripes, that he "was the opposite of a dandy whose stylishness would remain imperceptible to Americans. Boni's style was highly visible." The condemnation was not directed exclusively at de Castellane's cravats, but they certainly contributed to what Morand saw as the tasteless figure he cut. Twenty years later the range of viable colors and motifs grew suddenly larger—as compensation for the inexpressive rigor of the four-in-hand. Today, as professional dress codes have loosened to the point where it is no longer indispensable to wear a tie, the extraordinary range of design options is practically limitless.

THE PLACE OF THE DESIGN MOTIF

For demanding amateurs anxious to enhance their appreciation of ties by acquiring some relevant expertise, design motifs constitute the most precise subject matter in the field we might call "cravatology." Since they began to flourish in the 1930s, motifs have been inventoried, analyzed, and grouped in families by tie enthusiasts with a rigor worthy of the entomologist. For the specialist, a motif is first classed not in accordance

The classic and the modern, the sober and the audacious—patterns created by designers are a response to the vast range of tastes among today's men. Giorgio Armani ties in printed silk, from the Emporio Armani line, aimed at a young clientele (preceding double page).

At Lanvin in Paris, a rich choice of exquisite motifs and fancy patterns is offered (left).

The playwright and scriptwriter Noel Coward (1899–1973) brought to variety theater the vitality of the English music hall. He was equally noted for his subtle elegance, which was classical, but could at the same time be audacious. Here we see him in 1936, wearing a tie with small geometric patterns, which has been a popular design since the late nineteenth century (left).

Since the 1980s there has been a fashion for small figurative motifs, often amusing, surprising or exotic, and "all over" repeating patterns, covering the entire surface of the tie. Each evokes a universe, tells a story. We each find in them our own need to dream, our need for fantasy. Ferragamo ties in printed silk (left).

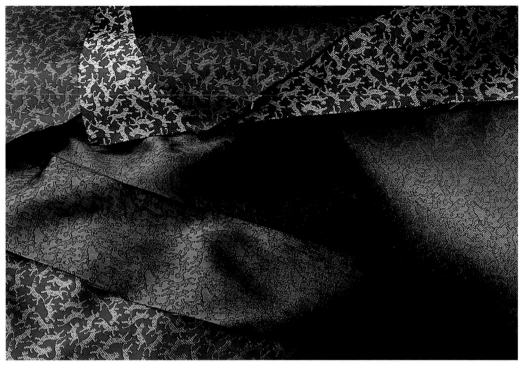

The vogue for little animals has given rise, since 1990, to two kinds of motif: the amusing and the classical. Charvet permits two classic, refined animals to appear on their ties: the elephant, and the panther (right).

These bundles of fabric samples at Charvet show the extent to which an identical motif—here the small square—can give a different final effect to a tie, depending on how it is produced, and the interplay of its colors (right).

The Macclesfield, one of the oldest tie patterns, which was a speciality of the textile producers of Macclesfield at the turn of the century, derived its name from the town. It became particularly fashionable in the 1920s. Its small, geometric figures give an effect of marquetry across the entire surface of the tie (right).

with its genre or style but with the nature of its execution and its placement on the tie. Motif placement in part determines the weave, and in certain cases the printing and manufacturing processes. Furthermore, a motif's placement is often at least as important for a tie's final look as the motif itself. The term "flowered tie," for instance, can designate both an inconspicuous design with tiny daisies all over it or a flashy one decorated with one large sunflower.

All-over ties. Throughout the world the term "all-over" is used to designate one of the most widely used design configurations: one covering the entire surface of the tie with single or multiple motifs. These repeating patterns can feature just about anything in the way of pictorial elements—small geometric shapes, Christmas trees, polka dots, animals, tennis rackets . . . you name it. Such motifs can be linked or free floating. The overall dimensions of a pattern's motif—known as the

"repeat"—can vary considerably from one model of necktie to another.

The success of repeating patterns with tie wearers certainly derives in part from the prestige historically associated with such designs. From the Middle Ages on, the use of small, identical figures, known in heraldry as "semé," has been symbolic. It was understood to evoke, in the words of Michel Pastoureau, writing in *L'Etoffe du Diable,* "something solemn and majestic, even sacred. Thus its use on royal insignia, coronation robes, liturgical objects, and in images depicting some aspect of the divine." The most famous example of this kind of historic motif is the fleur-de-lys, the emblem of the French monarchy still found on ties today. All-over configurations can bestow a certain dignity on even the most eccentric forms. Tiny lambs, for example, straight out of Saint Exupéry's book *The Little Prince*—recently featured on an Hermès tie—can create, when repeated 200 times at regular intervals, a very dressy impression.

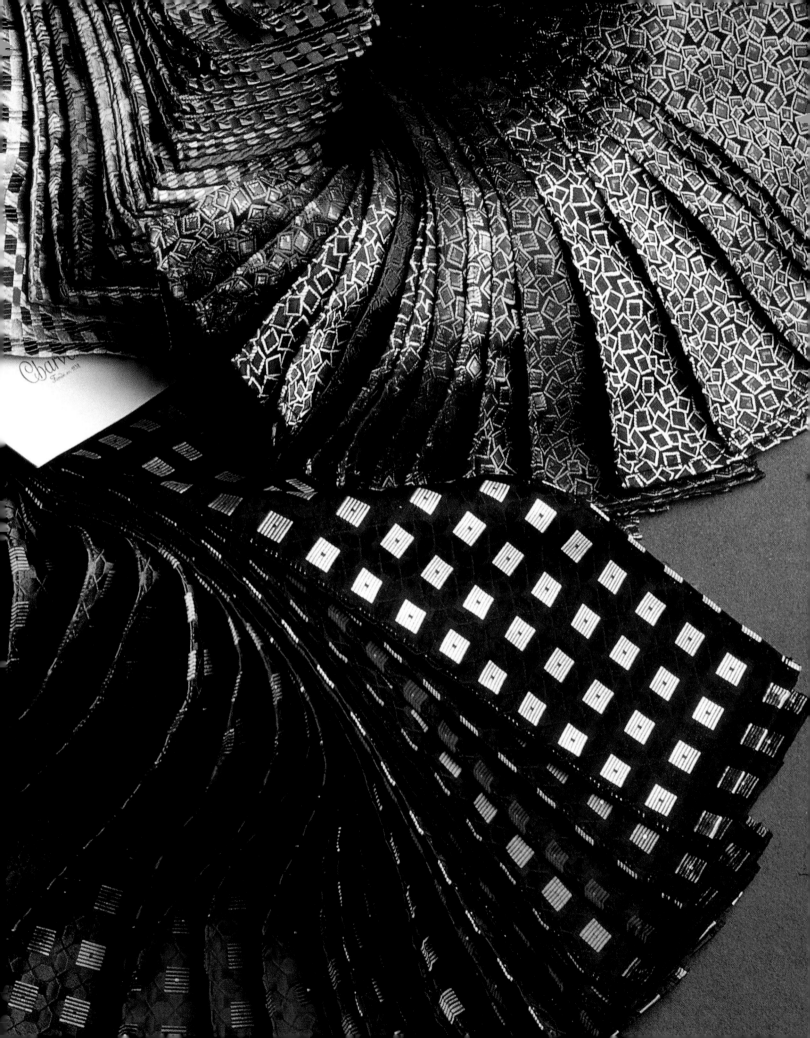

An engineered motif appears in a particular position on a tie, and usually only once. For example these flowers at the center of a Japanese tie produced by the Kyoto Necktie Association (right).

The American "bold look" of the 1940s had many antecedents. In Paris, between the two world wars, artists were in the habit of sporting clothes, and particularly ties, with multicolored geometric, jigsaw, or zigzag patterns, which were inspired by Futurism and Cubism. The painter Foujita, photographed in 1927, was one of the boldest devotees of this style (below).

Another more prosaic factor helps explain the success of the all-over: motifs can be aligned or placed from top to bottom or from left to right. This possibility of weaving and cutting the fabric in any direction lowers production costs considerably.

The diversity and fantasy in contemporary all-overs have not eclipsed the oldest and most classic of such tie-fabric designs: the Macclesfield. Weavers in the small town of the same name in Lancashire England—where silk fabric has been produced for centuries—have specialized since the 1920s in geometric repeating patterns. Ever since being introduced, such designs have been widely used on both woven and printed ties. But not every all-over motif is a Macclesfield, which features a tiny repeated pattern set against a background woven or printed with similar shapes. The resulting effect is often reminiscent of marquetry. The diminutive size

of Macclesfield motifs is easily explained: in the 1920s ties were shorter and narrower than today's models. Neither four-in-hands with short ends nor bow ties, were receptive to large design shapes.

Large motifs. The use of large motifs occupying all or most of the face of a tie's broad end is another design approach. These over-sized motifs first appeared in the 1930s when tie-silk manufacturers began using designs initially developed for upholstery fabric. In the course of the following decade this practice was taken up and transformed by American designers with their whimsical ties, as well as by Europeans, who favored over-sized paisley patterns. After being out of fashion for some time, such large motifs are now returning to favor thanks to a few particularly audacious designers like Kenzo, Versace, and Léonard. In a more classic vein, Hermès ties, inspired by their well-known square scarves, also belong to this category.

Underknots. Single motifs, carefully placed on the tie's face so that they appear only once the knot is tied, are relatively rare today. The design motif on an underknot is situated just below the knot or a bit lower down where the jacket lapels would cross. It can take on many forms including geometric figures, shields, and medallions. Silk weavers producing fabric with underknot designs must adopt the largest possible repeated pattern: since the motif appears on the tie only once, it is usually woven into the material at about twenty-seven-inch intervals. As woven silk ties are enjoying something of a renaissance, it would not be surprising if designs of this kind were to become fashionable once again.

Placement also plays an important role in certain all-over designs featuring repeated motifs which appear at specific locations on the tie. In a multi-colored repeated pattern featuring flowers, for example, it might be stipulated that red flowers should only appear in the center or on the edges. Whatever the case, all positioned or "engineered" motifs call for careful

An "all-over" design, on a Christian Lacroix tie (below).

A fine example of the large-scale fancy patterns that increasingly feature on today's ties. Hermès silk ties cut from their famous square scarves (right).

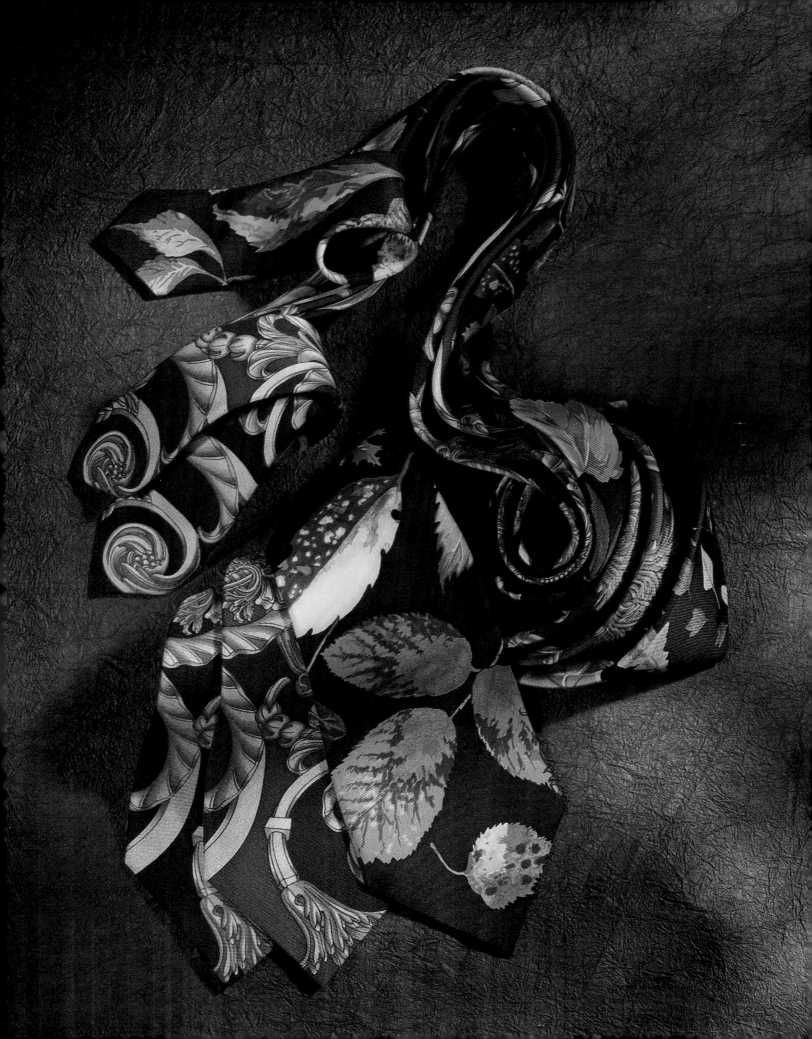

advance planning which takes into consideration the critical production phases of weaving, printing, cutting, and assembly of the tie.

CLASSIC DESIGNS

Seven to eight million ties are sold annually throughout the world, and it seems reasonable to estimate that new motifs developed in the same period are to be counted in the tens of thousands. But in the midst of this teeming invention certain motifs—which we might term classic—remain more or less constant, or return to favor in cycles. Some of these designs were first devised a century ago and are preserved in the form of fabric samples in the archives of weavers and printers. They need only catch a tie designer's eye to return to the forefront of the fashion scene. A great many ties are reeditions or slightly revised versions of these older motifs.

It is worth taking a moment to consider the phenomenon of the classic motif reappropriated from fabric-sample archives, which are an invaluable resource for designers. This is the case for Bianchini Ferier in Lyons, Mantero in Como, or David Evans in Kent, to mention only three of the most prestigious houses, but all manufacturers of tie fabric maintain such company archives. Some firms purchase stocks of samples from companies no longer in business, often at exorbitant prices. When tie designers decide to propose a new version of a classic motif to one of their clients—either *haute couture*, ready-to-wear, or department store—they often enjoy the considerable pleasure of losing themselves in large albums of old fabric samples. Here they can feast their eyes on every imaginable kind of geometric design, on thousands of stripe

and dot patterns, and on hundreds of paisleys. Once they have selected a pattern, they can ask the manufacturer to alter certain details, changing a color here or adding a shadow there. In certain design houses—Ratti, for example —where many old samples have been stored on computer disks, designers have the luxury of being able to instantaneously visualize the effect of their proposed changes. But even Ratti is not prepared to digitize its entire archival catalogue, which boasts of some 10,000 fabric designs.

Geometric designs. One need only flip through a few old department store catalogues to see that the first four-in-hands from the end of the last century often featured tiny all-over geometric motifs. In the 1920s Macclesfields started being widely worn in both Europe and the United States. Their diamonds, circles, squares, ovals, and rectangles can still be seen today—alone or in combination—on a great many ties and bow ties, but most often in enlarged, simplified, and brightly colored variants.

Among geometric motifs, diamond or lozenge shapes have always enjoyed a privileged status, doubtless because they harmonize particularly well with the pointed tips of current tie cuts. Striking designs such as checkerboard patterns can be obtained not only by printing, but also through a basket weave (a plain weave with two or more yarns woven together, resembling that of a basket). Because of their pure, beautiful lines and the wonderful results obtained by combining them, the classic geometric patterns transcend the ephemeral dictates of fashion.

All the traditional houses offer their clients a large range of classic motifs. A display cabinet at Hilditch & Key, London (left). These include small geometric designs, perennial motifs which already featured on ascots and four-in-hands at the end of the last century. A silk ascot woven in Como *circa* 1900 (below).

The archives of Lewin & Sons in London, a company specializing in club and regimental ties. In this album of samples collected since 1913, insignias are woven in a repeating pattern on a solid-color background, or between stripes, a characteristic of the style. Such ties, necessarily rare, since they could only be worn by members of the club or regiment concerned, are nowadays sought after by collectors (right).

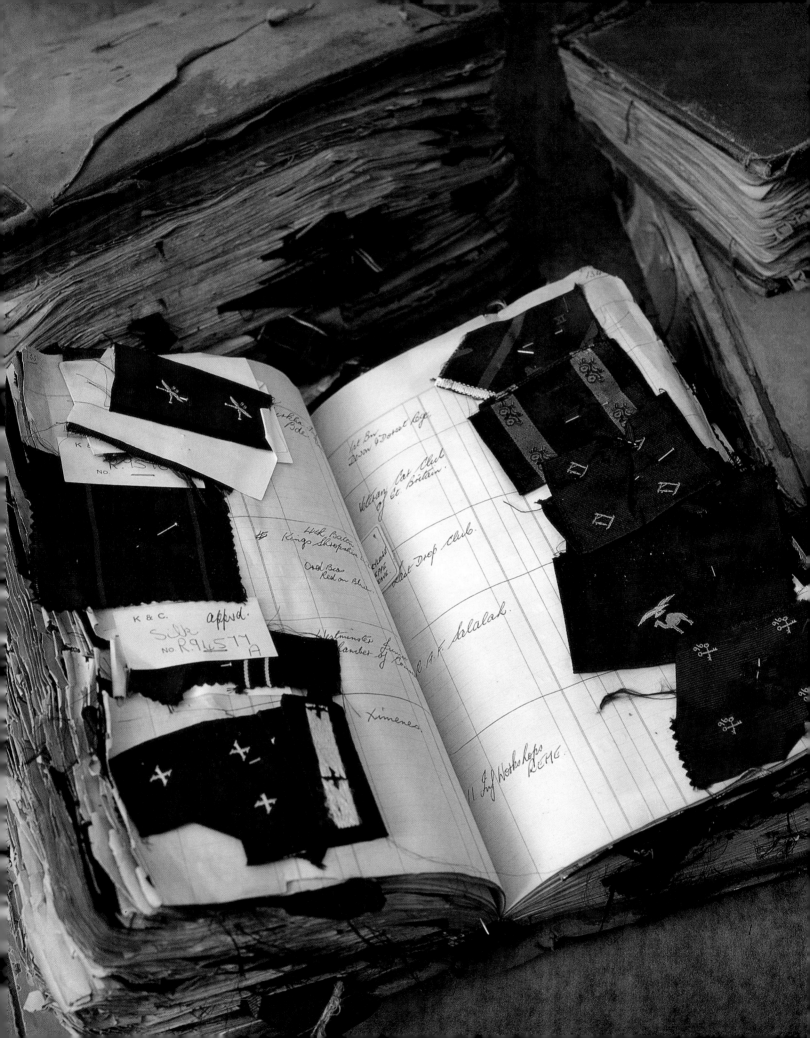

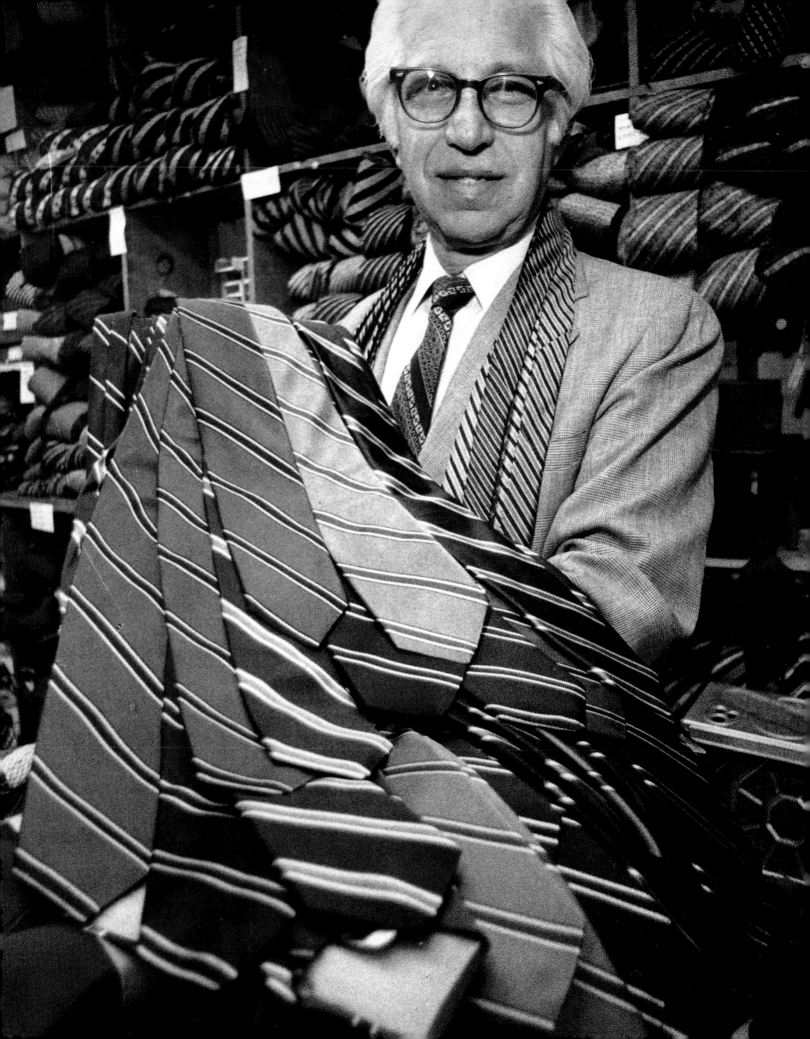

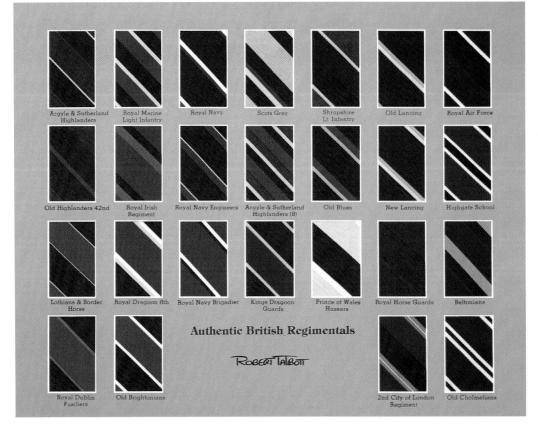

Argyle & Sutherland Highlanders | Royal Marine Light Infantry | Royal Navy | Scots Grey | Shropshire Lt. Infantry | Old Lancing | Royal Air Force

Old Highlanders 42nd | Royal Irish Regiment | Royal Navy Engineers | Argyle & Sutherland Highlanders (B) | Old Blues | New Lancing | Highgate School

Lothians & Border Horse | Royal Dragoon 8th | Royal Navy Brigadier | Kings Dragoon Guards | Prince of Wales Hussars | Royal Horse Guards | Beltonians

Authentic British Regimentals

ROBERT TALBOTT

Royal Dublin Fusiliers | Old Brightonians | 2nd City of London Regiment | Old Cholmelians

The Robert Talbott company of California has, since the 1950s, offered "authentic regimental ties" with the stripes reversed (right).

The tie which launched the international fashion for regimental ties: the Grenadier Guards tie popularized by the Duke of Windsor when he was Prince of Wales after the First World War. This one is made in woven silk by the London company Lewin & Sons (above).

The British regimental or club ties, also launched by the future Duke of Windsor involuntarily as a fashion after the First World War, are divided between authentic ones, reserved for members of the institution concerned, imitations, which can be worn by anyone, and the "genuine fakes," which are American copies of the authentic originals, but reversed with the stripes running from upper right to lower left. An authentic woven silk tie of the famous MCC—Marylebone Cricket Club (below). American "regimental" ties by Schreter & Sons, presented in 1981 by the company's chairman, A. Harvey Schreter (left-hand page).

Stripes. An unavoidable element of the classic sartorial lexicon, stripes, British by derivation, have been continuously used in tie designs since the 1920s. Earlier in history, however, striped clothing had been viewed consistently as the mark of something infamous or deserving of mockery. Until recently, stripes have been most widely associated with the uniforms of prison convicts. This use should be understood in the context of a tradition dating from the Middle Ages (at least), according to which, as explained by the author and medievalist Michel Pastoureau, there were numerous "individuals—both real and imaginary—whose clothing was striped because of some social, literary, or iconographic convention. In one way or another, they all happened to be excluded or marginalized—from Jews and heretics to jugglers and jesters."

Given this lineage, how did stripes manage to acquire their current prestige?

First, the success of stripes is explained by the fact that they are not, technically speaking, a motif: weaving them requires nothing more than changing the color of the thread on the loom. This means that they are cost effective, and it also accounts for their aura of simplicity. But

military dress, which has so often figured in the history of ties, has played a perhaps even more decisive role in this success. Colored standards, coats of arms, and uniforms have always served as identifying markers on the battlefield. England provides us with the earliest recorded instance of a particular color being used to distinguish one regiment from another: the day of James II's coronation (23 April 1685), each of the three participating squadrons of the equestrian Life Guards sported a ribbon of a different color—blue, green, or yellow—on their caps. Later, different English regiments wore cravats decorated with stripes in their regimental colors. This gave rise to what is still known as the regimental tie which is decorated with colored stripes on the diagonal, a feature inseparable from British uniform design. After returning to civilian life, British men occasionally wore the ties of their former regiments—and no other. When in 1919 the young Prince of Wales—the future Duke of Windsor—made his first visit to the United States, he was preceded by his reputation for elegance, which was a matter of contention in England. In his memoirs, *A Family Album*, the Duke wrote as follows about the trip:

"As a former officer of the Grenadier Guards, with whom I had served during the war, I had the right to wear this tie, and often did so. The fashion spotters were quick to notice this, and within a year of the Armistice the tie, with its broad blue and red stripes, had become the rage in America. It is still popular among Americans, who like to wear British regimental and old school ties, blissfully regardless of any right to do so." It was this trip, in fact, that initiated the universal taste for regimental ties, then for club ties and old school ties using the colors of colleges and universities such as Oxford and Cambridge. This indiscriminate appropriation often understandably irritates the British, for they hold that only members or former members of such institutions ought to wear them. In *A Moveable Feast*, Ernest Hemingway recounts how one day in 1925 he ran into Scott Fitzgerald in a Montparnasse bar—the Dingo—wearing the famous Grenadier Guards tie popularized by the Duke of Windsor: "I thought I ought to tell him about the tie, maybe, because they did have British in Paris and one might come into the Dingo—there were two there at the time—but then I thought the hell with it and I looked at him some more. It turned out later he had bought the tie in Rome."

Synonymous with British elegance, regimental ties have since conquered the world and are especially popular in the United States. Certain models have been particularly successful in America, like those featuring the colors of the University of London, graduates of Eton, and veterans of the 17th Lancers. However, there is something that clearly distinguishes the American copies from their models: the

diagonal stripes are drawn from upper right to lower left, the reverse of British usage. This curious switch might have resulted from the tendency of early American tie makers—unlike their European counterparts—to cut the fabric after having placed it face down.

It must be conceded that appropriating ties like this is in questionable taste. Certain designers therefore use stripe configurations similar to those of regiments and universities but which are in fact complete fabrications, lacking institutional affiliation.

Furthermore, those with a penchant for stripes need not limit themselves to regimentals. So-called heraldic ties—inspired by medieval coats of arms and featuring stripes arrayed either vertically or horizontally—first appeared in the 1950s. Rarer and a bit more exotic, mogadore stripes imitate those on Moroccan djellabas (Mogador is the previous name of the Moroccan port city now known as Essaouira): a broad band flanked by two narrower ones. There are many other options as well: bandolier stripes—diagonals which appear only once below the knot (panel stripes are their horizontal equivalent); ribbon stripes—isolated diagonal bands (single or separated from one another by the ground color); titan stripes—in the form of large chevrons; bengal stripes, which, evoking the tiger of the same name, are of equal width and in alternating light and dark colors; and shadow stripes, whose colors shade off into one another.

But today stripes are on the wane, at least outside the office, perhaps because their regimented patterns are at odds with a prevailing taste for whimsy. There is, however, one notable exception: woven ties with stripes of different weaves, which are characterized by rich textural and coloristic effects. Charvet has enjoyed great success with striped ties featuring three variations on rep weaves and allowing for a subtle variation of the two hues making up their color schemes.

Dots. Along with small geometric shapes, dots were among the first motifs to enliven ties. Edouard Manet, for example, posed proudly for Nadar wearing a dotted ascot around 1870. At

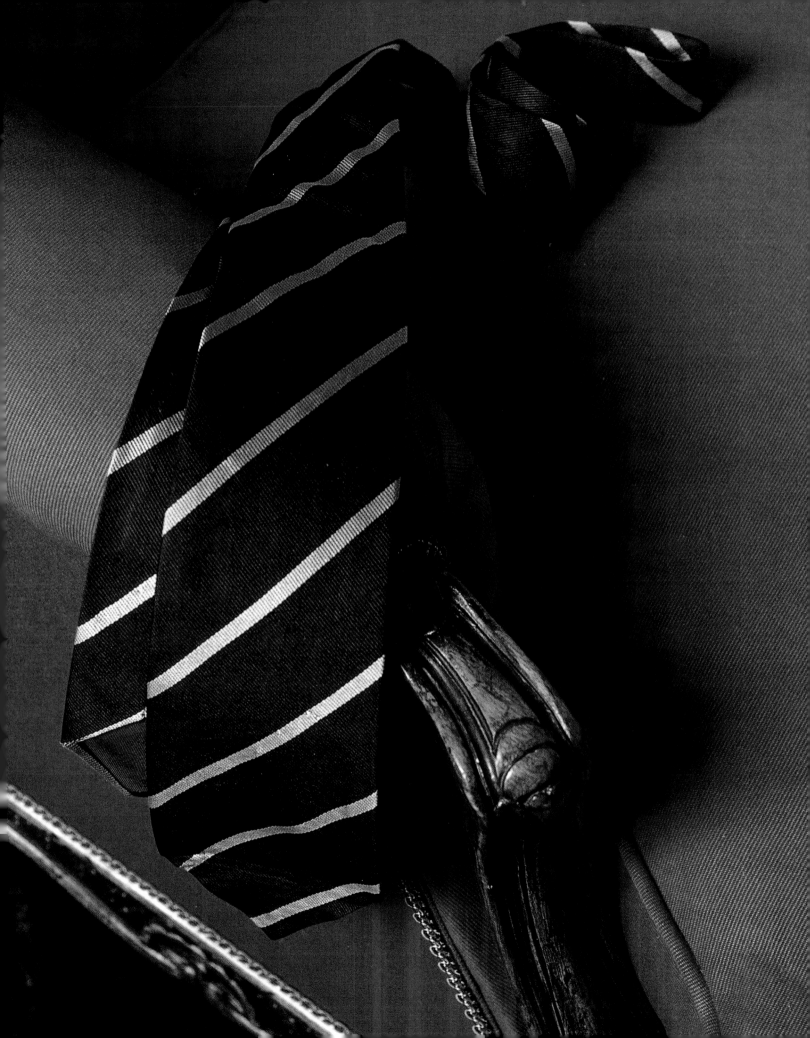

Among classic motifs, dots are the most common. They look wonderful on this ascot, worn, together with evening dress and top hat, by Clark Gable as he makes his Hollywood debut in the 1920s. At the age of 23 or 24, he is not yet wearing the slim mustache for which he was later to become famous (right).

that time a certain sense of chic, or perhaps a certain lack of taste, was required of any man daring to sport such neckwear, for such exuberant patterns had previously been the exclusive province of female dress. The metamorphosis of the dot into an acceptable male motif, and subsequently into a classic one (it was first widely seen on men's clothing in the 1920s), owes a considerable debt to Sir Thomas Lipton, who always wore a blue bow tie with white dots of his own design, an accessory soon dubbed the "Lipton." The ennoblement, so to speak, of the dot paralleled the social ascent of this small shopkeeper from Glasgow, born in 1850, who owned three hundred grocery stores by the age of forty, was emperor of tea and an English lord at fifty, and

who was an inveterate yachtsman throughout his life. Today the dot has acquired such classic status that professionals classify it as an "omnibus" design, a category also encompassing various stripes.

The dots on Lipton bow ties were, and remain, the size of confetti. Dots on this scale are the oldest and most classic variety. But Charvet has successfully revived a larger format about the size of a coin, current in the 1930s and known in French as *pastille* dots since they resemble small round candies of the same name. They are generally multicolored and executed in contrasting weaves. The polka dot is a third, intermediate size which in principle should be arrayed in a quincunx, an arrangement composed of four dots surrounding a fifth

Sir Thomas Lipton, the "emperor of tea" whose celebrated bow tie started a fashion for dots in the 1920s, would probably have appreciated this modern female version of his preferred neckwear. The model Gail Elliot, photographed by Albert Watson for the American magazine *L. A. Style* (right).

Like all other classic patterns, dots have their fanciful interpretations. Polka dots and *pastille* dots on Charvet woven silk ties (right).

80

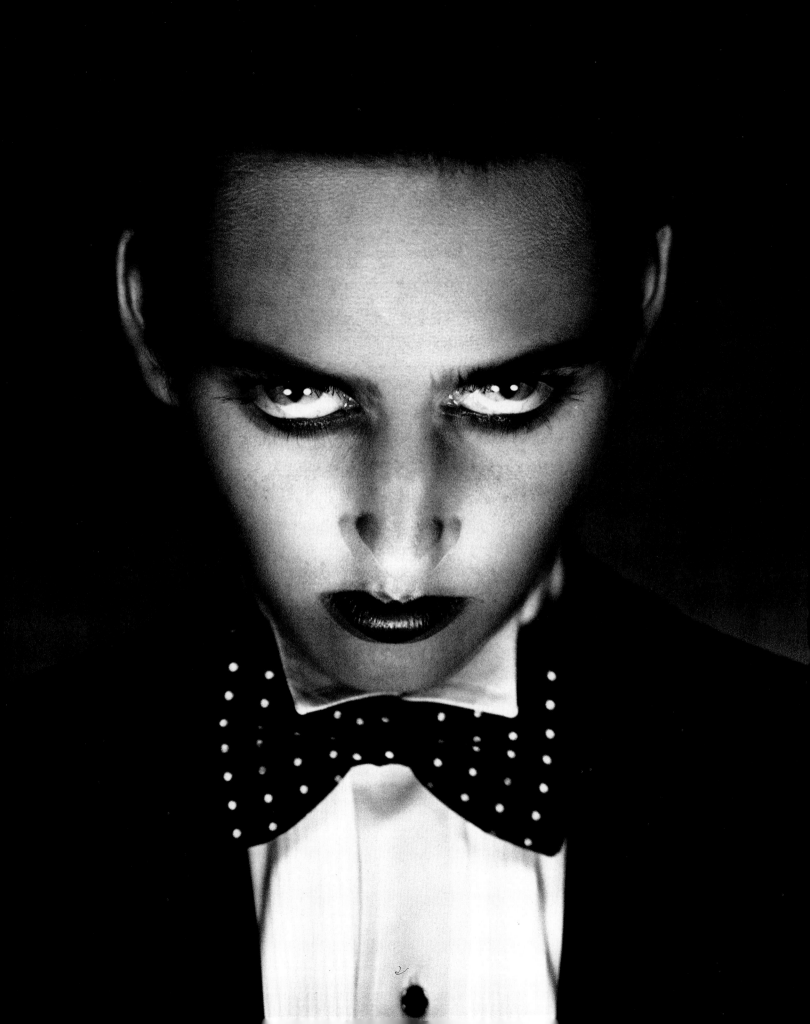

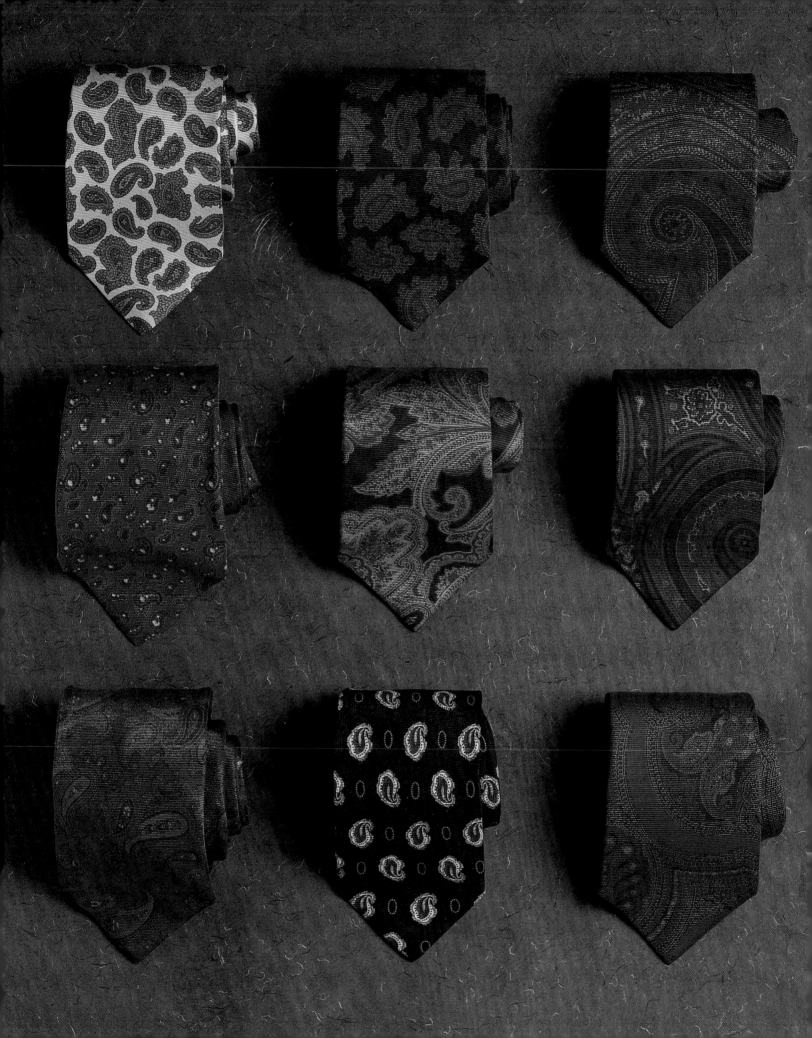

The silk-printing company David Evans is one of the great specialists of the paisley pattern, which is usually produced in madder. In these two silk samples for ties printed at Crayford in Kent, the deep, dense colors are perfectly suited to the subtlety of this age-old motif (above and center).

With its origins in Babylon more than three thousand years ago, the paisley pattern has the most fascinating history of all the classic motifs. In its principal form, a stylized palm shoot, it has been decorating ties since the 1930s. Paisley has been a constant source of inspiration for designers, and the variety of its interpretations is considerable. Etro ties in printed silk (left); Joseph Abboud tie in printed figured silk (center of bottom row).

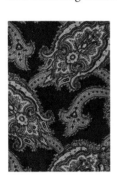

in their center. The dance from which polka dots derive their name is structured around the quincunx. Polka dots have been used on male neckwear for almost a century. Less classic ties can feature irregularly scattered dots of varying sizes. Of recent vintage, such designs have breathed new life into the motif. They appeal to the growing number of men favoring a blend of classicism and poetry.

Paisleys. Wearers of paisley ties, decorated with patterns whose dominant motifs take the form of drops or tears, are participants in a tradition extending thousands of years into the past. The origins of paisley, which enjoys ultra-classic status in the world of ties, date back to the ancient Babylonian civilization. Paisley is a stylized variation on the shape of young shoots of the date palm, then a powerful fertility symbol because it provided all the essentials for survival: food and drink, raw material for making useful objects, and wood for construction. Appearing on textiles, reliefs, and metalwork, this emblem of life spread throughout the Indo-European world and beyond, even leaving traces in Celtic art. Although it soon disappeared from the Greek and Roman worlds it continued to thrive on the Indian subcontinent, especially in the region of Kashmir. In this province's deep valleys in northern India, weavers—probably in the seventeenth century—started producing sumptuous wool shawls decorated with the paisley motif and combined with all sorts of vegetal forms. In the mid-eighteenth century the first cashmere scarves appeared in England, and soon thereafter they were also imported to other European countries by the East India Company. Their success with fashionable women was such that beginning in the 1780s manufacturers in Edinburgh, Paris, and Vienna began to produce variants with a European inflection. But it was in Paisley, Scotland—a small weaving town near Glasgow—that most of these scarves were

produced, and the motif came to be known by the town's name. Paisley in both woven and printed form has long been used as a decorative motif not only on scarves, but also on neckerchiefs, whether of pure silk or wool, or in blends of silk, wool, and cotton.

While single "drop" shapes were already used on the first four-in-hands, large, intricate paisley designs became widespread on ties only in the 1930s, when some were produced in a light twill fabric decorated with a type of paisley previously only used on scarves (which is why the French sometimes call them *motifs foulards*). In response to changing fashion, paisley is constantly being up-dated: hundreds of new paisley motifs make their appearance on ties every year. The motif provides rich opportunities for coloristic nuance and formal invention, but it also calls for complicated weaving techniques, and today's weavers generally limit themselves to simplified versions, sometimes using only single drops in repeating patterns. Paisley motifs now attain their full complexity only on printed ties. Two silk printers are universally admired for the beauty of their

In 1988, to show his confidence in his company's future, the American manufacturer Robert Talbott produced an advertisement using the founder's grandson, the young Robert Logan Talbott, wearing a tie decorated with a paisley motif, the symbol of life and longevity (below).

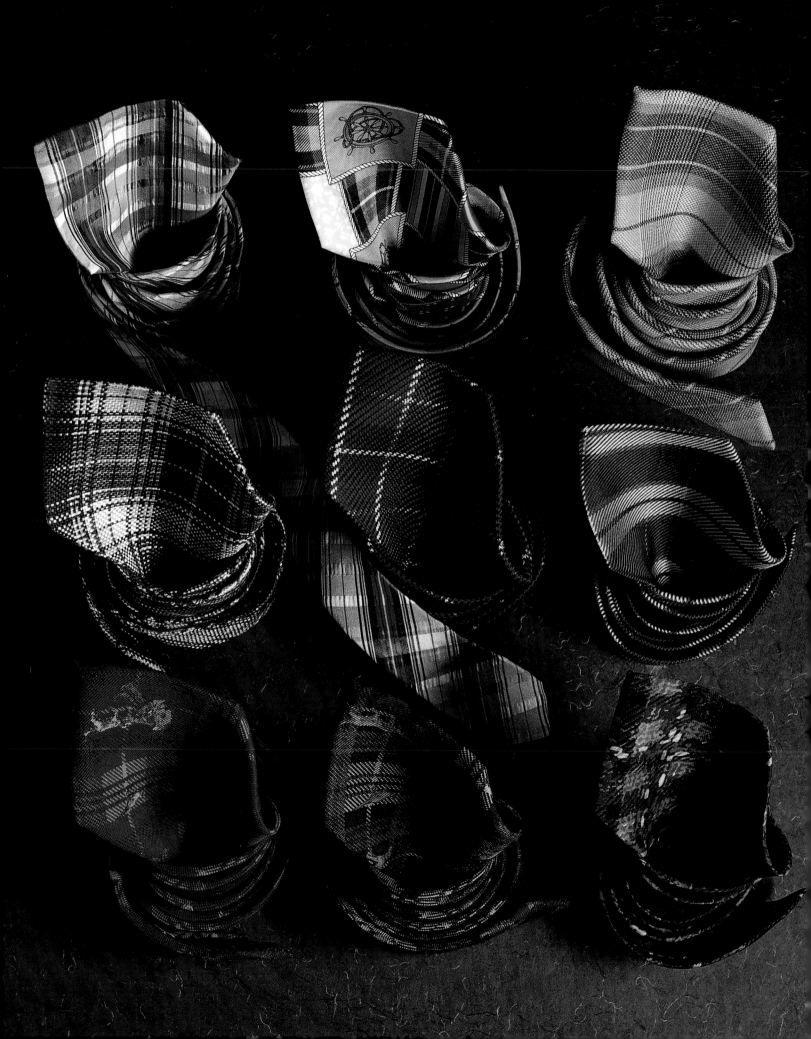

While in Scotland it is still possible to find ties decorated with the traditional clan tartans, most Scottish ties now originate in the fertile brains of designers, stimulated by the fine interplay of colors which plaid permits. Plaid ties (left-hand page, from left to right and top to bottom) by Robert Talbott, Richel, Ermenegildo Zegna, Etro, Charles Hill, Richel, Etro, Etro, and Richel.

paisleys: David Evans of England, specializing in classic versions, and the Italian firm Ratti, which favors more sophisticated forms and color schemes. This refinement is rooted in Antonio Ratti's affection for this motif, as can be seen in his magnificent collection of antique cashmere and paisley scarves.

Plaids. Frequently used on ties, plaids were originally worn only by members of the Scottish or Irish clan they represented. Most of the plaids developed by today's designers, however, are not affiliated with any clan and thus can be worn without fear of giving offence. Plaid ties survive all changes of fashion. They are often made of wool—in all likelihood because of the motif's association with kilts—and for some reason they are frequently worn by young boys. Recently there seems to have been a renewal of interest in plaids which have begun to appear on woven silk ties, often in combination with other motifs—in patchwork patterns, for example.

FIGURATIVE MOTIFS

Audacity and invention in tie design can be seen most clearly in that category of ties decorated with figurative motifs. Generally, members of three different professions collaborate in the production of such new motifs: the entity whose label is to appear on the tie (a shirt maker, a couturier, a ready-to-wear line, a department store chain, etc.); the tie designer (who devises the models for his client firms and often oversees the actual production process); and the fabric manufacturer. Each of these groups has designers who are entrusted with inventing new designs. Relations between the three can vary considerably: the initial impulse for a new motif can come from any one of the groups; this impulse then leads to creative exchanges between them. Freelance designers, who exhibit their prototypes to other professionals at trade shows, can also offer their creative services.

Sports and hunting. Another category of motifs with a British inflection that originally signified one's social status involves hunting and sporting themes. These are the most classic of all figurative motifs. They first entered wide use on ties at the beginning of the century, usually in small editions of refined all-over patterns. Hunting, fishing, and certain British sports such as golf, riding, and polo provided an excuse for

their devotees to wear small figures depicting related subjects: stirrups and saddles, horses, ducks, woodcocks and pheasants, fish, golf clubs, etc. This family of motifs would never have spread beyond Great Britain if Anglomania—a constant factor in male fashion—had not led to worldwide acceptation. Like the stripe configurations identified with regiments and British schools and universities, these motifs lost much of their original meaning when they crossed the Atlantic. In Chicago or Los Angeles one need not be a huntsman to sport a few grouses on one's tie.

As for France, it was Henri d'Origny, a passionate horse lover and a designer for Hermès, who released his celebrated equestrian motif designs on Hermès ties in the 1950s. But it was the intensifying Anglomania of the 1980s—best exemplified, perhaps, by America's Ralph Lauren and his numerous imitators—that inundated the world with polo players (Ralph Lauren's emblem), tiny ducks, and tennis rackets.

Animals. All animals not associated with sports and hunting are considered as novelty motifs. In the tie lexicon the term "novelty" refers to anything that is not classic but rather trendy and new—in a word, audacious. Archives

It was natural that their two traditional pastimes—hunting and sports—would feature as the principal figurative motifs on men's ties. They make an ideal accompaniment for sportswear outfits. Italian printed silk tie from the 1970s, preserved in the Krefeld Museum (above). Ascot tie in printed silk (left).

are of little use here: fabric manufacturers, tie makers, and couturiers all attempt to invent entirely new motifs. One of the iron laws of tie design is to create ties that are lighthearted in times of crisis, and serious in times of prosperity. This is why novelty designs are on the rise today—especially those featuring unusual animals, some of which are in the process of becoming classics. Since the beginning of the 1990s, repeating patterns featuring small animals have proliferated to such an extent that every known species must have had its moment, extinct species included. Before becoming a worldwide phenomenon, this zoological passion, from the mid 1980s on, was given free rein in Italy by Gucci and Ferragamo, and in France by Hermès. It took several years for Hermès to woo its classic-loving customers, but they finally succumbed to the turtles, storks, puppies with balloons, tiny birds, and squirrels invented by the Hermès designers. The two elephant motifs they devised—one spraying water from its trunk (1985), the other standing on its hind legs against a background of palm trees (1987)—immediately became objects of an infatuation which remains undiminished to this day: the firm has not reissued these designs, and the resulting scarcity has only further intensified the interest of collectors. For its regular clients, Hermès is willing to undertake a worldwide search for the odd example miraculously still in stock at one of its boutiques.

Why this craze? The rise of ecological awareness is certainly a factor. Another important reason is perhaps women's fondness for these cute little animals—they love seeing the charming creatures running down their husbands' chests. The fashion is now winding down in Paris, but it persists in the rest of Europe and the United States and has just taken hold in Asia.

Plants. Flower motifs have classic status when they are small scale and stylized, which is to say when they cast no doubt on the wearer's virility. Such flowers first appeared on male neckwear at the end of the nineteenth century, at the same time as leaf motifs. More exuberant and brightly colored flowers, however, enjoyed a first moment of glory in the 1940s in the United States, and a second one with the advent of the hippies in the 1960s. The latter's "flower children" took "peace and love" as their motto, embraced an emphatically feminized mode of male dress, and made flowers their emblem. No real hippies wore ties, of course, but many young, middle-class men decked themselves out with clothing from the celebrated boutiques on London's Carnaby Street, or their imitators—extravagant flowered ties figured prominently in such dress. Once this style went out of fashion, flower motifs entered a prolonged period of hibernation. But spring has come again! Flowers have returned to the scene. Hermès now sells ties decorated with veritable gardens of fruit and flowers, and several other tie makers are adding to the profusion with baroque designs.

Humorous motifs. Sports and hunting motifs were originally devised to appeal to specific groups of men and small animals were intended primarily to please women. Humorous motifs, on the other hand, are designed to raise a smile, usually by parodying classic motifs. In America such ties are often called "conversation starters" because their unusual designs can prompt dialogue and thus facilitate social interaction. Possibly useful information can also be conveyed: instead of shields or stirrups, a tie might feature dice—one of Gucci's most popular motifs in 1993—or playing cards, perhaps to indicate that the wearer considers himself more of a gambler than a sportsman. On the occasion of its 1993 centenary, Dunhill devised ties featuring its trademark specialties: watches, pipes, old automobile accessories like lamps, racing goggles, oil cans, etc. Tie enthusiasts more concerned about broadcasting their sense of humor than their social pretensions, however, will find a prodigious variety of motifs to satisfy them: bank notes, revolvers, Christmas trees, skulls, polar

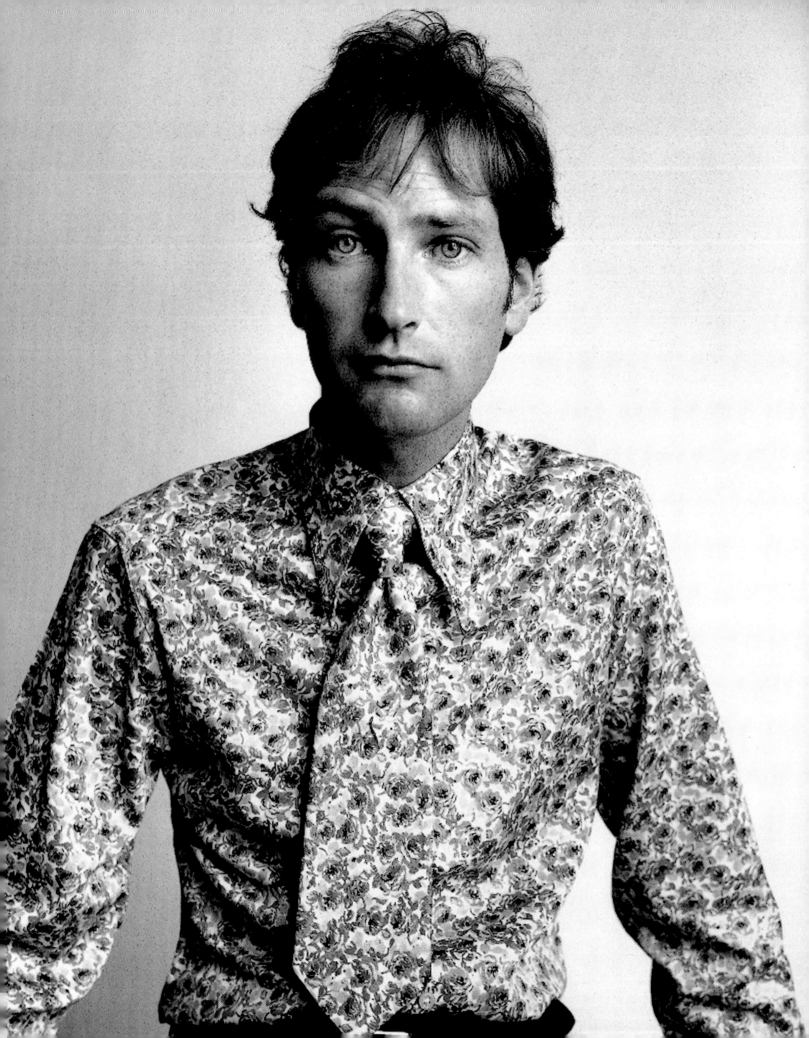

bears, and umbrellas are among the flood of tie images currently available to poke fun at the posturing of modern man. Even the most serious designers occasionally traffic in visual wit: in the 1940s Charvet sold ties decorated with postage stamps—the novelist Evelyn Waugh has his dandyish character Sebastian Flyte wear one in *Brideshead Revisited*. Today the first prize for humor must go to the French designer Claude Montana who creates disturbing trompe-l'œil designs that give the impression of torn silk or ironing burns on the tie.

Gag ties. It does not take all that much to transform a smile into a burst of laughter, but it does require a certain knack. Some designers —especially Americans—revel in the challenge. In August of 1950, a columnist in the eminently respectable magazine *Adam* wrote: "The American fantasy for such items knows no bounds. I thought I had seen everything in this line, but not so! I almost fell over backwards when I first caught sight of a tie in gilt lamé decorated with a green palm tree and a nude woman carrying a lamp, the better to find a man. . . . And the lamp was equipped with a working light bulb!" In the same vein of tomfoolery, Milwaukee-based

A trompe l'oeil tie by the designer Claude Montana. His creations are capable of seducing even sworn enemies of the tie (above).

The materials used may also give cause for laughter: metal, plastic, paper, and even mink have been employed (left).

Novelty ties are still the most peaceable and socially acceptable means for men to express their need for a little craziness. Some psychologists go so far as to say that it might be dangerous never to wear one. The Art of Ties, Fabien Ouaki collection (left and above).

88

designer Ralph Marlin sells fish ties whose fronts depict disconcertingly realistic trout, flounder, and even piranhas. There are also ties with transparent envelopes into which various figurines have been inserted. It should be noted that motifs are not the only vehicles for such gags: Jean-Paul Gaultier has proposed ties bearing cigar rings which he has had "cured" in Havana! And we should not neglect to mention those irresistible models equipped with hidden compartments making it possible to spray one's neighbor with water.

Artistic ties. The long-standing collaboration between art and ties assumes two forms. The rarest arises when a painter more or less spontaneously uses a tie or a piece of fabric as a support for his art, usually with commercial ends in view. Picasso, who almost never wore them, once found an abandoned tie in a closet, painted it blue, and then sold it. On a more industrial scale, in the 1940s Salvador Dali created a complete line of ties featuring large dream-like shapes in a surrealist idiom, and signed them as if they were paintings. Between 1912 and 1928, Raoul Dufy devised several thousand designs (with flowers, elephants, views of Paris, etc.) for the Lyons silk manufacturer Bianchini Ferier, some of which are still available on neckties today—as are Sonia Delaunay's alphabet motif and Jean Cocteau's goose quill design, both of which were originally created for use on ties.

The second sort of collaboration—by far the most frequent, having been a constant since the inception of ties—arises when designers appropriate ideas from painting or the decorative arts in devising their own models. Every tie maker and fabric manufacturer must have a library of art books. The one in Ratti's offices, in Como, boasts of several hundred volumes. And when I recently visited Jean-Claude Colban in Charvet's offices, a magnificent volume on the San Marco mosaics in Venice was lying open on his desk.

The phenomenon became especially pronounced in certain American ties of the 1940s: some featured large geometric motifs inspired by Art Deco ornamentation or abstract-expressionist painting, while others featured shapes and symbols derived from Aztec, Indian, Egyptian, or Japanese artifacts. In subsequent years tie makers have sought inspiration in Gothic art, oriental carpets, the Italian Renaissance, and French Impressionist painting, among others. The Turkish designer Vakko has proposed a beautiful line dubbed the "Art Collection" which is based on motifs taken from the rich Ottoman decorative arts tradition: geometric mosaics and vegetal patterns redolent of Sulieman the Magnificent's sumptuous palaces, motifs inspired by Iznik pottery, designs featuring lotus and peony blossoms characteristic of the Saz style, and so on. Givenchy's 1995 spring–summer collection features motifs cribbed from Etruscan mosaics, the Lascaux caves, and paintings by the Nabis.

As a general rule, designers prefer to focus on small details of an extant work, which they then use in repeating patterns. But some audacious ties reproduce large segments or even entire works: there is nothing like the Mona Lisa's smile to brighten up a gray winter day. And there can be no better way to express one's love of culture: the increasing success of this kind of tie runs parallel to an increasing taste for museum-going. In fact, gift shops of some large museums sell ties linked to collections and exhibitions. Since the extraordinary success of the recent Toulouse-Lautrec show, the Louvre has consistently carried ties decorated with his monogram. The Metropolitan Museum in New York sells ties linked to the traveling Tutankhamen exhibition as well as its oriental carpet holdings. The Rodin Museum in Paris sells a beautiful tie on which Rodin's celebrated *Thinker* meditates, comfortably ensconced

At the Guy Savoy restaurant in Paris, waiters, maîtres d'hôtel and wine stewards all dress in black. But they wear brightly colored ties, as if in homage to the culinary image of this establishment, which is noted for both its classicism and its inventiveness. A wine steward, and his Big Ben Club tie in printed figured silk (above).

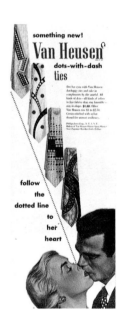

The American "bold look" of the 1940s gave rise to some audacious ties, and to advertisements that were equally creative (above and left).

between ribbon stripes set against a bronze-green background.

American ties of the 1940s. Mixing all kinds of themes and images, the crazy American ties of the 1940s constitute a class apart. Although they date from a single decade and originate from a single continent, they have nonetheless enjoyed considerable success. In 1947 the magazine Esquire coined the phrase "bold-look ties" to characterize them. The Second World War was again partly responsible for this reckless fantasy. First, consistent with the law already cited—that in economically depressed times, people seek out cheerful neckties—it was only natural that ties be employed to help alleviate the anguish felt by American soldiers and their families. And second, once Europe was convulsed by war, American tie makers were on their own—deprived of their classic British suppliers and models. They delighted in their new-found independence. Rayon and dacron replaced silk. Regimentals were banished in favor of ties featuring motifs of enormous diversity: almost anything was considered fair game, provided it had the requisite gaiety and brilliant coloring.

Initially large geometric patterns dominated the field (often inspired by cubism or the Indian and African decorative-arts vocabularies), although characteristic Art Deco vegetal designs were also used. Then came a flood of flamboyant, exotic imagery such as Hawaiian beaches with palm trees, Aztec pyramids, and the snows of Kilimanjaro. The staples of America's national iconography were also widely used: covered wagons, rodeos, gold prospectors, the first railroads, oil wells, skyscrapers, and pink convertibles. There was much sympathy with bootleggers during prohibition—so even mug shots of gangsters were prominently featured! Certain ties bore abstract designs whose colors were suggestive of some indefinable dish—they were dubbed "scrambled-egg" ties.

Since the 1920s ties and art have often come together. Sometimes an artist creates a motif especially for a tie, but more often tie designers borrow motifs from existing works of art. Whether ancient or contemporary, paintings and artifacts are a continuing source of inspiration for tie motifs. Byblos tie in figured printed silk, after Magritte (above); a unique tie model embroidered in point de Kiev, after Malevich (below); Flammarion 4 tie with a specially created motif by Arman (right).

Bold-look ties were the delight of collectors —including Dany Kaye and Frank Sinatra—and made the reputation of certain designers. Those in greatest demand were of course the rarest, and most of these were painted by hand. The most celebrated creator of such ties was Countess Mara who produced models in limited editions of 1,800 or less, each one signed with her initials. She is said to have come up with the quip: "Tell a man you like his tie, and you'll see his personality open up like a flower."

Bold-look ties found a limited secondary market in Europe just after the war, but they disappeared altogether in the early 1950s. Thanks in part to the current economic crisis they are now making a comeback in a somewhat watered-down form in Europe, and in the United States with all their characteristic exuberance—as can be seen in the line of Nicole Miller, for example.

Many ties elude easy classification. Ties can feature several motifs—flowers arranged between stripes, for example or patchwork ties, both of which are now fashionable. Half-and-half or double-life ties devised by Sulka are actually two ties in one: the two strips are of equal width, each one bearing a different design. Reversibles are a great specialty of the Italian designer Mila Schon. Terrace motifs are formed by interlocking z's. Bird eyes appear as clouds of tiny specks suggesting caviar. A thousand pages would be insufficient to list the possibilities. And even such a long list could not encompass all the variations workable on a given motif by changing the weave. Nor could it communicate the degree to which a motif's success is determined by its color scheme. For the right colors can temper the audacity of an extravagant design, just as they can liven up a more classic one. What is more, by varying the colors that are used, the same model can be given many different casts, many different personalities. Finally, any tie maker will tell you that a beautiful color scheme can save a poor design, but never the other way around. It is subtleties like this that make the world of ties so wonderfully fascinating.

Between 1912 and 1928, the painter Raoul Dufy created furnishing fabrics for the Lyons silk manufacturer Bianchini Férier. Flammarion 4 designers are now using some of the motifs created during that period on their printed silk ties (right).

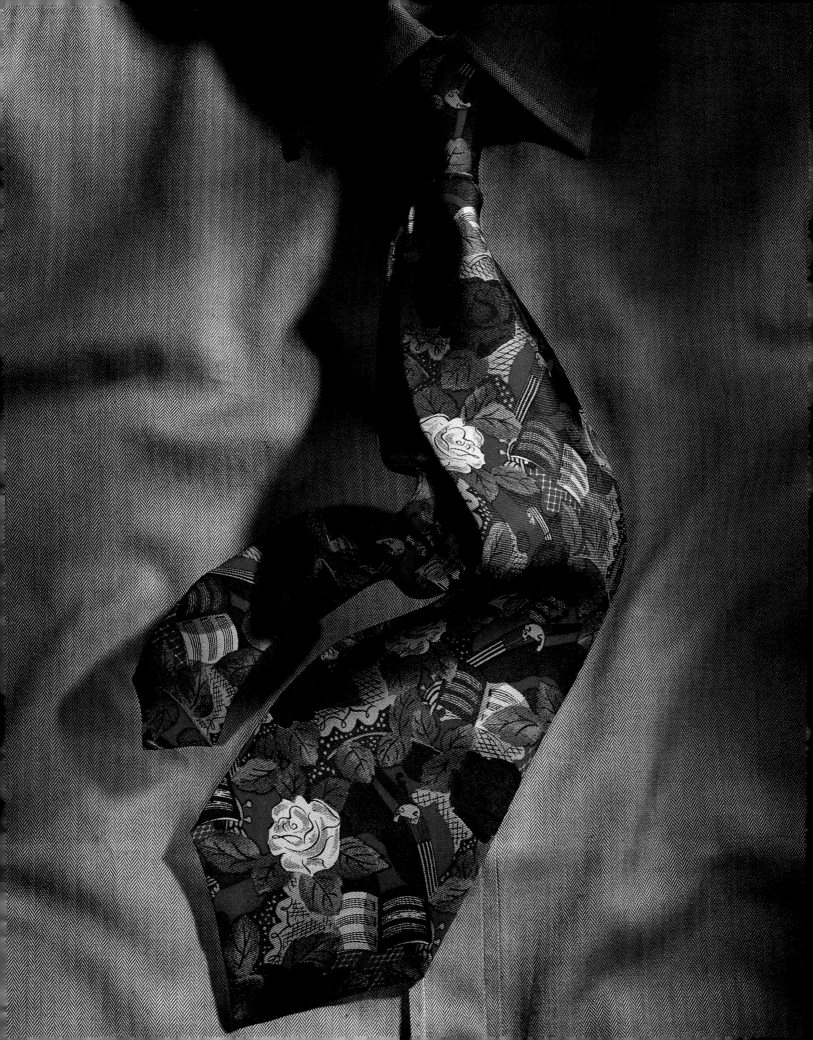

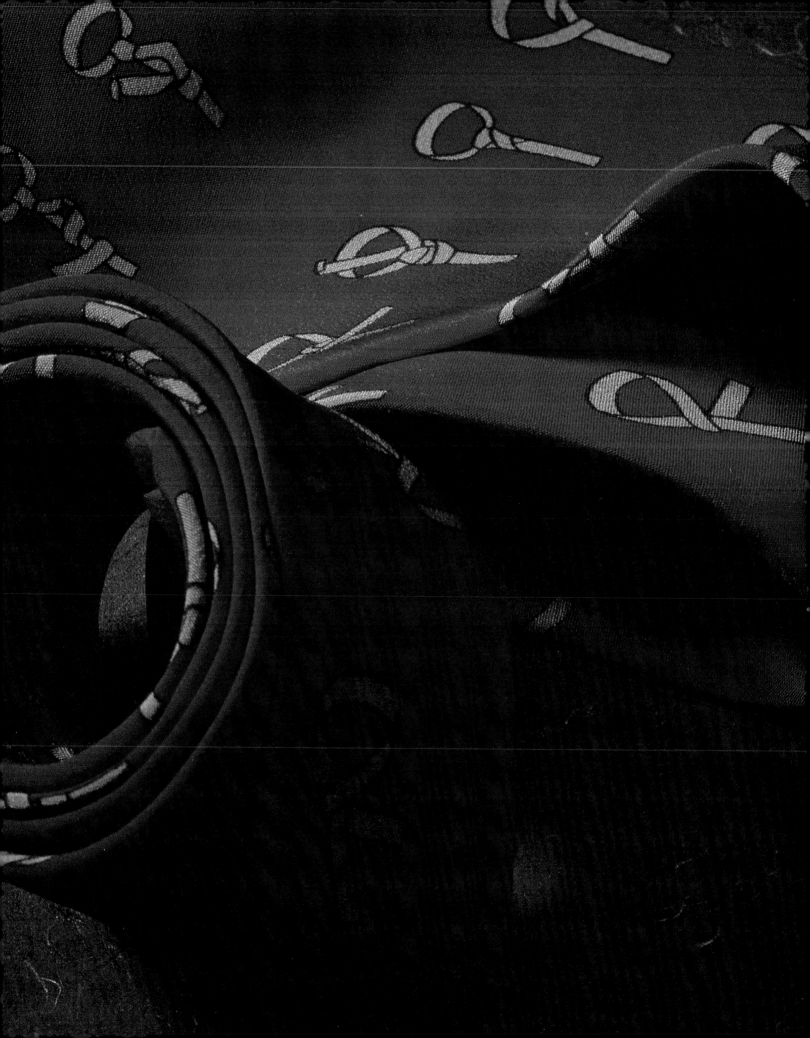

TYING
THE
KNOT

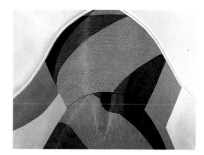

If the 600 million men worldwide currently wearing knotted ties could retain only one thing from this book (which I hope many of them will be inclined to read!), I'd like it to be an enhanced sense of the symbolic, magical, and mythological value in the act of knotting a tie. To knot a tie is, in essence, to perform an action whose origins are lost in the mists of time, but which has long been attributed symbolic significance. In human symbolism, knots represent union, marriage, and fertility, and thus life. "A holy knot will unite us tomorrow," Léonor tells Ariste in Molière's *School for Husbands.* The *ankh*—also known as the "knot of Isis"—which bears a curious resemblance to late seventeenth-century male neckwear, was regarded by ancient Egyptians as a symbol of life and eternity. In Japan, knotting is an art every bit as prestigious as flower arranging. The first two Japanese divinities to unite and thereby to give birth to the world are called *Musubi*, which literally means "knotters" or "knotted." Tying one's tie, then, is not as insignificant as it may seem. Not only is it a cru-

cial factor in determining the wearer's elegance and seductive allure, it is also charged with magic and historical significance. Whether we like it or not, it is a sacred act which may indeed protect us from harm. Given this tradition, we should at least attempt to perform it with the requisite skill.

But what knot are we to use? In absolute terms there are some 4,000 different knots. In a book on certain aspects of ties, two Italian experts, Davide Mosconi and Ricardo Villarosa, have counted *188 Ways to Tie One's Tie.* While this may seem like quite a lot, it is not really so many, if we bear in mind that, theoretically, there is nothing to prevent us from inventing a new tie knot every day. Of the 3,800 knots inventoried by the specialist in the field, Clifford W. Ashley, a good thousand of them would probably be viable for use under a shirt collar. If we consider that in practice no more than three or four knots are in general use 188 is actually quite a large number. Contemporary time constraints and the narrow parameters of acceptable professional dress can be cited as reasons for this.

"Brummell would then settle himself in front of his mirror, with his chin pointing in the air, and accompanying his actions with slight movements of his jaw, he would reduce his necktie to suitable proportions, while at the same time arranging its folds." This little scene, described by Brummell's biographer, William Jesse, is today repeated several million times a day all across the planet. President Vaclav Havel at home on 2 February 1993, the day of his inauguration (left).

Father's Day is always a good day for fathers, children, and tie salesmen. A 1960s poster by Jean Effel for the Fédération française de la cravate (below).

Even in the first half of the nineteenth century, a veritable golden age during which a certain Stefano Demarelli gave tie-knotting lessons in Paris, the pseudo-baron de l'Empesé enumerated no more than fourteen principal knots and eighteen derivations. Admittedly, his book was based on a rather parsimonious English treatise.

Three years after the 1827 publication of *L'Art de mettre sa cravate*, the more complete *L'Art de la toilette* appeared, which described seventy-two different knots. "It is the dandy's task to imagine the seventy-third," wrote Roger Kempf in his *Dandies, Baudelaire et Cie.* Today's dandies, however, make their mark with colors, and motifs, and the way in which their ties coordinate with their suits and shirts. Three or four despotic knots now hold sway over the entire world, and affecting to wear a fifth now smacks of the self-consciously bizarre. But it is still possible to diverge from the norm without seeming to dress like a clown.

Whether classic or unusual, the essential thing about a knot is the care and attention with which it is executed. Nothing is more vexing than a careless and sloppy knot which reflects badly on the wearer and abuses the poor defenseless tie. Let us try to avoid behaving like those men vilified by the anonymous author—perhaps Balzac—of the *Physiologie de la toilette*, "who wear cravats without feeling them, without understanding them, who throw a piece of fabric around their necks each morning as if it were rope; then spend the day walking, eating, tending to their affairs, and in the evening go to bed and sleep soundly, free of remorse, perfectly satisfied with themselves, just as though their cravat had been flawless."

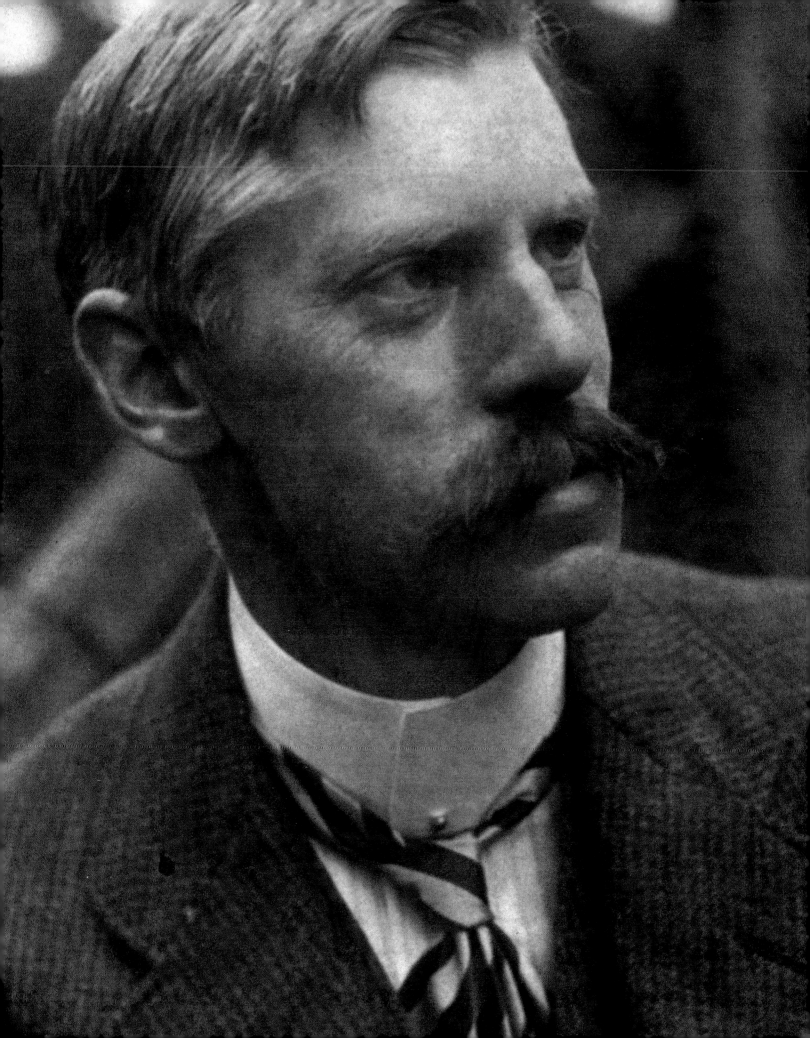

THE FOUR-IN-HAND

Three types of neckties are currently in use: the modern version of the four-in-hand, the bow tie, and the ascot.

Each has its own history and set of forms. Since its inception circa 1870, the four-in-hand, today's most widely worn style, has been associated with sports and virility, with movement and speed, as suggested by its alternative English names, the sailor or yachting knot. The four-in-hand is eminently practical as sportswear because it does not come loose, it is more masculine than the gracious bow tie, and it can be quickly knotted. Marked by rapid technological and industrial advances, the modern world has fostered the emergence of a new kind of professional: the man in a hurry who works long hours and exercises regularly. And this new creature seized upon the four-in-hand with such enthusiasm that half a century

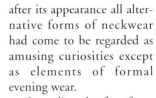

after its appearance all alternative forms of neckwear had come to be regarded as amusing curiosities except as elements of formal evening wear.

In reality, the first four-in-hands had nothing in common with modern ties except the knot itself, which is easy to execute and does not come undone. These models were made from strips of fabric intended for bow ties, and were much wider than those worn today. They were also shorter than we are now used to, extending no lower than the sternum, because of vests, which were standard wear. We have already seen how the principal drawback of the four-in-hand—the havoc this tight knot wreaks on the material—prompted the American Jesse Langsdorf to devise the modern tie in the 1920s. Cut on the bias and sewn from three segments of fabric, these early models were of more or less the same dimensions as we are accustomed to today:

A four-in-hand, together with a high turned-down collar (sometimes a stiff collar) and vest: this was the town dress of our great-grandfathers, up until the 1930s. An elegant young man, *circa* 1900 (left).

The main point in common between the nineteenth-century four-in-hand and our modern tie is the knot, which is directly inspired by a sailor's knot. Hence its alternative name: the sailor-knot tie. Extremely sober, and without a bow, it was first adopted by sporting types and men of action. Alfred Dunhill, the founder of an empire that had its origins in horses and cars, photographed at the turn of the century by Cecil Beaton (left). The Dunhill company, which celebrated its centenary in 1993, presents a collection of some hundred ties, in woven or printed silk, each season.

Since it was more or less standard, allowing for few variations, the four-in-hand tie was soon being sold ready-tied. Catalogues of the major department stores of the time indicated which ties were ready-tied. Late nineteenth-century catalogue for the Grands Magasins du Louvre, offering ties "to knot oneself" (right). English four-in-hands of the 1920s (far right).

A late nineteenth-century four-in-hand: its convenience and its sobriety were the source of its success (above).

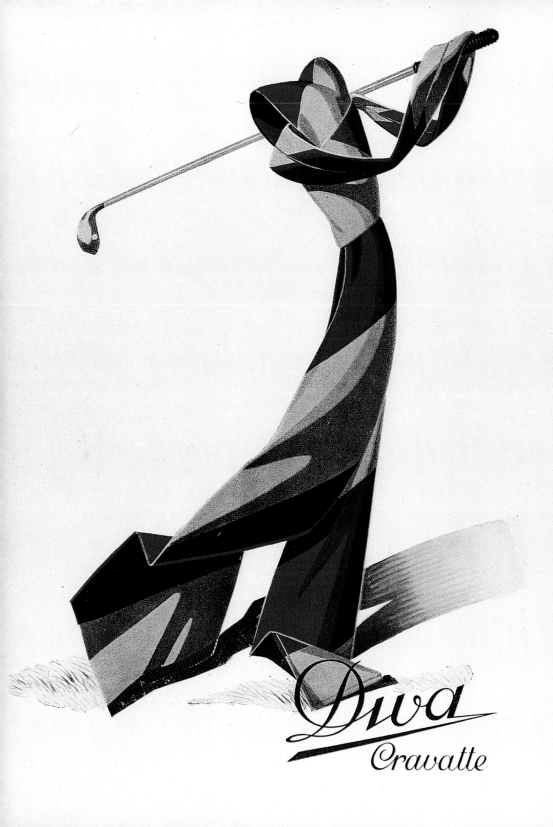

Diva

Cravatte

Invented by an American tie-maker, Jesse Langsdorf, today's four-in-hand began to become popular in the 1930s. Its principal characteristics were a broad end and a narrow end, both with pointed extremities, a neck band, an interlining, and the fact that the fabric was cut across the bias. These characteristics have remained unchanged. An advertisement for the Italian Diva tie in 1950 (left).

At the end of the 1960s, tie-makers felt under threat, because the young were becoming disaffected with ties. They attempted to rejuvenate the tie's image by making it brighter and cheekier, and by employing up-to-date marketing techniques. A poster for "Tie Night" a promotional event organized in May 1970 by the Fédération française de la cravate (above).

from 2 to 3 inches across at their widest point (the current average is 3 inches) and some 55 inches long, sufficient to reach the belt of a man of average height.

Some designers have altered these dimensions over the years, even proposing completely new shapes in hopes of catching the public's fancy. The styles of the1950s—marked by the emergence of rock-and-roll and an explosive increase in the number of dress-conscious urban youths—were characterized by narrow ties with squared ends, a style probably launched by England's Teddy boys. But these postwar rebels, who mockingly appropriated the style of Edwardian suit associated with Savile Row (the London street famed for its tailors and considered the prime emblem of British sartorial conservatism), were most partial to bow ties, which will be discussed later. In any event, these narrow ties became quite popular and continued to be worn until the social and political upheavals of the 1960s, which saw the emergence of a new style of dress associated with hippies. This development threw everything back into question, and its "revolutionary" agenda prompted two different reactions relating to ties. The most pervasive was also the most radical: because ties were standard wear, and because they symbolized middle-class convention, in certain circles ties were simply banned. In cold weather, wool turtlenecks and Indian scarves were worn instead. The other reaction was more moderate: given that the prevailing format was a narrow one, many decided it would be an appropriately "rebellious" gesture to wear really wide ties. Credit for having invented this wide four-in-hand usually goes to the iconoclastic bard of London hippiedom, Michael Fish, who in 1965 inundated Savile Row (more precisely, Turnbull & Asser on Jermyn Street) with Indian silks and "kipper"

ties before opening his own shop, Mr. Fish, on Clifford Street in 1966. His clients included the likes of Mick Jagger, the Beatles, Lord Snowdon, and actor Terence Stamp. A few months later, but in a very different spirit, the American Ralph Lauren launched his Polo line (predicated on the appeal of a certain rugged-American look), which included his unusually broad ties, which were more than four inches across. Wide, big-knotted ties disappeared from the scene at the same time as hippies, acid rock, and bell-bottoms in the late 1970s.

Since its invention by Jesse Langsdorf, revisions of the modern four-in-hand have been devised that are far subtler and much more sophisticated than the kipper tie, a few of which even today's dress-conscious men might feel comfortable wearing. Among them are the split

The wide tie—from five to six inches across—that became fashionable in the 1960s and 1970s was launched in London by the designer Michael Fish, and shortly afterwards was taken up in Paris by Pierre Cardin. Nicknamed the "kipper" tie by its inventor, it was often decorated with flowery or psychedelic patterns, although occasionally it had more sober motifs. The singer Adamo on the cover of Salut Les Copains in February 1967 (left); English kipper ties from the 1970s, in printed silk (below).

En toutes saisons les cravates de Twill de
SALEZA

Given that it seems ideal for all occasions, the modern four-in-hand has few variants, and such as there are have tended not to last. However some of them deserved a better fate—for example, the split tie, invented by the Saleza company in 1955. An advertisement for Saleza ties dating from 1948 (above). Another exception is the "Fourtie," a reversible tie with four separate motifs, which the Dutch company Chapon & Haar has been taking legal steps to protect since 1988 (right).

or vented tie and the pleated tie. Created in 1955 by the Parisian Saleza, the split tie has a vent running down the length of the principal face rather like those on the backs of some sports jackets. The interior is lined with fabric of a contrasting color, creating a kind of vertical stripe effect.

The pleated tie is somewhat reminiscent of the jabot and was invented by a Berlin designer in 1951. Here the silk is folded over repeatedly like a fan so that five bands are visible on the tie's face. Both its cost and its inhospitability to classic motifs (dots excepted) have limited its appeal. Mention should also be made of a tie model that marvelously complements the narrow jacket sleeves and pants legs that were fashionable in the 1950s: the drop-line tie, which instead of widening becomes slightly narrower toward the bottom, its broadest point being just below the knot. This odd design was introduced by the Swedish designer Amanda Christensen in 1955 and though it was initally well received, its success proved short-lived.

Some designers with an acute sense of the ridiculous have devised alternative models that poke fun at traditional ties: Angelo Tarlazzi recently proposed a "shrunken" version extending no lower than the sternum (rather like early four-in-hands), while the Spanish designer Gene Cabaleiro tries to persuade his clients to wear reversible ties with undulating edges and eccen-

tric motifs. But these isolated efforts are more like practical jokes than serious attempts to overthrow tradition. In the end, is not caricature a form of flattery?

As we have just seen, the four-in-hand tie, whose basic design was set some seventy years ago, remains more or less a prisoner of its own classic status. It is as though its form has been fixed once and for all and every attempt to change it is doomed in advance. But some variety remains, thanks to the many ways in which it can be knotted. The final appearance of any knot is a function not only of its form but also of the tie's width. In addition to the traditional model and in order to increase sales, some makers issue what are known as bottle-shaped ties. These models are cut narrower at the point where the tie is to be knotted, resulting in smaller, tighter knots. Bottle-shaped ties were also used when voluminous knots were fashionable, but their narrow segments were higher, at the collar, widening again at the level of the knot. One should take care to distinguish between low–bottle-shaped ties, for small knots, and high–bottle-shaped ties, now out of fashion, for large knots. Sticklers can also opt for the half–bottle-shaped, which produces precisely the same effect but to a lesser degree.

How does one tie a four-in-hand? The knot is the most important part of the four-in-hand, for its ends are often hidden behind a jacket or vest. It offers the only true means of imposing one's individual stamp—for a tie's motifs and design are ultimately the signature of the designer and manufacturer. So it is crucial that the knot be both well-chosen and properly executed: in the case of error only the wearer, or perhaps his wife, can be held responsible for the walking disaster that is a poorly tied or

Even more spectacular, other variants are the work of creators eager to ban once and for all the conventional aspect of the tie. Their efforts prove that in material matters there is always room for invention. Reversible and wavy-edged ties, by the Spanish couturier Gene Cabaleiro (left); Thierry Mugler tie in Shantung silk, reversible and double-faced, with oblique ends, from his 1987 collection (right).

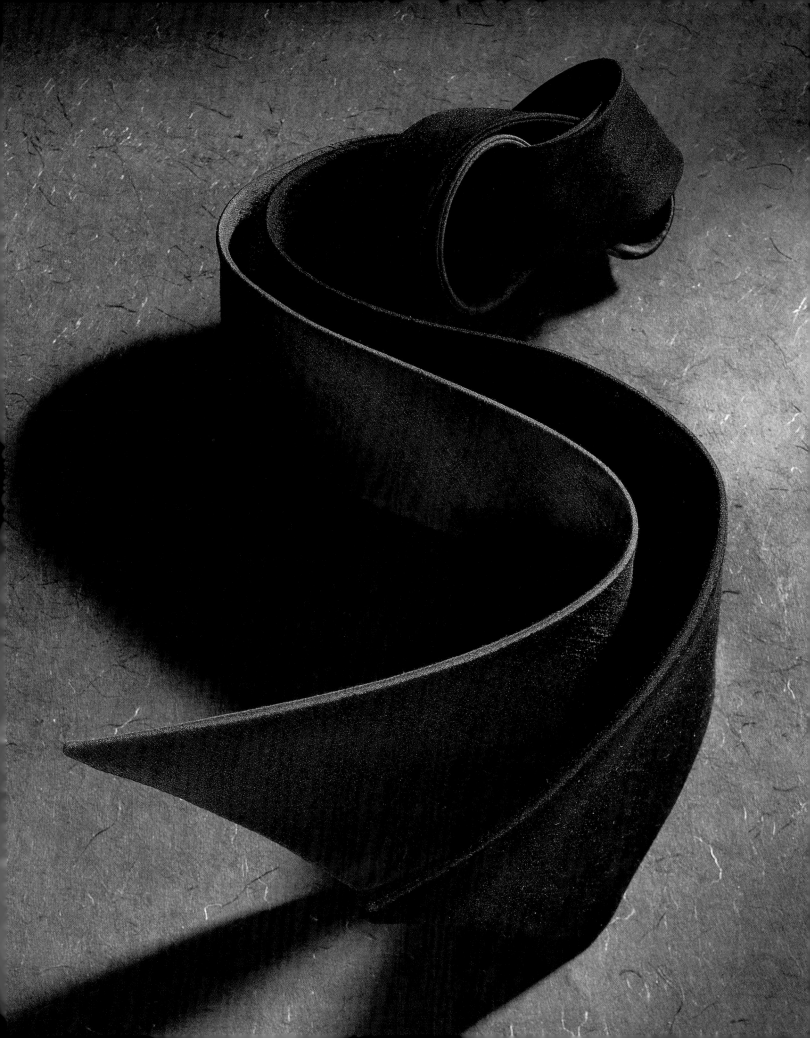

inappropriate knot. But there's no need to panic: like all more-or-less agreeable human activities, with a little practice an attractive four-in-hand can be executed in a flash.

Not every knot has a universally accepted name. On the following pages I will be using the names and terms which are most widespread or which seem the most readily understandable.

The four-in-hand proper. This is the knot that is first taught to little boys in tie-wearing countries, and the one they inevitably associate with their initiation into the world of men. Unfortunately, they frequently never learn any others. This knot's principal advantage is its suitability for almost all tie models and shirt collars. Inspired by a sailor knot, it is simple to execute, solid, and easy to loosen. First arrange the tie so that the narrow end is just above the belt, with the wide end extending about ten inches farther down (an estimate, variable according to the tie's length and the physical characteristics of the wearer). If right-handed, place the wide end on the right; if left-handed, vice versa. This principle of left versus right holds for all tie knots. The next step is child's play (see illustration p. 163).

This knot, like all those for four-in-hand ties discussed below, is not properly executed unless it fits comfortably into the shirt collar; it should not be half hidden by its flaps, and the segment circling the neck should always remain invisible.

The knot should not be overly triangular: a dash of asymmetry adds a salutary touch of poetry. On the other hand, one should start over if the tip of the wide end isn't at belt level—ideally, the tie's widest point, just above the tip, should coincide with the belt's upper edge—and of course, one must begin again if the narrow end falls lower than the wide one. Slipping the tip into one's pants should be avoided, if only to prevent unnecessary wear. Some corpulent men think this tends to downplay their bellies, but this is surely not the case.

When the fabric of the tie permits (if it is silk twill or a supple Jacquard silk, for example), a beautiful effect can be obtained by using the index finger to press a slight convex cavity into the tie just below the knot. The French call this little hollow a *cuillère*, which means spoon or scoop. Finally, and although some dispute this, it is a good idea to slip the narrow end through the label or the bar tack sewn onto the back of the tie's wide end.

The small knot. Although this is incontestably the most elementary of knots, it is not the one most widely used. Less voluminous than the preceding one, but also more difficult to loosen, it does not suit every collar, nor is it right for every tie. It should not be used with bottle-neck ties. But it is quite useful for models that are wide or thick and which therefore produce four-in-hand knots which are too bulky. Unlike the above description, here the wide strip is passed over the narrow strip only once. As a result, it can only be executed if the wide strip is turned 180 degrees at the beginning of the operation (see illustration p. 163).

The full-Windsor. Contrary to what is usually maintained, this knot was not invented by the Duke of Windsor anymore than was the Prince of Wales check. But it is true that the former Edward VIII launched the fashion for the knot in the 1930s and that it has remained popular ever since. "Don't use the Windsor knot any more, I've been copied too much, and badly," the Duke counseled Count Nuvelotti twenty years later on a beach in front of the Excelsior Hotel on Venice's Lido (Nuvelotti himself prefaced a book entitled *In Praise of Neckties*). Good advice, because the Windsor had been discredited due to its having been worn in mindless imitation of the duke himself, without any other justification. In his humorous guide, *Le Chic*

"In an elegant world, an irreproachable tie knot is an essential part of one's toilette; it does not matter whether the knot is simple or complicated, because the art is what counts. There are some knots which seem casual in appearance, but which have taken considerable labor before the mirror, and many a stamped foot, many an exclamation of impatience." (Doctor A. Debray, *Hygiène vestimentaire*, 1857). The artist Balthus photographed by Man Ray in 1933: his large tie knot must have seemed rather eccentric at the time (right).

The Duke of Windsor did not invent the large knot which bears his name, and which was already known to his father George V before him. But he was the origin of its popularity, after an American journalist noticed him wearing it in July 1935, when he was still Prince of Wales. It seems that the success of the Windsor was linked to the popularity of shirt collars with wide openings (the "Kent" or the "Italian" style), and that it only got its name after the Second World War. In the beginning this knot was admired not so much for its volume, but for its extreme solidity: since it was a double knot, it would never work loose. The Duke of Windsor knotting his tie, photographed by Lord Lichfield (left).

Anglais, James Darwen asserts that this knot—like all the fashions launched by the trend-setting Duke of Windsor—is the height of vulgarity: "I recommend that it be worn only by those wishing to look like a public relations specialist, a British Airways pilot, or a supporter of Margaret Thatcher." Others will tell you, with an air of distaste, that the Windsor knot is now worn only in South America. So now you have been warned. If, however, you should ever need to fill a wide collar opening on an Italian shirt using a lightweight tie, then the Windsor will come in handy, because its essential characteristic is its large volume. At the outset, the wide end should hang about fifteen inches below the narrow one (see illustration p. 163).

The half-Windsor. More attractive than the full-Windsor, this knot has an intermediary volume: one that is smaller than the full-Windsor but larger than the four-in-hand. It also has the advantage of giving a discreet fullness to very thin ties (see illustration p. 163).

The Prince Albert. This knot derives from the four-in-hand proper, to which it adds a second loop. This feature makes it especially attractive to short men, because it results in a tie length that is more consistent with their stature. The knot should be tied tightly, and should be long and narrow. It is recommended for use with soft, narrow ties and long collars. The Prince Albert is the prime example of a highly original knot which never seems ridiculous—quite the contrary. To tell the truth, it is my favorite knot for four-in-hand ties. To begin, the wide end should be made to hang about fifteen inches below the tip of the narrow end. When looping it over the narrow strip, care must be taken not to pull the knot too tightly, otherwise passage of the second loop will be difficult. The necessary opening can easily be secured by the insertion of two fingers after the execution of the first loop (see illustration p. 163).

The cross knot. Again, this is a very beautiful knot that is both original and elegant, though more complicated than the Prince Albert, which is described above. Ideally this knot's cruciform configuration should be readily apparent, a result which is not easily achieved. Like the Prince Albert, it should not be used with ties that are especially bulky, or those made of heavy woven silk, knits, or wool (see illustration p. 163).

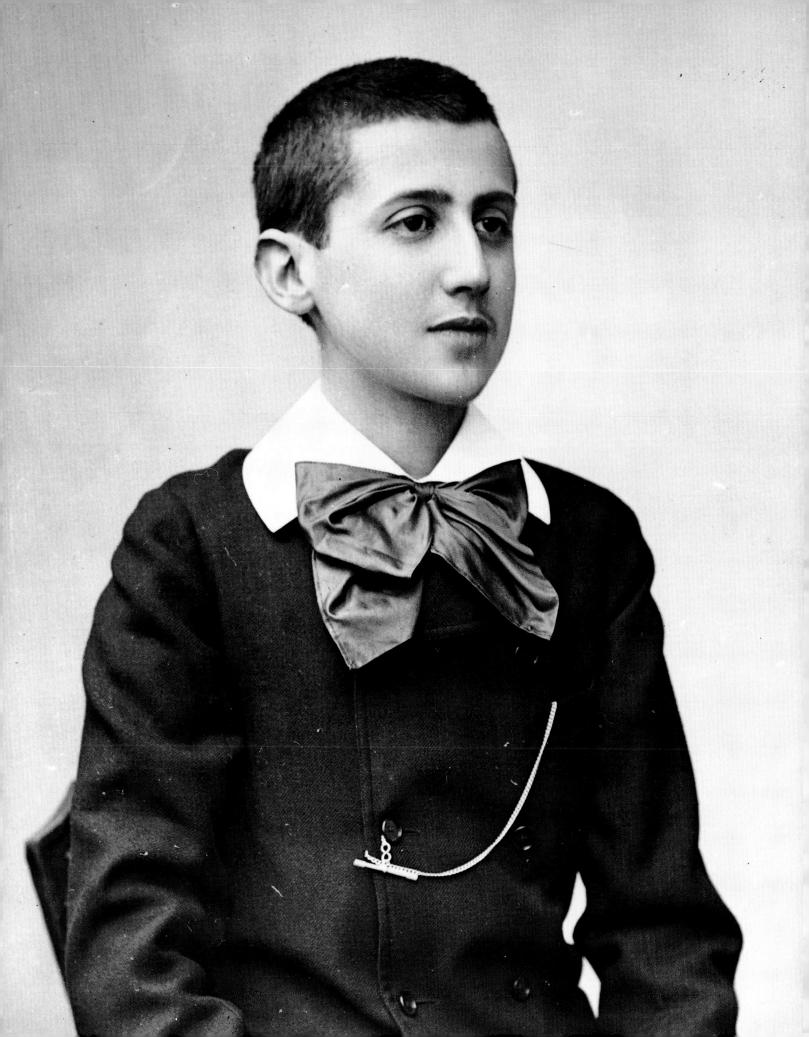

THE BUTTERFLY, OR BOW TIE

In France, before the advent of the four-in-hand tie, *papillon* (butterfly) was used to designate the well-known lepidoptera, a woman's hairstyle, a small sail, and a kind of gas jet, but never neckties. At that time they were known simply by the generic term cravats, because they had no competition from other types of neckwear. In these final years of the nineteenth century they assumed an amusing variety of forms. To get a sense of this one need only examine the neckwear worn by a few of the famous French men photographed by Nadar: Alphonse Daudet's large rectangular bow, Baudelaire's even larger asymmetrical one, Émile de Girardin's long thin bow decorated with chevrons, Viollet le Duc's white *lavalière*, Mallarmé's large wing bow, etc. A dozen different knots were current, each of which could be varied infinitely to express the full range of human emotions. Until the beginning of the twentieth century, even bow-like knots were called "ties" or cravats. In the wake of the immense success of *Madam Butterfly,* which was first performed at Milan's La Scala in 1904, this style of neckwear was dubbed the "butterfly" tie in Puccini's honor. Gradually the designation came to be applied to almost all ties that were not four-in-hands, even those with forms quite unlike those of the beautiful winged insects. In contrast to today, wearing a butterfly or bow tie signified nothing in particular. Although somewhat less than a century earlier it had represented an alternative to the middle-class rigidity of the stock, and so became associated with political liberals, romantic artists, and a Bohemian lifestyle, by the time the four-in-hand began to

dominate the field it was simply the most commonly worn model of necktie, whether by day or by night.

The triumph of the four-in-hand changed all of this. In a photograph from the 1930s, Sir Thomas Lipton, posing proudly in the famous blue bow tie with white dots that now bears his name, already seems a bit out of step, surrounded as he is by admirers wearing four-in-hands. Since then only the occasional passing fashion has revived the taste for bow ties. In the 1950s the British Teddy boys adopted an existing variant long worn in the western and southern United States called a string tie, which consists of a thin strip of black cotton or velvet whose long ends are left hanging over the shirt front. This fashion was picked up by rock-and-rollers around the world, including Bill Haley and Elvis Presley. In the United States it was also popularized in the 1960s by the astute businessman

At an age when he would have been going to bed early, like most boys of his time, Marcel Proust went to school wearing a necktie which, despite its shape in the form of a gracious butterfly in flight, was not yet called a "papillon." In France this kind of scholar's knot was worn right up to the 1920s. Marcel Proust at the age of fifteen, photographed by Nadar (left).

Along with tea, Sir Thomas Lipton also gave his name to a bow tie: a blue one with white dots, which he sported regularly on his yacht, the Shamrock, wearing it with a wing collar (right).

The painter of the most famous portrait of Marcel Proust, the artist Jacques-Émile Blanche, a "society portraitist," has also left us striking images of André Gide, Jean Cocteau, Claude Debussy and Igor Stravinsky. This gallery of portraits offers a precise vision of male fashions at the turn of the century. The great English designer and illustrator Aubrey Beardsley (who died in 1898 at the age of 25), painted by Jacques-Émile Blanche in 1895 (left). Together with the *boutonnière*, the bow tie in those days must have seemed the absolute antithesis of the austere four-in-hand.

All united against the four-in-hand: the artist in his *lavalière*, the bourgeois in his ascot, and the aristocrat with his bow tie. Caricature from the turn of the century, in *The Tie: a Breviary of Good Taste,* a 1912 guide published in Germany (below).

Many bow ties can be adjusted thanks to a graduated-band system in both French and English measures. Bow ties by Turnbull & Asser and by Lord's (below).

"The majority of men who wear a bow tie do it because the majority of men do not." Thus wrote Abbott Combes in the *New York Times* in 1986. With the onward march of the four-in-hand, the bow tie has become a way of making oneself stand out. An illustration from *Adam* magazine, April 1948. The bow tie with long, slim wings depicted here, sometimes called a "dragonfly," was fashionable in the 1950s, but is no longer worn (right). The "bow-tiful" Dolores Bichette, promoting "national bow-tie week" in 1954, for the manufacturers of American bow ties (below).

tently and exclusively (which a recent French study indicates is the case for eleven percent of its adepts), it clearly intimates that the wearer is a free-spirited non-conformist. The bow tie is especially favored by intellectuals and creative professionals: everybody knows a journalist or a lawyer who sports one regularly. But bow ties are also worn by those whose occupation obliges them to lean over frequently: doctors, architects, and waiters. Less virile than the four-in-hand, bow ties are likely to be read by straight-arrow types, despite the conspicuous example set by Winston Churchill, as indicating a certain lack of seriousness, and a tendency toward irresponsibility. Businessmen with limited imaginations are likely to say to themselves: "Better not trust a man with a bow tie, he's likely to be a bit scatterbrained." And John T. Molloy, author of the

known as Colonel Sanders, who from his flagship restaurant in Kentucky launched a successful campaign to make the entire globe clamor for his fried chicken. The emblem of his Kentucky Fried Chicken fast-food chain features the "colonel's" smiling face—and just below, this typically Southern style of necktie. Jacques Lacan—who as the inventor of the short session is to psychoanalysis what Colonel Sanders is to chicken—must have loved the string tie, for he wore one constantly. Also in the 1960s, both the clip-on, a kind of small detachable bow tie, and the "twist" became popular. Small boys often wore them proudly on festive occasions.

Today, owing to its now somewhat marginal status, a bow tie worn during the workday is a fail-safe way to set oneself apart. Donned consis-

After rock and roll, the twist: in the 1960s, this fashionable dance gave its name to a sober variant of the bow tie, in which the two ends were crossed and sewn. A boy at a wedding, very proud of his twist. The author in 1962, at his cousin's wedding (right).

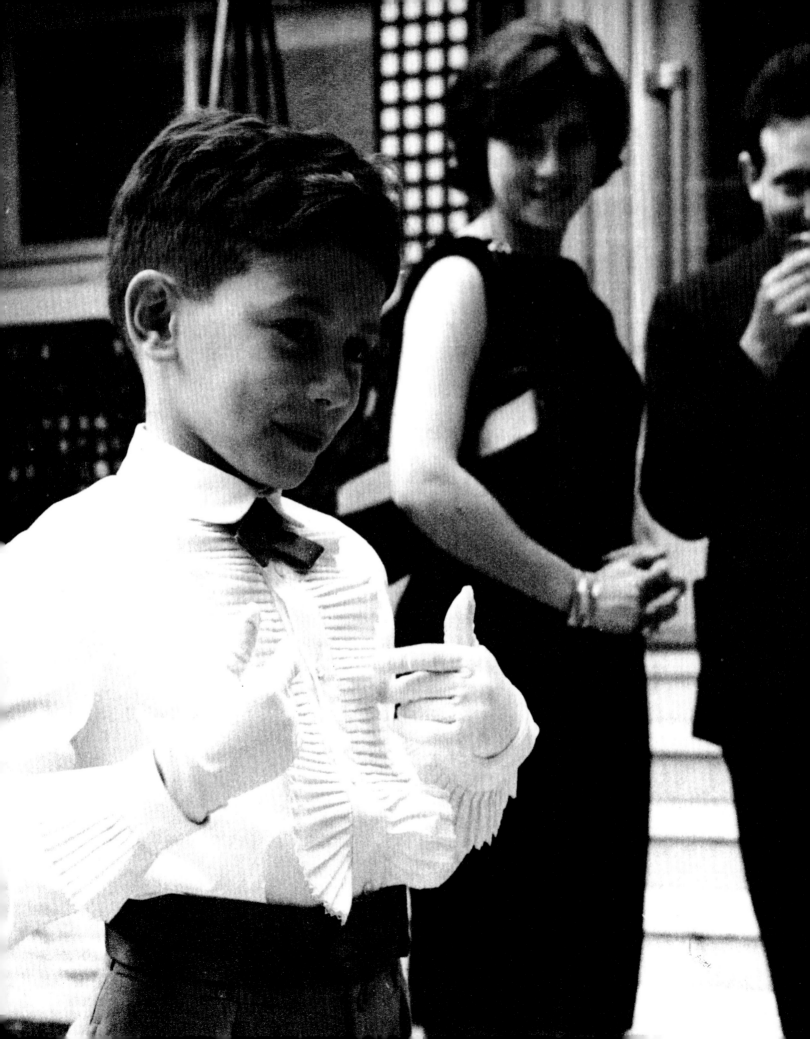

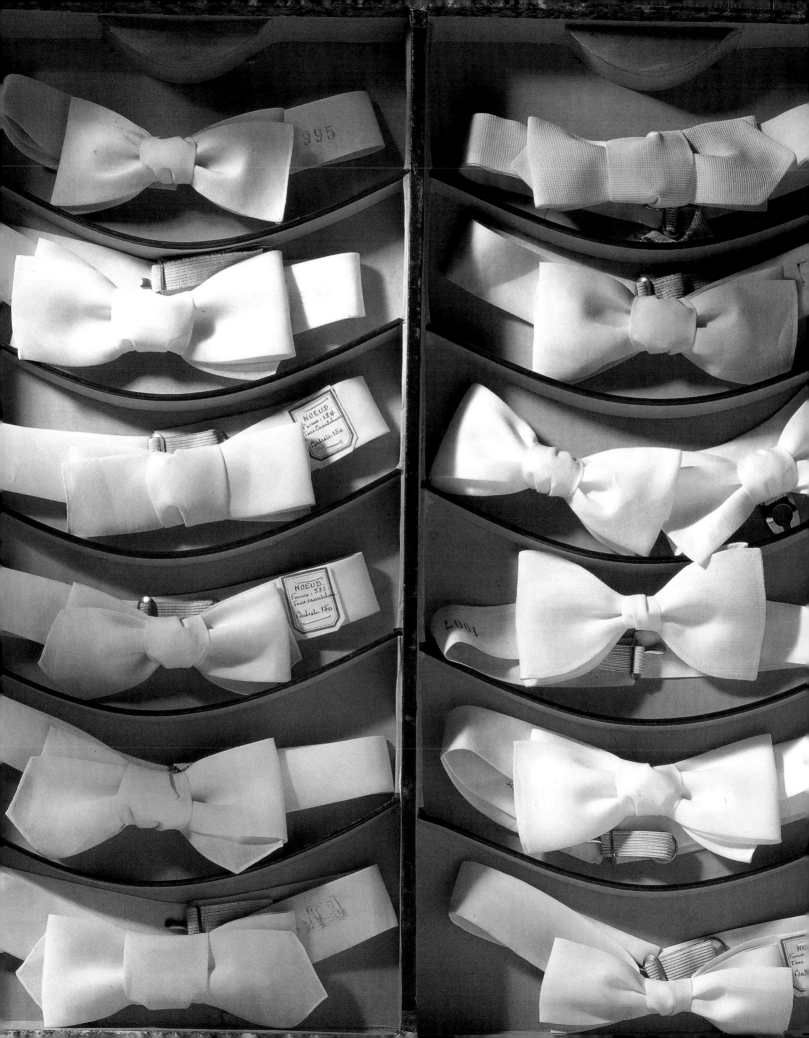

successful *Dress for Success*, advises his readers squarely against wearing one. Which may be the best reason I know to do just that!

The code of formal evening wear, however, makes the bow tie obligatory, whether with a tuxedo (usually black or some other dark color) or tails (always white cotton, and worn with a turned-down collar). The familiar phrases "black tie" and "white tie" can be recognized here. Precisely because they are required, and difficult to knot, bow ties are the exception to a rule that is too often ignored: once we have graduated from elementary school, ready-ties are prohibited. We will return shortly to this subject of burning interest.

What remains of the thousand-and-one bow ties of yore? Only two: the "bat wing" and the butterfly. The first has ends that are straight, while the second has curved ends. Today, all mass-produced bow ties must adhere to one or the other of these basic designs. Even their dimensions are pretty much standardized: about 4 inches long by 2 to 3 inches wide. But there is another crucial alternative to consider: whether or not to wear a bow tie one has to knot oneself. Current reality may well discourage readers tempted to take up the bow tie challenge—more than 90% of bow ties currently on the market are ready-tied. The explanation usually given for this is both simple and mysterious: no one knows how to execute the knot. The mystery derives from the fact that the knot itself is remarkably easy to execute; even a chimpanzee can master it in less than an hour. This being so, why is it that bow tie wearers—who want to set themselves apart by means of this charming touch of fantasy—do not learn to tie it themselves? Is it not just a bit contradictory to declare one's originality by means of such a prefabricated product? The gesture has something hoax-like about it.

There are two kinds of such convenience bow ties. Some—the least dishonorable—are simply pre-tied by the manufacturer (they can be loosened), while others have knots that are sewn in place. But both types have a fastening and adjustment system of some sort: either a simple hook sewn on the inside of the band, or—what is much worse—two strips of velcro. Wing collars, which leave the band of the tie exposed, prompted the development of the hook system, which is completely invisible. It is used in even the finest, top-of-the-line ready-ties.

The few remaining classic bow ties take the form of a ribbon whose wide ends are cut into the requisite bat wing or butterfly (also known as thistle) shapes. Some are made in once piece, but these are rare and must nearly always be made to order. If not custom made, these models must be selected in a size corresponding to one's neck size. But today, in most cases bow ties are composed of two pieces which, thanks to an ingenious hidden sliding system, can be adjusted to the necessary length.

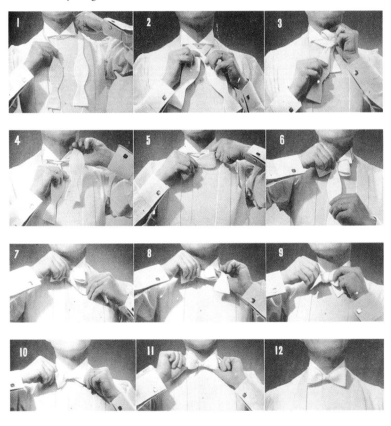

How does one tie a bow tie? Tying a bow tie is one of life's great pleasures. Contrary to rumor, this knot is no more difficult to achieve than the four-in-hand. The only real challenge of the operation arises in step five, which will take a neophyte several minutes and a bit of patience to execute properly. The trick is to keep the whole construction somewhat loose through step four by slipping a finger under the loop during the second step. As a bow tie's length is generally adjustable, one can easily honor a long-standing rule: the distance between the two tips of the tie should be the same as that between the outer edges of the person's eyes (see illustration p. 163).

The tying of a bow tie is child's play, requiring only a bit of instruction. A demonstration by the tie-maker R. Richard, for the readers of *Adam* magazine in 1951 (above).

The ascot, which became fashionable at the end of the last century, is rarely seen today. It is worn with formal dress or, particularly in England, at hunting parties.

In town its flaps are generally crossed, but they may also be worn parallel. A ready-tied late nineteenth-century ascot (above); Two ready-tied 1883 ascots preserved in the Krefeld Museum (below).

THE ASCOT

The third and last type of tie still in use, the ascot, with its wide flaps crossed over the chest, is worn only on festive occasions, usually with tails: at marriages, elegant horseraces, or other hippic events. It was the Ascot race, held annually in April since 1771, that gave the ascot its name. Although it became standard wear for certain occasions only in the early twentieth century, the ascot existed much earlier, appearing as the first cravat in books on male neckwear published in the 1820s. It was called a "Gordian-knot cravat," after the complex knot which, according to legend, only Alexander the Great was able to untie with a blow of his sword. But this moniker is paradoxical, for as we shall see the ascot knot is about as easy as they come. We should, however, bear in mind that the tying and loosening of cravats in this period was considerably complicated by the starching of the fabric, to such an extent that some impatient young men, upon returning home after their nocturnal revels, simply cut them off with a pair of scissors.

The ascot became the mode in upper-middle-class and aristocratic circles during the 1880s. It was worn on important occasions as well as at dinner parties and on Sunday walks in the fashionable Bois-de-Boulogne on the outskirts of Paris. The dimensions of those admissible at the Ascot races were once strictly regulated: 50 inches long, 3 inches wide flaps, and less than an inch wide at the neck band. These rules are no longer enforced, and today ascots are usually worn with their ends crossed and the whole secured by a tie pin with a pearl—preferably a

real one. But there is nothing to prevent the ends from being arranged side by side in parallel falls. An imaginative Englishman dubbed this variation the "Athenian" way of wearing an ascot, after its supposed resemblance to the columns of the Parthenon.

How does one tie an ascot? The fact that the type of neckwear easiest to knot is also the one most frequently sold in ready-tied form is a pointed reminder—should any of us have forgotten it—that absurdity is endemic to human affairs. Like the tuxedo bow tie, today the ready-tied ascot is not only tolerated but actually considered perfectly acceptable. Its apologists would have us believe that on his wedding day a man's fingers tremble so violently—if they are not completely paralyzed—that he is incapable of tying a simple knot. And why not ready-tied four-in-hands for first dates? As the reader can see, the simplicity of the ascot knot disproves such far-fetched notions and renders all further commentary superfluous (see illustration p. 163).

Given its shape and the location of its pin, the ascot provides a suitable vehicle for a spy camera. The "necktie detective camera," an illustration from *Albert Hopkins's Magic* (left).

"In order to wear the plastron properly, an elegant bearing and much natural presence are indispensable, and while, by the nobility of his manner, the authority of his gait and the volume of his torso, M. le baron de Grandmaison, for example, has the right to sport a plastron in whatever manner he will, the same cravat would, needless to say, have a completely other appearance on the intimates of M. Fallières." Thus the journalist R.B. de Monvel evoked, in 1913, in *La Gazette du Bon Ton*, the aristocratic nature of the plastron, which could also apply to the ascot. A demonstration from a small manual dating from 1906 (top, right); a gentleman wearing an ascot, *circa* 1900 (bottom, right).

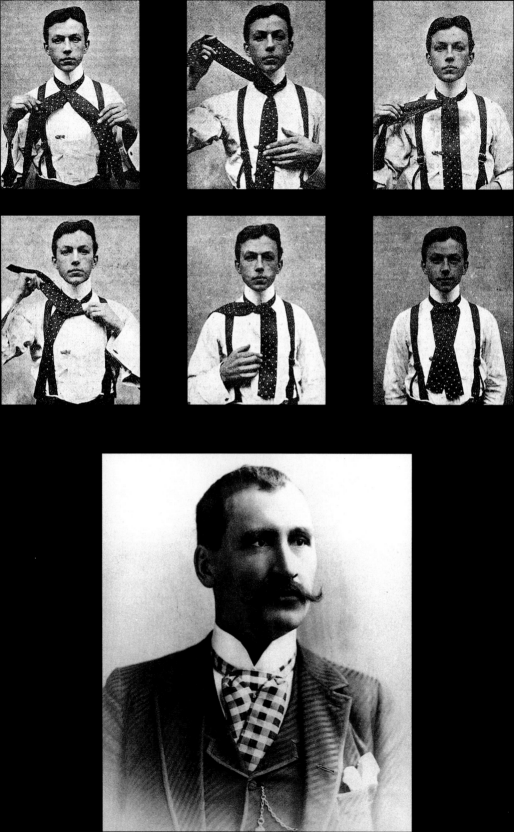

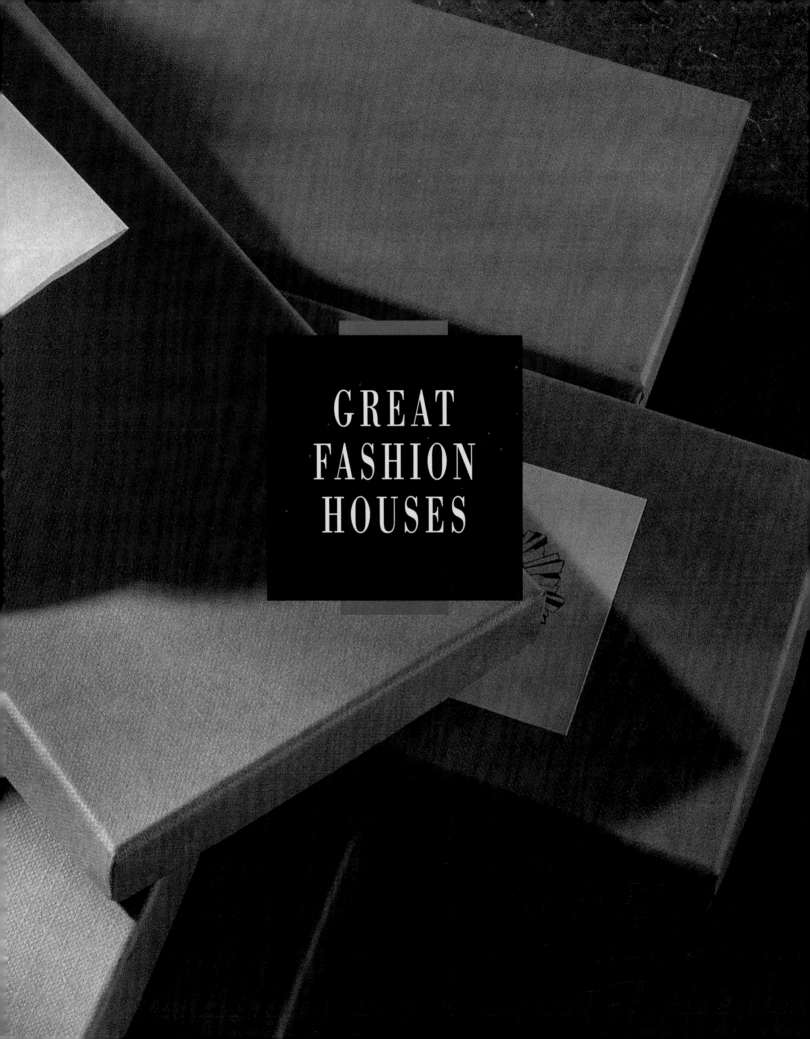

GREAT
FASHION
HOUSES

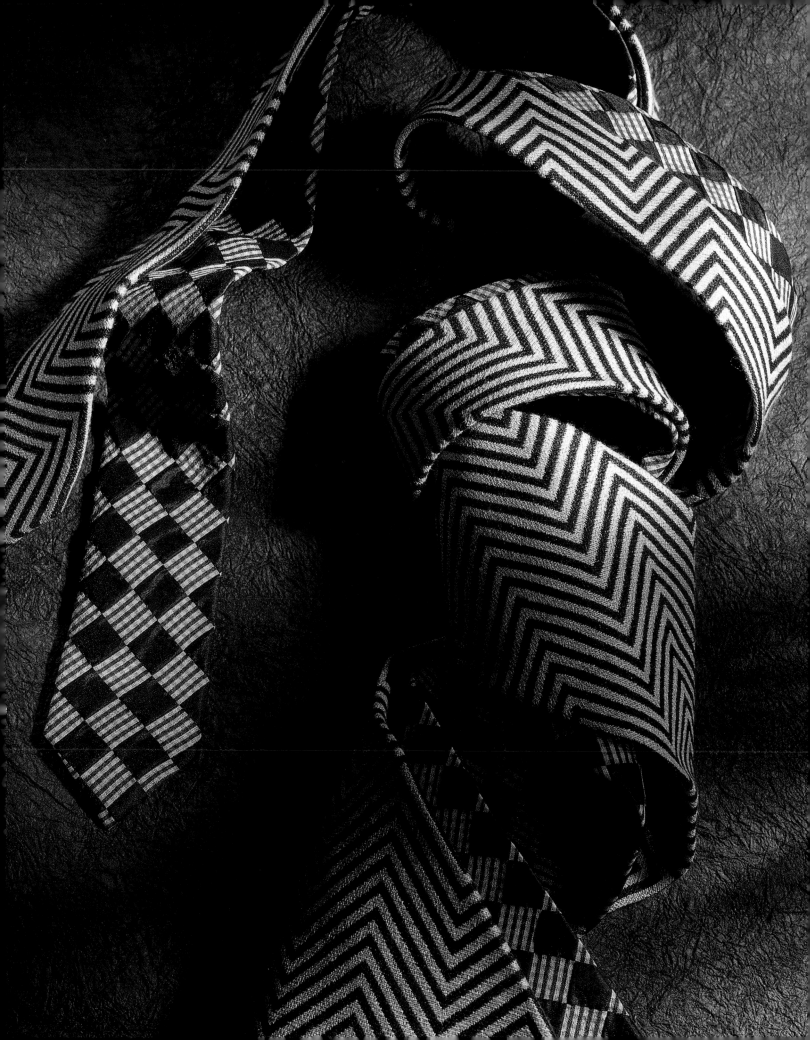

It is difficult to imagine the degree to which some men are enamored of their ties. The will of one distinguished Canadian, for example, stipulates that he be buried in a shroud made of Hermès ties. He wants his favorite, well-worn ties to be sewn into a kind of patchwork quilt. An unusual case? Not at all. Only the absolute discretion dictated by Japanese etiquette prevents me from divulging the name of a very famous man who, before his recent death, left instructions that he be buried with six Charvet ties chosen especially for that purpose. This is a sentiment I can fully understand. Some ties have a quality that others lack, a certain something that prompts us to consider them among our most precious possessions. This elusive quality can be an extreme refinement, an exemplary originality, or the perfect expression of a certain tone or temperament. It is a function of individual taste. Fortunately, design houses with offers capable of satisfying demanding customers are not rare, and perfect examples of all styles, from the most classic to the most audacious, can be purchased from one of them. I would have liked to mention here all the firms and fashion houses throughout the world that, under the aegis of a single label, draw on the skills of designers, weavers, printers, and manufacturers, coordinating their efforts to produce ties which leave us spellbound. I would have also liked to discuss the many French *haute-couture* houses: Christian Dior, Lanvin, Yves Saint Laurent, and Chanel to name only a few.

I would have liked to dwell on certain Italian tie lines, like those by Prochownick, Armani, and Ricci, on numerous British tie makers, including Holliday & Brown, Michelsons, and Michael Drake; on the German Hugo Boss; and the American firms Garrick Anderson, Gene Meyer, Calvin Klein, and Brooks Brothers. Unfortunately, I had to make more or less arbitrary choices in order to convey an accurate idea of the current range of beautiful ties available. The group brought together here constitutes a vast array of professional tie makers who, from the strictly traditional to the wildly unconventional, demonstrate the richness of today's world of ties. Here, then, from A to Z, are a few of the great tie designers whose ties I deem worthy of paradise. Alphabetical order has its advantages, it turns out

One of the elements characterizing the clothing produced by the Italian couturier Giorgio Armani has been the search for the finest silks, and a choice of deep, neutral colors. Emporio Armani tie with chevron pattern, in woven silk and Giorgio Armani tie with a square motif in embossed silk (left).

Anthime Mouley

The famous Jeanne Lanvin blue rules in the couturier's shop in Paris. Today, Lanvin ties are designed by Dominique Morlotti, in collaboration with the French tie maker Anthime Mouley. An Anthime Mouley advertisement published in *Adam* magazine in 1950 (above). One of the handsome tie display cases in the Lanvin shop on rue du Faubourg Saint-Honoré, as seen from above on carpeting with a "wave" motif designed for Jeanne Lanvin by the interior decorator Armand-Albert Rateau (left).

In the leading establishments, the finest ties sometimes merit a special box of their own. Pepper-and-salt tie (preceding double page).

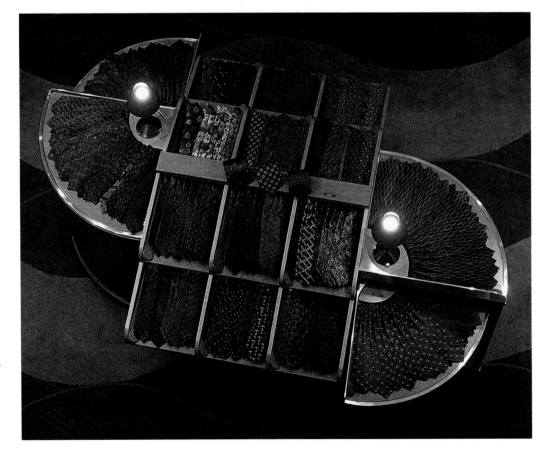

115

Germany is a major tie producing country, and many German tie makers produce wonders. Ascot, founded in 1908, is known among professionals throughout the world for its sublime knit ties, the excellence of its assembly, which is entirely by hand, and the quality of its washed and madder silks. The company's "hand-sewn" label (above); An Ascot printed washed silk tie (bottom, right). A more recent arrival on the scene—its first collection of ties dates only from 1982—the Hugo Boss company nevertheless offers both printed and woven silk ties of an irreproachable quality (center).

that I will begin with a designer whose ties instill in me a feeling of perfect harmony and well-being. There are a thousand reasons to love the ties of **Joseph Abboud**. One of the principal being that his creations disprove the assertion that there is no middle ground in the United States between screaming bad taste and puritanical conformism. While his American counterparts invented the bold-look tie, Joseph Abboud —born in Boston and now based in New York—takes great pleasure in subtle Mediterranean nuances, and in refined patterns with soft contours and burnished colors suggestive of Italy. He established his own men's clothing firm in 1986 after having worked for three years as an assistant to Ralph Lauren.

Joseph Abboud's creative process differs from that of most tie designers, who tend to work in close collaboration with other professionals and graphic artists: Abboud conceives his own motifs, fine-tunes them with his assistants, and then sends his designs to silk fabric manufacturers in Como for production. He draws constantly and never goes anywhere without a sketchbook and pencil. One day while vacationing with his family in Palm Beach, he telephoned to tell me about a motif he had designed that morning while basking in the sun. All of his collections feature some 250 completely original designs, each interpreted in five different colors.

Perhaps it was his study of comparative literature in the United States and in Paris that led to Abboud's fascination with classic European style. He frequently works variations on classic motifs, such as small geometric shapes or paisleys, to come up with new forms which are then rendered in exquisite colors. His tie with three paisley drops arrayed in a circle is one such example. Abboud ties are celebrated for their rich neutral tones that are suggestive of earth and wood. From his weavers and printers in Como, Abboud obtains beautiful silks carefully made to his specifications and often featuring special effects such as pleats and flocking. On rare occasions he has them blend the silk with merino wool, Egyptian cotton, or linen.

Designers such as Joseph Abboud are like painters who lavish particular care on their

motifs; others are like sculptors who are preoccupied above all with working the material. Ascot of Germany is more of the latter type. This family firm was established in 1908 by Karl Moese and is based on the banks of the Rhine in the city of Krefeld, which has been Germany's principal silk manufacturing center for three centuries. Karl's grandson, Wolfgang Moese, heads the firm today. This affable and witty Francophile goes about his work with a mixture of pragmatism and devotion. The pragmatism is evidenced by how consistently he manages to satisfy the changing demands of fashion. The devotion can be observed in his commitment to perfection. And perfection itself can be witnessed in his chosen fabrics and production methods.

All ties bearing the Ascot label, several hundred thousand per year, are sewn entirely by hand. The firm employs sixty people who work out of their homes and who never go near a sewing machine. Wolfgang Moese simply smiles when he is told that excellent results can be obtained today by machine sewing with hand finishing. He knows that only crafting ties entirely by hand can guarantee a perfect result, especially when it comes to fitting together the envelope and the interlining. The composition of the interlining is one of Ascot's trump cards: the firm uses an American-made blend of wool and polyester which helps insure that the tie will maintain its shape. The slip stitch is another distinctive feature of Ascot's assembly process: having noticed that some of his clients think this thread is a flaw and therefore cut it, Wolfgang Moese had it placed inside the envelope where it is invisible and protected.

Neophytes are perhaps more likely to be impressed by Ascot's fabrics: one of the firm's specialties is knitted silk which is available in solids or decorated with stripes and dots. Then there are Ascot's many wools, some of pure cashmere and others of silk-and-wool blends. And finally, the firm creates sumptuous woven silks with subtle variations in the weave. Ascot also offers admirable imitation wools and tweeds made from washed silk. A similar velvety result can be obtained with madder. Demanding silk enthusiasts find the result extremely attractive.

Joseph Abboud, an extremely refined designer, has, in the space of a few years, contrived in magisterial fashion to impose an alternative image of American ties. He defines this style as elegant, romantic and serious, quite the opposite of the "conversation-starter" novelty ties which he considers "contrary to the dignity of the tie and of male dress in general." Abboud's sensibility fits well with the tradition of the best silk producers in Como, to whom he entrusts his designs. Joseph Abboud ties in printed silk, woven silk and printed figured silk (right).

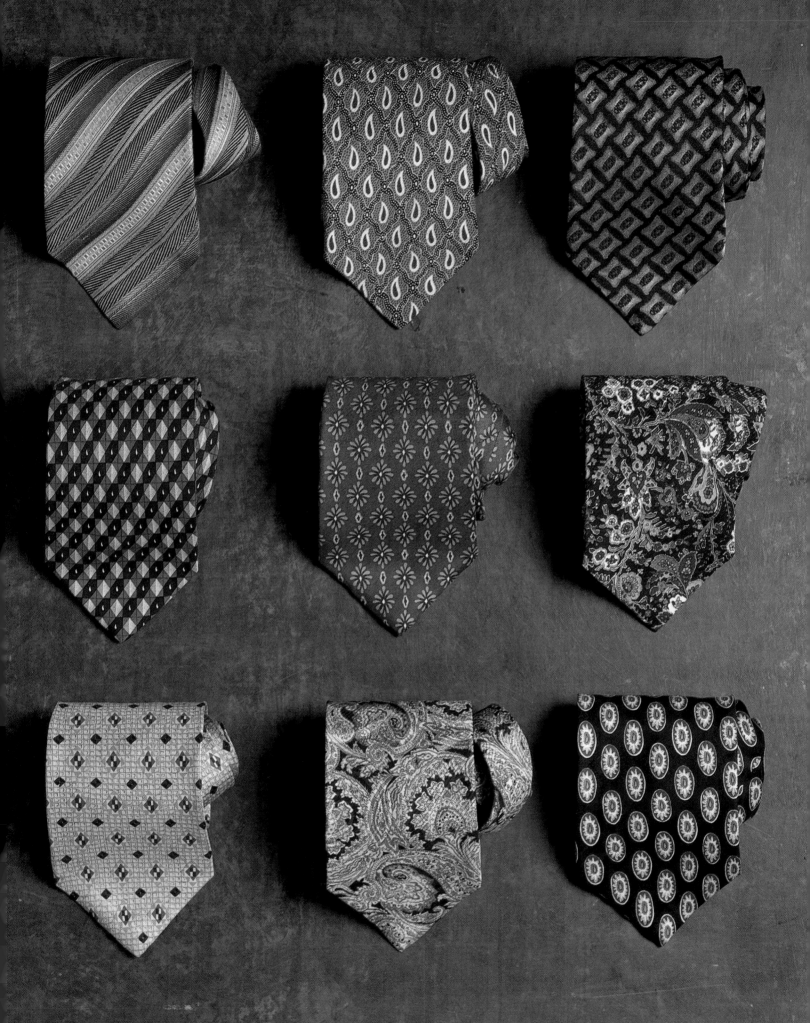

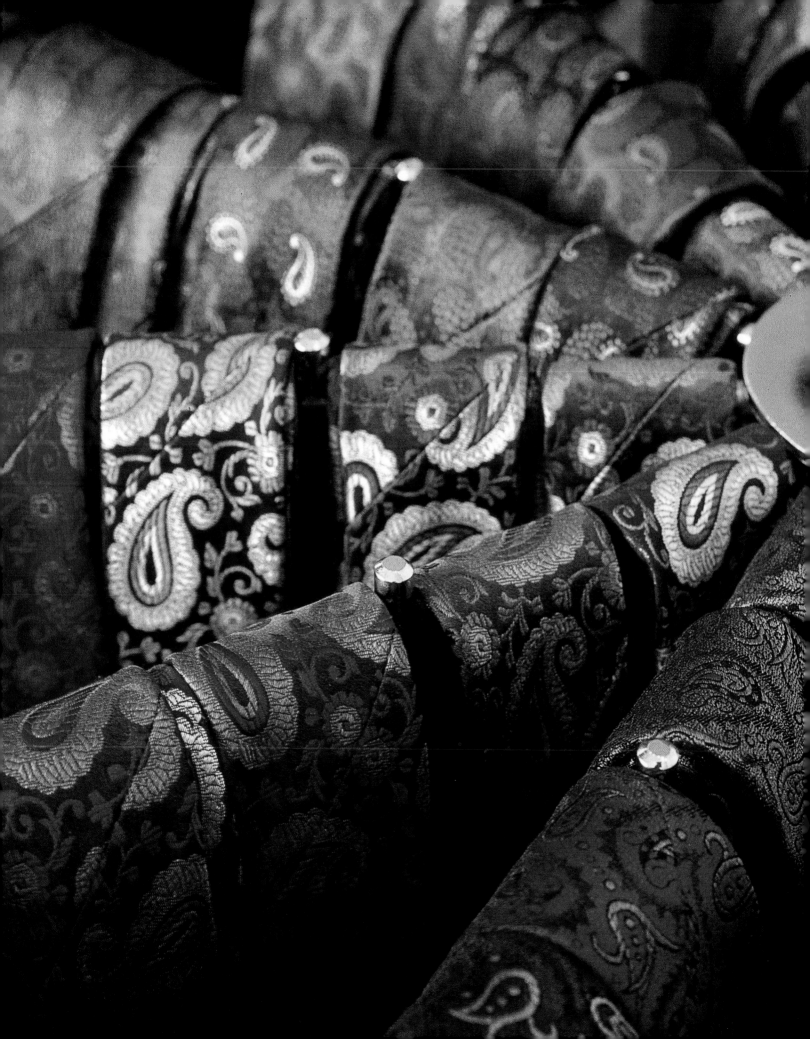

There is no place in the world with a greater selection of classic silk ties than Charvet on Place Vendôme in Paris. The tie lover will find a classicism in patterns, which does not at all exclude a boldness of color—colors that often shimmer in the light, thanks to special effects in the weave. Like precious stones, Charvet woven silk ties offer a lively, changing beauty that is revealed in movement. A display of Charvet paisley patterns in woven silk (left).

If they have not already done so, these same enthusiasts will find much to inspire them by crossing the threshold of the great temple of the Jacquard silk tie: **Charvet**, on the Place Vendôme in Paris. Pronounce this name anywhere in the world before a tie lover and you will see his face light up like the sun which is the firm's emblem. Founded in Paris in 1838 by Christophe Charvet (son of a keeper of the Imperial wardrobe), and situated on the Place Vendôme since 1878, early in the twentieth century this sanctuary of the custom-made shirt also established its international reputation as a maker of fine ties.

One can get a sense of Charvet's distinguished history from a partial list of its customers: Edouard Manet, Claude Debussy, Valéry Larbaud, Jean Cocteau, Coco Chanel, Gary Cooper, Yul Brynner, and John F. Kennedy. But it was Marcel Proust who immortalized the Charvet tie with a single adjective in a passage of *A Remembrance of Things Past*. Waiting for the appointed hour of his luncheon engagement at Swann's house, the narrator whiles away his time "tightening from time to time the knot of my magnificent Charvet tie and taking care not to soil my polished boots, I wandered up and down the avenues waiting for 12:27." Regarding its current list of famous customers, the firm is a model of reticence—their names are a zealously guarded professional secret. But it is known to include a sizable number of prominent French politicians. And not so very long ago one of its most eminent clients made a decisive intervention in the firm's history: none other than General Charles de Gaulle, whom Charvet served as official haberdasher for half a century. When in 1965 the Charvet heirs sought to sell the firm they were contacted by an American buyer. The French government grew concerned: was it even conceivable for the General to visit an American tailor? The French Minister of Industry instructed Denis Colban, who sold fabric to all the fine haberdashers in France, to locate a French buyer. Colban made his first visit to Charvet and purchased it himself that same day. General de Gaulle could sleep in peace.

Under Denis Colban's guidance, the firm's line of ties has assumed increasing importance. An expert in the art of color, Charvet's new owner sees ties as the most elegant forum for exercising his gifts. His first business decision was a spectacular one. He produced a line of Jacquard ties in almost a hundred different solid colors, as well as other original multicolored designs which the client could readily coordinate with the firm's thousands of shirt fabrics. This decision illustrates one of the ruling principles at Charvet: the customer cannot be satisfied unless he has real freedom of choice. Today, tie lovers visiting the ground floor of this spacious shop, whose calm atmosphere seems designed to foster contemplation and meditation, will find the world's largest selection of ties, made exclusively of silk. A veritable Ali Baba's cave, the ground floor has several hundred models on display, each available in at least twenty different colors. And this is but a small portion of the possibilities: should a customer not find something that strikes his fancy, he can place a special order on the basis of a fabric sample. Two weeks later his dream tie will be ready, and the surcharge for this remarkable service is only ten percent.

But freedom of choice does not mean that anything can be found at Charvet. Passing fashion is proscribed—Denis Colban characterizes it as planned obsolescence. Anything judged to be in poor taste—regimentals and small golfers, for example—is forbidden. Favor is reserved exclusively for simple, beautiful designs. In a word, timeless. Most Charvet ties are conceived by Denis Colban, in collaboration with his children

Satin, twill, rep, ottoman, crêpe, taffeta, faille, ribbed, flecked, basket weave, grenadine—every weave can be found at Charvet. This, combined with the finest silks, and a perfection of assembly, make Charvet ties the most luxurious of masculine accessories. Bow ties in basket weave, which are sold ready-tied—but not sewn—and in three sizes (above).

"Look here! I want a Chinese necktie for my dog." Since 1838 the Charvet house has sought to satisfy the most demanding of clients. Drawing by Sem from the 1920s (left).

Twill weave silk printed with small figurative repeating patterns has conquered the world, and Ferragamo has been both initiator and unrivaled master in its refined version. Designers of this Florence-based house create their motifs with all the care of miniature-painters drawing on art of every epoch and continent. Painstaking color separation, a silk that is heavy and often gummed, an interlining in lightweight wool, and a hand finish for the final product, provide a fitting outcome for the work of the designers (right and below).

Anne-Marie and Jean-Claude, in audacious color schemes and subtle weaves. Another characteristic of Charvet ties is the extraordinary quality of the silk fabric used in their manufacture. Early in the twentieth century, King Edward VII of Great Britan, a friend and customer of the firm's founder, put Charvet in contact with the finest English silk makers. Charvet is now the only house to use a Lyons silk-weaver, one worthy of the distinguished French tradition. It goes without saying that production is supervised by Charvet and the ties are sewn entirely by hand.

In the realm of printed ties, a comparable love of perfection can be found at **Ferragamo**. The Neapolitan Salvatore Ferragamo was one of the great shoe designers of the twentieth century. It was after his death in 1960 that his widow Wanda decided to diversify operations by establishing a ready-to-wear line. Ferragamo's first tie collections appeared in 1972, under the supervision of Wanda's daughter Fulvia Visconti. Ferragamo is the real instigator of a tie fashion which is now a worldwide phenomenon: the craze for small animals in repeating patterns. A widely used scarf design, such motifs were featured in its very first collection. But the directors at Ferragamo—who cultivate a certain elegance—are averse to silly and naive designs. Over the years Ferragamo has come to dominate the field of printed ties with figurative motifs—as opposed

to traditional abstract motifs of dots, stripes, paisley, and so on. In addition to animals, the firm's designers are partial to sports themes as well as to motifs ingeniously adapted from the traditions of ancient or exotic civilizations. Chinese tea porters, Indian elephants, panthers perched atop ancient Egyptian columns, and medieval troubadors, have all figured in recent collections. The most striking feature of this flood of images is the subtlety of the color schemes and the remarkable finesse of the miniature-like precision in the rendering of details. A five-color tea chest, a lute with delicate marquetry decoration, a bird cage with elaborate trellis-work—in addition to exceptional silkscreening, such refinement is the result of a special printing technique which is a closely guarded secret.

Let us remain in Italy. Still in the domain of printed silk ties, another firm has distinguished itself over the last quarter century through its subtle handling of a theme usually associated with England and France: horesback riding. The firm is **Gucci**, and the company's history provides an explanation for the phenomenon. At the beginning of the present century, the luxurious Hotel Savoy in London hired a young Italian immigrant born in Florence with the mellifluous name of Guccio Gucci as its *maître d'hôtel*. In the splendid lobby, the young man was able to ponder the ostentation of the hotel's rich clients, who frequently arrived with mountains

of expensive luggage in tow for a single horse race. Such was the apprenticeship of an empire builder. Upon returning to Florence in 1920, Guccio Gucci used his savings to open his first shop for saddlery and fine leather goods Its sign featured a horse's bit which was to become the house emblem. The store was successful, and a few years later Gucci opened another in Rome, on Via Condotti, then a third in Milan, on Via Montenapoleone. His four sons soon became involved in the business. Guccio Gucci died in 1953, the very year his house gained an international reputation by opening a shop in New York.

The first Gucci ties appeared in the spring of 1968. The initial model devised by the designers was a silk twill printed with a horse's bit in a repeating pattern, available in four color schemes. Other motifs associated with horsemanship followed—riding whips, spurs, stirrups—but a discreet penchant for humor soon manifested itself in the use of crossed pipes, bent nails, and old firearms. Today, the 200,000 Gucci ties sold yearly throughout the world continue to honor this double tradition. House standards are very high when it comes to silk, which is most often woven and printed in Como. Recent bestsellers are an all-over with pairs of dice and another with bear cubs. Crisp details and sophisticated color schemes make the smiles raised by such Gucci offerings all the more pleasurable. The most distinguished of men have been seen wearing Gucci ties featuring playing cards, Gypsies, and bank notes. However, on

more momentous occasions, Gucci-wearers such as the President of the United States, Bill Clinton will opt for a more traditional Gucci design, for example a repeating pattern with yellow hunting horns against a sky blue ground.

There are many similarities between the business histories of Gucci and **Hermès**. Hermès also began as a saddle and leather specialist, diversified activities by working with silk, and eventually offered twill ties printed with an equestrian emblem which recalled the firm's beginnings. But Hermès has a particular specialty: it is probably the only house in the world to control the entire process of manufacturing printed ties (excluding the execution of the silkscreens). Hermès and its subsidiaries weave a magnificent, incomparably soft twill which they also print; they then lavish great care on the final stages of production.

I have already evoked the intensely passionate attachment some men have to their Hermès ties, and further evidence can be collected any Saturday at the Faubourg-Saint-Honoré store where dozens of tie lovers crowd around its famous stirrup-shaped display racks, all trying to get closer but inevitably brushing up against one another, with the utmost politeness, of course. Yet another phenomenon illustrates the strong attachment some customers feel toward their Hermès ties: many customers return to the shop carrying ties they purchased some fifteen to twenty years earlier which are in need of repair. It is as though these ties had become a part of themselves, as though the thought of losing a Hermès tie were as painful as losing a limb.

The world-famous Hermès tie was created not in Paris but in Cannes, just after the Second World War. The Hermès store in that city was located right next to the casino, whose dress code stipulated that ties were to be worn. Would-be, tie-less gamblers, having been politely shown the door, often went into the shop in hopes of buying a tie, only to meet with disappointment. Around 1947 or 1948, the store manager, Bobby Breward—the life story of this very British saddle maker, an intelligence agent during the war,

Fine lines and bright colors, traditional motifs related to horse-riding or small, light-hearted designs, combined with deeply colored brilliant silks processed in Como—since 1968 Gucci has combined the classical and the fancy with a firmly-stated philosophy: "a tie is not a complementary accessory, but a contrasting accessory." Gucci goes to great lengths to ensure that its clients' ties, while not breaking the delicate balance of elegance, do not go unnoticed. Two printed silk ties, featuring dice and a magician's hat with dove (right).

United States president, Bill Clinton chose this Gucci tie with a motif of yellow hunting horns on a blue background, created at Como by the designer Albertina Porro (above).

would make a terrific novel—suggested to Robert Dumas that he consider satisfying this demand. Emile Hermès' son-in-law, his assistant at the time, gave the go ahead.

The first ties to bear the Hermès label were purchased from Italian and English tie makers and appeared a few months later. They sold well, and in 1953 Robert Dumas decided to bring some of firm's expertise in silk products to bear on their production—Hermès had been making square silk scarves since 1935. The first ties dec-

Hermès tie, instantly distinguishable from its many imitators, was to be born on the drawing table of d'Origny, who was a passionate horseman. Bits, stirrups, and spurs—not to mention the oft-repeated chain links—were scattered over twill ties in cleverly conceived, seemingly abstract patterns.

Henri d'Origny is still a mainstay of the Hermès tie department. He is an exquisitely courteous gentleman who receives guests in front of the drawing table where a thousand motifs have been designed—motifs worn the world over, and recognizable at a glance. Yet he remains unim-

Across five continents, the famous stirrup-shaped racks (left) present Hermès ties to enchanted clients. Magnificent twills, sumptuous colors, exquisite printing, assembly that is attentive to every detail: these are some of the ingredients of the company's international success.

The pencil behind the Hermès name: that of designer Henri d'Origny, originator of the classic Hermès designs based on horse-riding themes. D'Origny's style has been imitated around the world, with greater or lesser degrees of success, and is recognizable at a glance. It is a subtle alchemy of motifs ranging from figurative to geometric and abstract, with an occasional dash of humor, that merits the title of art. The modest Henri d'Origny at work, photographed by Édouard Boubat in 1985 (right).

orated with motifs by house designers, and with the Hermès name printed on the back of the wide end, went on sale the following year.

Hermès ties became internationally renowned in the 1960s under the guidance of Patrick Guerrand (one of Emile Hermès' grandsons). In 1958 he had the excellent idea of hiring one of his old schoolmates who also happened to be a superb designer: Henri d'Origny. The classic

pressed by his success and describes his work as though everything were done without him, as though he could not take credit for this gift from heaven: "Everything happens very quickly. I design my motif; I color it; I have it reduced to make sure it will look well on a tie; I send it to the silkscreen artist; and there it is!" He has long since widened his range to include animals, and flowers, as well as hunting and sailing imagery. But over the last ten years other designers have been crafting a different version of the Hermès tie, using more whimsical motifs featuring a variety of small animals in striking colors, naive flowers, and multicolored clouds.

Almost one million Hermès ties are sold each year, 80% of which are made of printed twill. In terms of quantity, ties outsold the famous Hermès square scarves in 1991. The two collections that Hermès presents each year both feature thirty-five models, each available in a dozen different color schemes. Swiss fabric is most often used in ties made of Jacquard silk. Hermès purchases exclusive models from its weavers, or, more

Since around 1985, the classic image of Hermès ties has been accompanied by a proliferation of amusing little creatures in repeating patterns. Hermès, who launched the fashion in France, saw their sales advance by leaps and bounds. A few of Hermès best-selling birds and beasts in woven silk (below).

Christian Dior, one of the first major couturiers to put his label on ties designed for him, in the company of his muse, Mitza Bricard, *circa* 1950 (left). Today, the house of Dior offers ties more in touch with its own identity and history, such as the *toile de Jouy* motif, designed by Christian Bérard, inspired by the original decor of its Parisian shop.

rarely, has them produce woven versions of the most successful printed designs. The president of Hermès since 1978, Jean-Louis Dumas has said that he intends to expand the line of woven ties, which are in increasingly greater demand.

With **Charles Hill**—whose line represents the *nec plus ultra* of English ties—we return to the richness and diversity of fabrics. In 1973, the tie specialist Charles Hill left Turnbull & Asser on Jermyn Street to head a new subsidiary of the famous clothier. His ambition was not only to produce ties for Turnbull & Asser, but also to expand his horizons by creating his own label. His intention was to make nothing less than the most beautiful ties possible. Twenty years later he has succeeded. Turnbull & Asser, whose clients include the British royal family, many members of Parliament, and quite a few celebrities, provides Hill with a prestigious sales venue. Many other fine stores now offer ties made by him—including Harrods in London, Old England in Paris, and Burberrys in New York. Meanwhile, Hill has managed to establish an excellent reputation for his own label, which is characterized by its serious tone, sumptuous materials, and remarkable inventiveness in a classic mode.

The easiest way to identify ties conceived and manufactured by Charles Hill, since they often

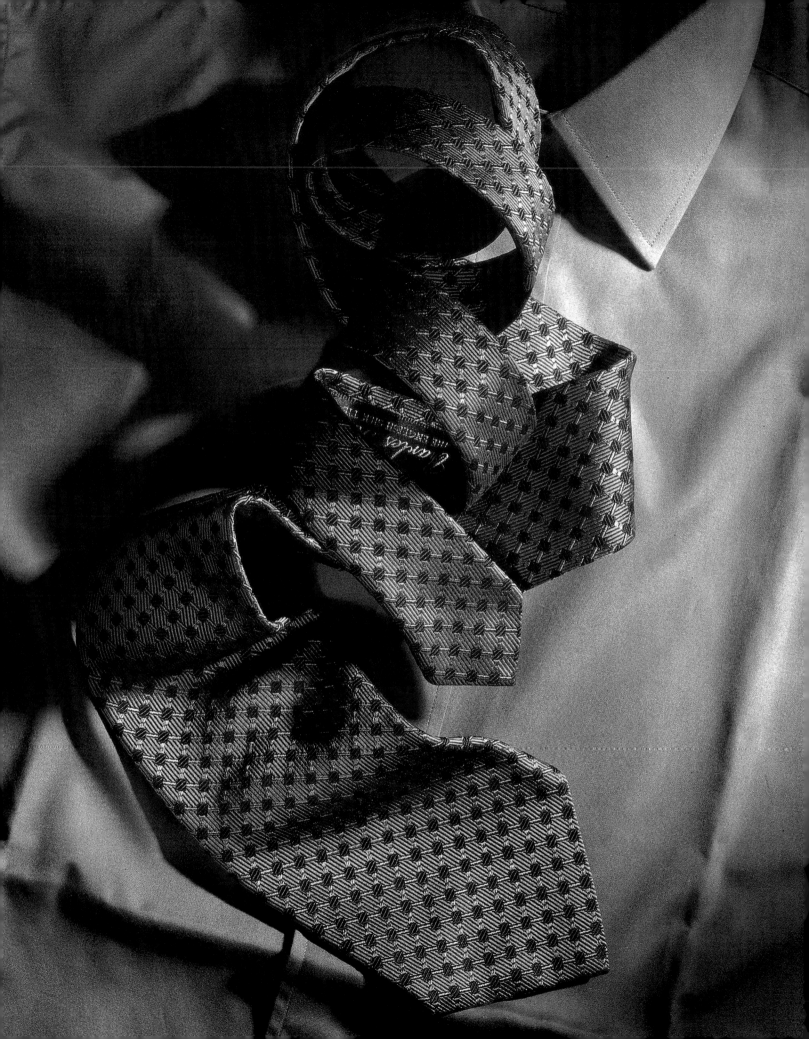

British tradition has something to be said for it, particularly when interpreted by designers such as Charles Hill: classic motifs that will never go out of fashion, a deliciously heavy silk, and ties that are entirely hand-sewn. Charles Hill is a great professional of the tie-making world, and his talents were for a long time employed by the London shirtmakers Turnbull & Asser. In 1973 he went on to start his own company. Charles Hill woven silk tie (left).

carry other labels, is to examine the small tag specifying the material on the back of the narrow end. His initials can be found there in very small print. But there are other, subtler signs. Few current tie makers use such heavy woven and printed silks (up to 50 ounces), or the beautiful madder silks of David Evans, Charles Hill's fabric printer. Hill often uses them when they are least expected: in designs featuring multicolored *pastille* dots, for instance, which are scattered over a 40-ounce silk. What is more, all Charles Hill ties are sewn entirely by hand.

He regards discretion as the supreme expression of elegance. His firm offers no publicity brochures, publishes no annual production figures, and his ties never indulge in "novelty." Charles Hill remains a temple of paisleys, stripes, regimental and club ties, dots, and geometric patterns. But the house is adept at introducing subtle color schemes suited to its clients' personalities. Hill himself is particulary enamored of Egypt, and he occasionally authorizes the use of motifs straight from the valley of the Nile: one such tie features a beautiful column inscribed within a cartouche, which the somber reflections of the madder silk plunges into mysterious obscurity.

As with painting, the breadth of expression encompassed by the universe of ties is so great that boredom is out of the question. What do Charles Hill and **Nicole Miller** have in common? Nothing much, other than their capacity to make us love a small strip of fabric. Once upon a time, then, there was a young New York designer named Nicole Miller who created an amusing and relatively inexpensive line of women's clothing with motley and playful motifs she devised herself. Through the promotion efforts of her associate Bud Konheim, her talent was soon recognized, and the first Nicole Miller boutique opened on Madison Avenue in 1986. Soon after the store opened, Bud Konheim noted that a certain model, a silk dress printed with theater and opera tickets in an all-over pattern, was not selling. The motif was droll and its colors perfect, but it obviously was not right for a dress. Kon-

heim decided to try it on scarves. When placing the order with his manufacturer, he asked that a tie also be made for his personal use. The manufacturer responded that given the realities of the production process he couldn't accept an order for less than thirty-six ties. Konheim gave the green light. He kept one of the ties for himself and placed the others in the boutique, pricing them at $45.00. On their first day in the shop, the security guard saw the ties, fell in love with them, and bought one. He wore it the next night at the Metropolitan Opera, where he also worked. Proud of his new tie, he showed it to the manager of the gift shop. He loved it too, and the next day appeared at Nicole Miller to purchase all thirty-four ties, which he then proceeded to resell for $90.00 a piece! They were gone within three days. Thanks to opera buffs, a star of the tie world had been born.

Immediately, Nicole Miller's "conversation starters"—basically a contemporary version of the bold-look tie of the 1940s —became known and sought after in New York. Ties decorated with opera tickets were followed by beer bottles, playing cards, Harley Davidsons, wine labels, and so on, all meticulously printed in striking colors, and always on beautiful silk.

Today, Nicole Miller sells more than ten million ties per year. When Bud Konheim is asked about the reason for this success, he answers: "Because our ties are funny, and we all need to laugh."

The ties of **Richel** are neither funny nor sad. They are simply beautiful. One wants to study and caress them, while the ease with which they can be perfectly tied is a pleasant surprise. The Barcelona-based Richel, the finest tie maker in Spain, could give lessons to the entire world. Meeting Michel Catris, Richel's founder would be a pleasurable experience for any lover of ties. He receives his visitors in a large office overflowing with sample silks and ties, and fifteen minutes later one finds oneself pouring over many magnificent models, whose beauty and quality Catris describes with the precision of an experienced professional and the fervor of a man who is passionately in love with his craft.

The premises of Turnbull & Asser in London's Jermyn Street, the shirt Mecca of London's political and artistic elites. Here one finds ties and bow ties of a supreme elegance, sold as Turnbull & Asser, but designed and made by Charles Hill (left).

The wild ties produced by Nicole Miller are direct descendants of the 1940s American "bold look" ties. By some miracle—perhaps having to do with the silk fabric, the quality printing, the fine detail of overlapping motifs, and the use of innumerable colors—they are never vulgar. In the United States, where her products are immensely popular, everyone knows that when you wear a Nicole Miller tie, even if it is printed with bottles of dishwashing liquid, boxes of laundry detergent, baseballs or even the left-overs from a dinner party, it will never be in bad taste. Two Nicole Miller ties in printed silk (right).

Some companies stand out for their strong individual stamp and inimitable style; others, such as Richel, offer a broad variety of styles destined to satisfy all tastes. To this eclecticism (ranging from the simple black tie, through dots and stripes, to big multicolored designs), the Barcelona company adds elements which make it one of the most dependable tie producers in the world today: on the one hand, sumptuous silks that are designed, printed and woven in Como, and on the other hand a guaranteed perfection of manufacture, under the control of expert hands in Spain. Richel tie in printed figured silk (right).

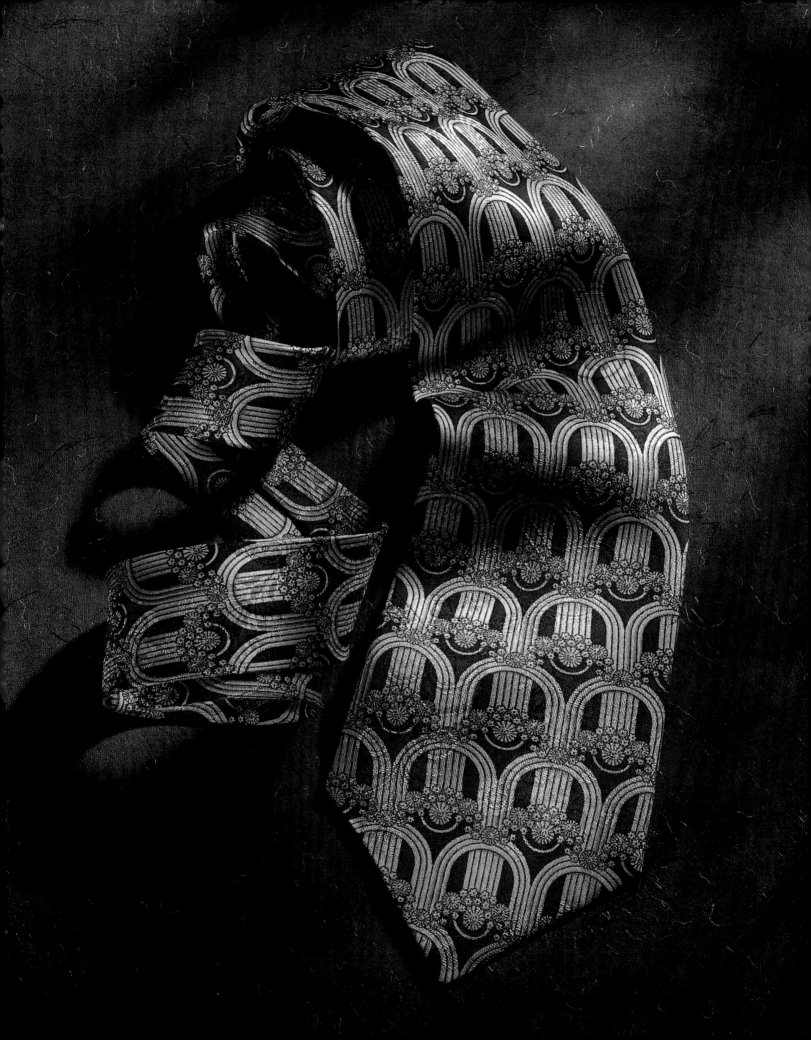

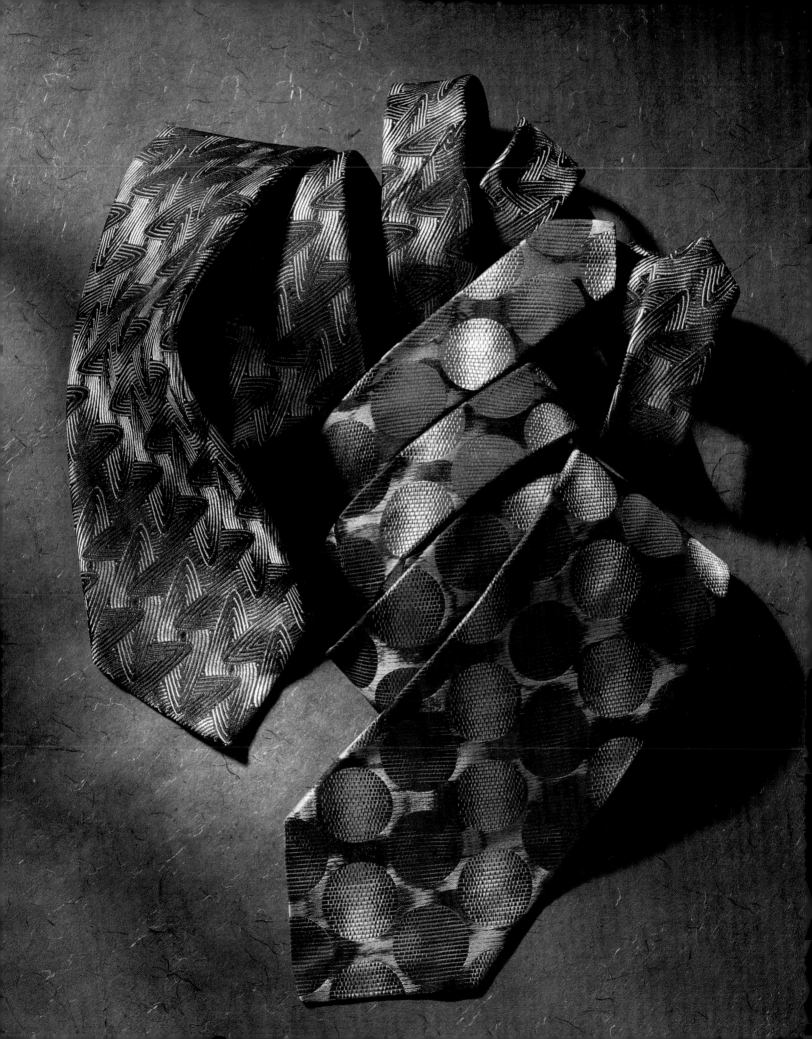

In the classic register, the Robert Talbott company is incontestably the most prestigious producer in the United States. "Invent colors, textures and designs; seek out the finest silks, cottons, wools and linens; create the best product possible, and then sell it at a fair price without worrying about what others are doing." This is how the company sums up its policy. Since 1950, the Talbott family has been scouring Europe in search of the finest fabrics, and transforming them into exclusively hand-sewn ties in its California workshops. The results come close to perfection.
Woven silk ties (left).
A 1981 advertisement displaying one of the company's specialities: the regimental tie (bottom, right).

In 1948 when Michel Catris started his business, Catalonia already boasted of a number of tie makers. But their offerings consistently suffered from two decisive defects: designs were suffocatingly banal, and production quality was inadequate. Catris set to work, and a year later Richel ties were famous throughout Spain. Today, after forty years of uninterrupted progress, Richel manufactures one million ties per year and is the official tie supplier to King Juan Carlos.

At first glance, Michel Castris's recipe seems simple: take the most beautiful printed and woven silks from Como, then transform them into ties with all the requisite care. In reality, however, the process is not that easy, because the art of the tie has much in common with alchemy. To obtain the best silks from Como weavers, for example, one must first win their confidence, even their friendship. Michel Catris speaks with emotion of the four "monarchs" of Como, his friends Antonio Ratti, Giovanni Campi, Gianni Binda, and Luigi Turconi: "They have always given me their best designs and their most beautiful silks. I owe everything to them." Such modesty is exemplary, perhaps, but it is common knowledge that the quality of the silk is not in itself sufficient to assure a tie's beauty. It must also be perfectly made, and it is in this department that Richel surpasses its competitors. The Richel factory assembles five thousand ties each day, sewn almost entirely by hand with meticulous details such as the slip stitch and a perfectly fitted interlining of wool and spun viscose.

Styles of all kinds are welcome at Richel, which makes it an ideal showcase for Como weavers in both traditional and innovative models: whether printed or woven, sober or sophisticated, their work will be made to look its best. But Michel Catris is especially fond of rep, fine mogadore, and above all grenadine, which is prized by connoisseurs for its rough-grained hand and the beautiful shape that it gives to knots.

Conceived in Italy and manufactured in Spain, Richel ties are Mediterranean through-and-through, much like the effusive personality

of Michel Catris. But the story behind **Robert Talbott** is archetypically American. Imagine a graduate of the prestigious Harvard Business School who, at age forty, cut a rather brilliant figure in New York high finance but who, one fine day, after a series of mishaps, found himself unemployed. In Paris or Rome this fellow would have sought out a position as a vice-president in a bank and calmly awaited retirement. But Robert Talbott was a New Yorker, and his enterprising spirit was irrepressible: every day brought thousands of new ideas. Talbott had two great loves in life: his wife Audrey and bow ties. In 1950 Robert and Audrey Talbott made the important step of leaving New York to settle in Carmel, California, where they set up a bow-tie business. At first things were simple: Audrey made the ties herself and Robert delivered them. Inspired by Charvet and Sulka models worn by the men in her family, Audrey's craft was of such obviously high quality that the Talbotts soon acquired a clientele. In 1953 they hired a few workers and added long ties to their line. Five years later they opened their first shop in Carmel and began to work with Italian and British silk makers, who wove silk for them based on their own designs. When Robert died in 1986, the house was producing and selling more than one million ties and bow ties per year.

Although founded in California, Robert Talbott ties are among the most traditional produced in the United States—they epitomize the snappy, all-American look. George Bush is partial to them, and his wardrobe perfectly exemplifies this style of dress. Robert Talbott's brand of traditionalism shows French as well as British influences—he never once disguised his admiration for Charvet. Talbott designs feature dots, geometric forms, stripes, and paisleys galore. It goes without saying that Talbott is the uncontested champion when it comes to American clubs and regimentals—the firm makes ties for Harvard, Stanford, and the very exclusive Bel Air Country Club, for example. Talbott ties are either printed or woven, and all of them are sewn entirely by hand. Since 1986, Robert Talbott has

Founded in New York in 1895, the Sulka company became internationally well-known between the two world wars, thanks to its Paris branch. It still remains one of the temples of the traditional refined tie. Neckties in printed silk, with a motif of neo-Gothic-style medallions (left).

"Talbott of course"

also offered seven-fold ties, a model long unavailable because of its high production cost.

Miraculous seven-folds are one of the rare things in common between the American Robert Talbott and the Italian **Ermenegildo Zegna**, who decided to include them in his 1994 fall collection. Here again alphabetical order proves fortuitous: it allows me to end this short survey with one of the most inventive tie houses, a firm which, in addition to traditional ties, offers its customers a symphony of motifs and materials as beautiful as they are surprising.

The Zegna firm was founded in 1910 in the major Italian wool-producing center of Biella, in the Piedmont mountains. In 1923 at age twenty, the founder's son, Ermenegildo Zegna, took over the reins of this small wool business. As the result of hard work sustained over the next forty years, Zegna became one of the great Italian textile firms. At the same time, Zegna himself, an enthusiast of wool, mountains, and nature, lavished much time and energy on a special passion of his: a natural park and tourist center created in 1938 on the slopes of Mount Rubello.

During the 1960s Ermenegildo's sons, Aldo and Angelo, diversified the firm's activities by creating a line of fine men's ready-to-wear. Thirty years later, Ermenegildo Zegna shops are to be found the world over—from Mexico City to Melbourne by way of Peking. They sell clothing celebrated for its refinement as well as for the natural characteristics of its exquisitely made fabrics: wool, of course, but also linen, silk, and ravishing cottons. Such scrupulous attention to the original, natural qualities of materials is altogether typical of this remarkable firm, born in the mountains, whose current directors still honor the ecological priorities of their grandfather Ermenegildo Zegna.

An affiliate of the Zegna group, Orsini participates in the design and production of ties not only for the Zegna label but also for Léonard, Givenchy, Paco Rabanne, Dunhill, Aquascutum, and more. Luciano Donatelli, Orsini's director,

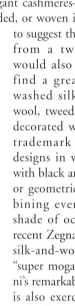

is one of the finest connoisseurs of both the industrial and artistic aspects of contemporary tie production. "A song is difficult," he told me when we met, "for everything must be said in three minutes. But ties are still more difficult, for all must be said in three seconds." For Zegna, Orsini has devised several modes of such instantaneous communication, but the most fascinating is without doubt the one that is also the most reflective of the firm's traditions, the one that delights in the attraction and natural beauty of noble materials. Personally, I will always first associate Zegna with wool. It would be difficult to find more elegant cashmeres—whether knitted, combed, carded, or woven in such a way as to suggest that they were cut from a tweed jacket. It would also be difficult to find a greater variety of washed silks that imitate wool, tweed, and cashmere, decorated with the house's trademark patchwork designs in warm colors, or with black and white stripes, or geometric patterns combining every conceivable shade of ochre. The most recent Zegna innovation is a silk-and-wool blend called "super mogadore" But Orsini's remarkable inventiveness is also exercised for Zegna on brilliant silks to achieve a multitude of special effects —embossed silk patchworks, patterned velours obtained by a process called *chenille*, and figured silk ties printed with large designs.

There we have it—from Abboud to Zegna—an overview of the great fashion houses that practice the art of tie design and production at its most exalted level. It is true that the art of making ties thrives on the passion and technical mastery of designers, but the enthusiasm of demanding amateurs is equally important in keeping the flame alive. When the manager of the Hermès tie department, Pascaline Bachelet, told me about a Canadian client who was madly in love with Hermès ties, I understood, detecting a hint of genuine emotion behind her smile, why she worked so hard to satisfy demanding customers such as he.

How can a tie be simultaneously highly sophisticated and sublimely simple? This is the secret of the Zegna company. The effect is achieved by searching out rare materials, and treating them with genius: soft wools, washed silks, velvety silks, mixtures of wool and silk, mogadore, and other noble fabrics give this company's ties their essential characteristic: a quality of naturalness. Ermenegildo Zegna washed silk tie recommended for wearing with jeans (left); Patchwork motif on silk tie (right).

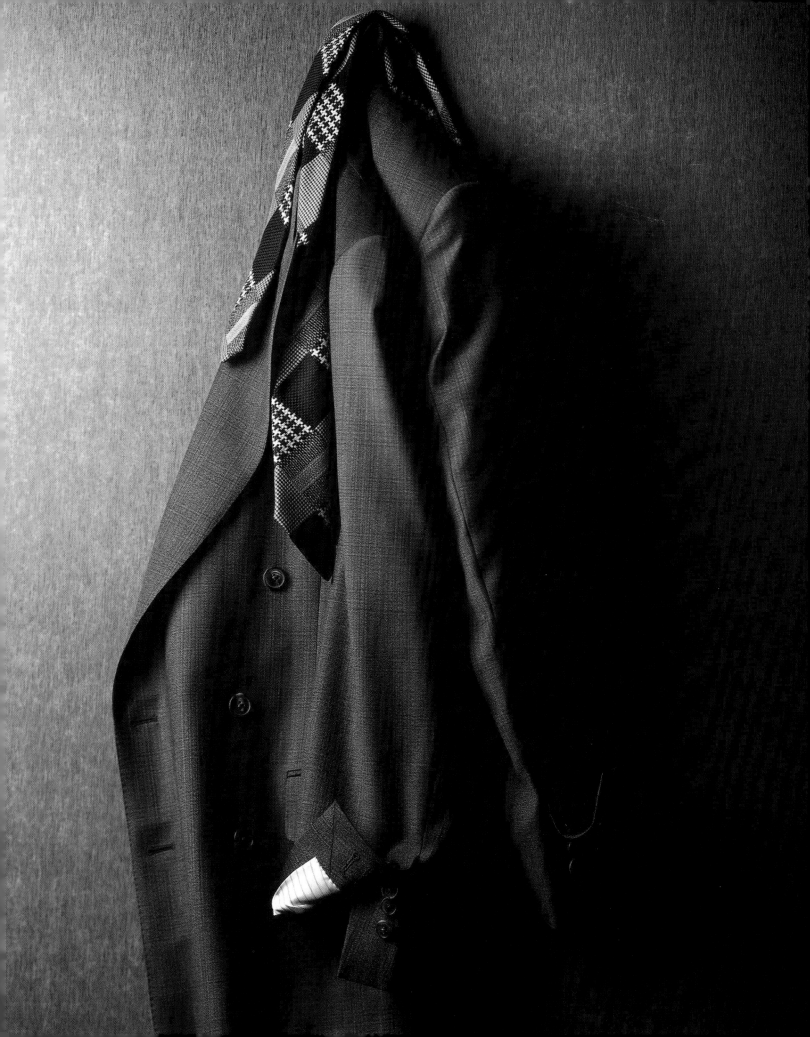

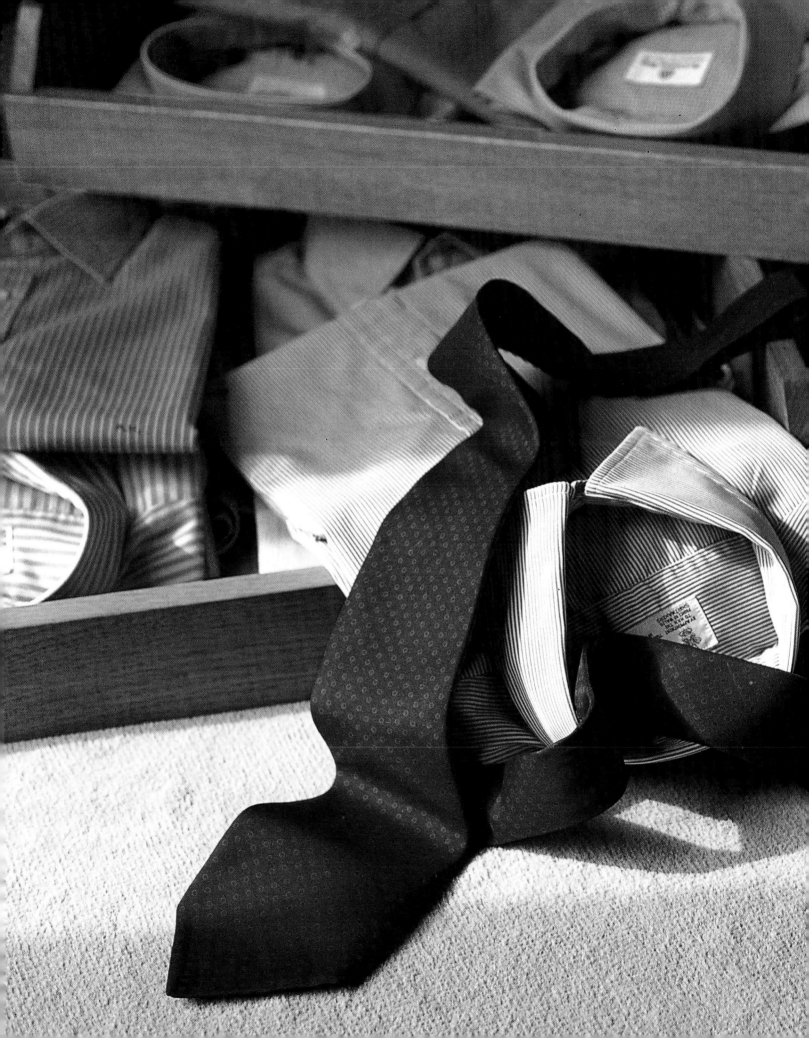

A MANUAL
OF STYLE

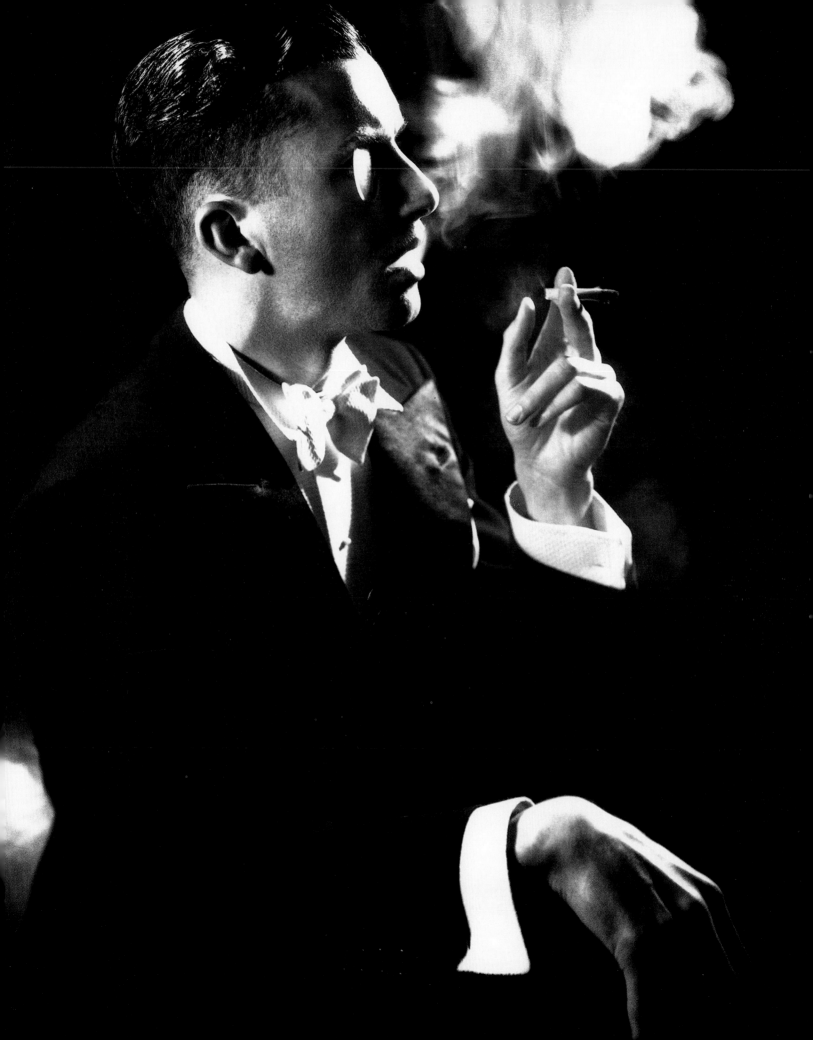

How fortunate are those men of British high society who employ a butler, one of whose duties is to oversee their wardrobe and to guard against lapses of taste. Such a one was Jeeves, P. G. Wodehouse's unforgettable fictional "gentleman's personal gentleman," who never let his young employer's would-be sartorial eccentricities go unremarked. His master Bertie Wooster was especially prone to failures of judgment when it came to socks, but ties were also a matter of contention. One day, when the young man insisted on wearing a bizarre tie recommended to him by a friend, Jeeves declared, in his habitual detached but cutting tone, that had a friend of his told him that such a tie suited him, he would, whatever that person's age or station, strike him smartly on the head. Fortunately most employers place their entire confidence in their butlers. "One of his first morning duties," confides Ivor Spencer, founder of a prestigious school for butlers, "is to present his employer with two complete suits of clothes for wear in the city. One will be chosen and worn, while the other will be returned to the closet. A large selection of ties must also be presented which are coordinated with one or the other of the suits. Very often these are ties they themselves have chosen from the best shops."

Alas, the world's injustice is such that there is no butler or valet at your beck and call. You yourself must decide which tie to wear every morning of your life, and quickly too, for you are always in a hurry. On some days you dress to seduce, on others to reassure or pass unnoticed. On occasion you must consider important business meetings or social outings with friends. Yet whatever the specific circumstances, your tie must harmonize with your shirt and jacket.

Some men remain serenely calm in this moment of decision. This is the case for men who let their wives decide for them, and have never regretted doing so. They are rare. Or those who wear the first tie they come across, refusing to take the matter seriously. One does not know whether to envy or to pity them. Still others place all of their faith in the three basic rules they learned from their father, who in turn had learned them from his father. Their lives are often the image of their clothing, as monotonous as a flat stretch of highway. Then there are those with a sure sense of color and fabric, whose awareness of the potential pitfalls allows them to

One tie that is absolutely obligatory: the bow tie in white cotton piqué, accompanying formal evening dress. Charles Boré in 1930, photographed by François Kollar (left).

A certain conception of male elegance, as seen by the artist Gruau (above).

True elegance is never far from simplicity, according to Marcel Proust. Simplicity in coordination: a red tie with blue confetti dots on a blue-striped shirt (preceding double page).

Would a true butler trained in the British school have tolerated his master sporting an American "bold look" tie? Certainly not! The English valet presents his master each morning with a selection of ties that excludes any hint of fancy. But we are in the United States—more precisely, in Hollywood. Cary Grant, Edward Fielding and Larain Day in *Mr. Lucky*, an RKO film production by H.C. Potter in 1942 (left).

reach their decision in a minute or two. This marvelous moment is consecrated to selecting the one tie, among all the possibilites, that makes them smile that day. These men are the artists of the tie whose knowledge serves their imagination and whose imagination champions elegance. If you aspire to join this select company, and have no butler at your service then this chapter is especially for you.

TO WEAR OR NOT TO WEAR

To wear or not to wear a tie, that is often the first question to be pondered. It should be noted immediately that wearing a tie has become largely a matter of personal choice, although some obvious exceptions include very expensive restaurants, certain society circles, a few casinos, official ceremonies, and, of course, many workplaces. But there are also occasions when, although not mandatory, such wear is to be recommended. Everyone knows that ties—unless they are decorated with naked starlets or laughing giraffes—confer an impression of dignity and respectability on the wearer. Such an impression can be quite useful, especially in professional life, where one must win over and maintain the confidence of one's colleagues. But such attire has its uses in other contexts as well. John T. Molloy, the author of *Dress for Success,* suggests that delinquents should wear ties to prevent the police from suspecting them. Molloy also draws our attention to another interesting phenomenon: in restaurants where ties are not compulsory wear, the *maîtres d'hôtel* instinctively seat tie-less customers at the worst tables, close to the kitchen or entrance.

On the other hand, there is still reason to rejoice: there remain virtually no situations in which ties are completely out of place, except perhaps the Sahara in mid-August or at varsity football games. The rugby team of the Racing Club de France once wore bow ties during a match. They lost, but no one held the bow ties responsible. In temperate climates, the only disadvantage to wearing a tie would seem to be pre-

cisely the impression of respectability it creates. Men do not always want to appear stiff, stilted, and respectable. But should they want to wear a tie when inclined to strike a more relaxed note, there are plenty of models to choose from: "conversation starters," and a wide variety of novelty and joke ties. Many men think that ties do not go with jeans. They could not be more mistaken. Hermès salesmen recommend that customers buy ties cut from the celebrated Hermès scarves for wear with jeans. The element of fantasy in such ties with large motifs is wonderfully suited to the casual appearance of a pair of jeans. Charvet suggests its sportiest silk ties, woven in a large, irregular grain called "hopsack" that perfectly complements the texture of denim.

Another question often arises in cold weather: is it permissible to wear a tie with a sweater? The answer is yes—if the sweater is a V-neck. Many, myself included, feel that bow ties should be worn. But Italian trend-setter Gianni Agnelli—one of this century's great dandies, and president of Fiat—often sports long ties with crew necks. The Italians have named this eccentric uniform a *golfatta,* a compound of the words *golf* (from the Italian for sweater) and *cravatta.* Like his habit of wearing a watch over a sleeve cuff, the *golfatta* has become part of the legend associated with this great industrialist, art lover, and philanthropist.

The tie question is a bit more delicate when it comes to women. I am not speaking here about the various knots devised for them, most notably the gracious *lavalière,* but rather about

men's ties. On women a tie most often prompts the wearing of shirt, jacket, and pants as well. Women achieve both superb and awkward results in this typically male uniform. Sometimes the intent is precisely to wipe out all traces of femininity, which such garb is certainly capable of doing. But then there are those superb instances when this sartorial strategy results in an ambiguity that is mysterious, troubling, and seductive. How is it, exactly, that certain women achieve this effect? What was the secret

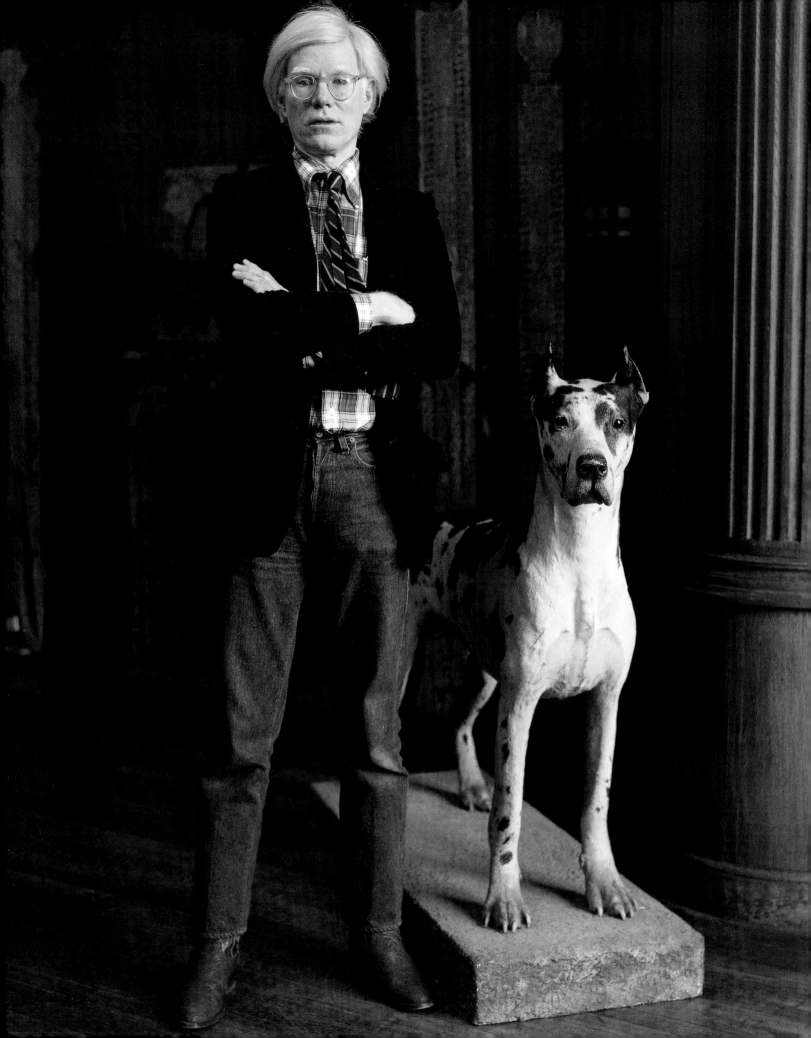

People often used to ask Marlene Dietrich why she liked to dress like a man. She replied that the best songs were written for men. The seductively ambiguous Marlene Dietrich in full masculine attire (left).

Over the years, the meaning behind ties being worn by women has radically changed. *Pantalonnades*: great-grandmother and her great-grand-daughter, taken from *L'Illustration*, 1939 (below).

of Marlene Dietrich, for example, who used such dress to transform herself into a fascinating image of irresistible allure? Doubtless her gaze, her silhouette, her face, and her voice contributed much to the ultimate effect, because instead of giving her masculine airs, her clothing made her seem almost divine; she was a creature transcending familiar human categories, inaccessible and so all the more desirable.

FIRST ENCOUNTERS

Let us come down to earth again. A few years ago *Playboy* magazine published a cartoon that said a lot about a man's relationship to his tie. In the image two couples greet each other on the sidewalk, and by chance, the women are wearing identical dresses and the two men identical ties. The eyes tell the whole story: the two women are furious, both consumed by mutual hatred while the men are spontaneously drawn toward one

another. For a man, a tie is not so much an expression of his worth as an affirmation, conscious or other wise, of his deepest personality. Two men wearing the same tie are likely to find a kindred spirit, an accomplice, a person with similar opinions and tastes. It follows that there can be no universal guidelines for tie selection, for the choice is entirely dependent on the wearer's temperament.

Yet clear limits on choice are set by the assortment of ties in one's closet, from which one must choose when the delicious moment arrives. It is worth remarking that only those ties in good condition should be candidates; all too often a few wearings will suffice to turn a tie into a useless rag, a mere crumpled strip of fabric with split seams and a label hanging on by one end. Before buying a tie it is advisable to carefully assess its quality, however much it may fascinate you on the display rack. Such scrutiny is usually superfluous when buying from

The sober and sporting four-in-hand tie gives a woman an image that is energetic and determined, an image that it does not necessarily give to a man. The actress Norma Shearer in *The Snob*, a 1924 silent film by Monta Bell (right).

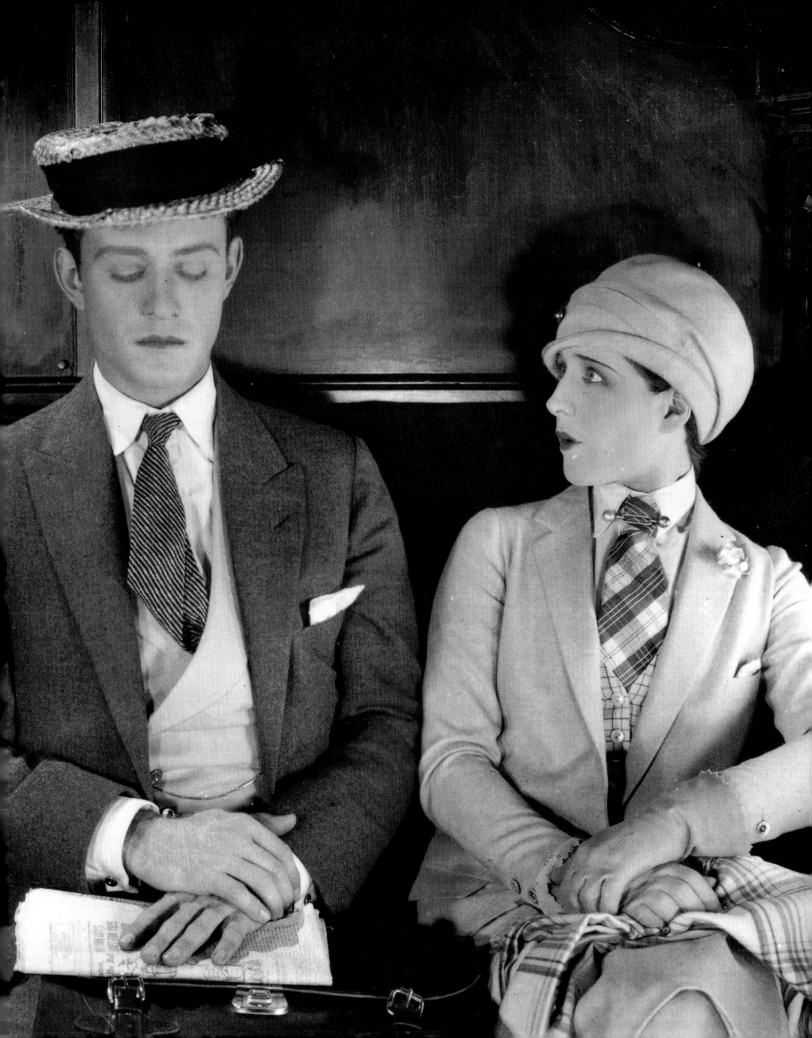

The jewel of a man's wardrobe must be chosen with love, but with an eye for quality, and then worn according to his humor, but with an eye for coordination. A group of well-tied friends, meeting in 1992: from left to right, the couturier Christian Lacroix, the writer Pierre-Jean Rémy, the model and designer, Inés de la Fressange, the Como silk-producer Ricardo Mantero, and the jeweler Alain Boucheron.

A sometimes delicate moment: the first encounter. 1912 illustration from a German manual: *The Tie: a Breviary of Good Taste* (below).

renowned tie makers whose quality-control procedures are exemplary. One should know that buying a mass-produced tie in a shopping mall is quite a different proposition from buying a tie on the faubourg Saint-Honoré, Savile Row, or Fifth Avenue. When in doubt, one can run a personal quality check.

Imagine for a moment that you are standing in front of a tempting specimen. You like the tie's motif, its color scheme, its texture, as well as that ever so elusive and mysterious *je ne sais quoi*. Before rushing to the cash register, the following five-step quality-control should be performed. First, verify the angle on which the material was cut. All fine ties are cut on the bias of the fabric. This oblique cutting angle, which increases the amount of wasted fabric, is a dependable guarantee of a basic level of resistance to wear and tear. On certain ties, those made of silk twill, for example, the angle of the cut can be discerned with the naked eye: fine ribs will be visible at a 45 degree angle to the tie's vertical axis. But more often you will need to perform the following simple test: grip the tie at its narrow end and let it hang freely. Should it twist or kink even slightly, you can be sure that it has not been cut correctly.

Second, verify the tie's elasticity by holding it by its two ends and stretching. A well-made tie will return at once to its original length. Third, verify the presence of the slip stitch. This length of thread is left loose at the end of the envelope's back seam in order to give it a certain "play." It is often hidden under the envelope but can be found with a bit of gentle probing—it is several inches long and often takes the form of a loop. Its presence allows the tie to be pulled and stretched—as when a knot is tied with it—without the seam coming apart. Fourth, closely examine the two seams which secure the lining at each tip—they should be tightly sewn together. Fifth, pull gently on the lining of each tip. The lining should not shift and should go high enough to completely hide the interlining.

These precautions may seem exaggerated, but surely confidence in a tie's longevity is worth the investment of a few minutes of one's time.

QUANTITY

How many ties should one own in order to be prepared for all occasions? In 1950, the unfortunately defunct magazine *Adam* asked six fine Parisian haberdashers the following question: "What should a male wardrobe include?" Regarding ties, Viley maintained that twenty-two were necessary: a dozen fancy silks, three pure wools, three silk twills, two for tails, and two for tuxedo wear. Representatives of the Dorian Guy fashion house suggested thirty-six: a dozen solids, a dozen prints, six clubs, and six

A tie is the frailest item of masculine dress, because most vulnerable. It must be made to perfection, to resist all assaults. Katherine Hepburn and Spencer Tracy in *Adam's Rib*, a 1949 George Cukor film (right).

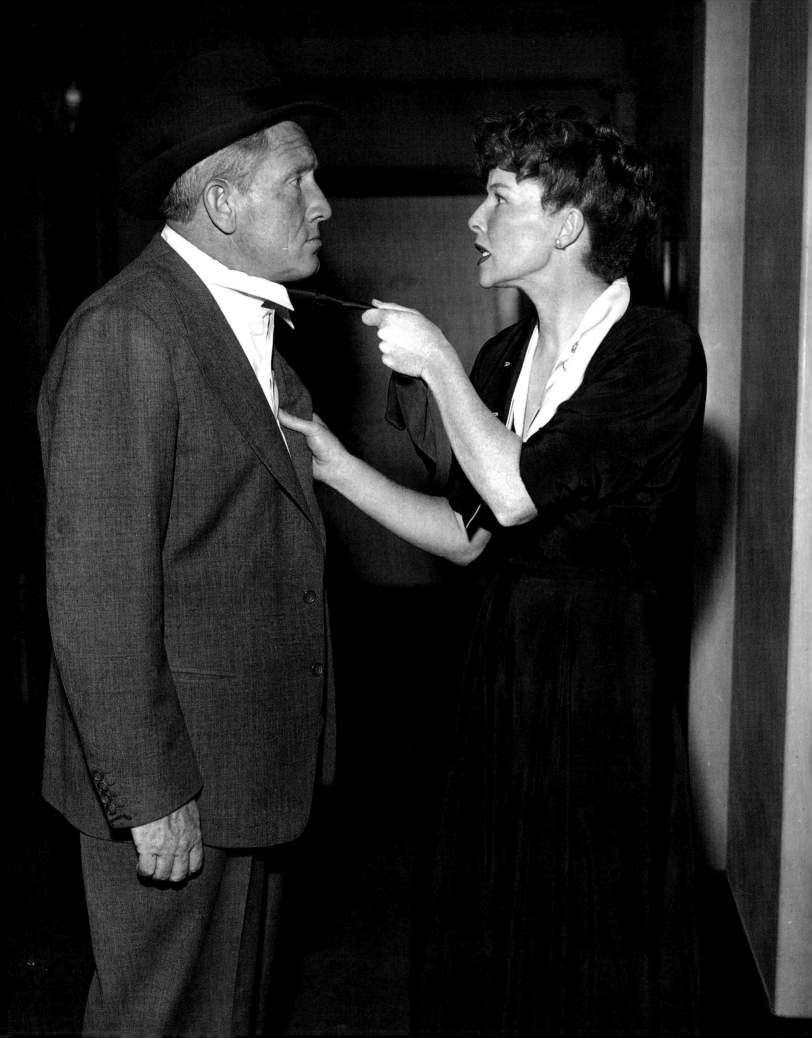

Ideally, a tie should be in keeping with both shirt and suit, but also with the personality of its wearer. Mademoiselle Carven trying ties on the actor Eddie Constantine in the 1960s (right).

The elegance of Gary Cooper (1901–61), a 1930s fashion trend-setter, had to do with a certain nonchalance, a relaxed attitude, which went with clothes that were loose-fitting and sometimes even slightly wrinkled. On the screen he was the perfect image of the middle-class American man, but he was actually of British extraction. Gifted with an innate sense of refinement, it would never have crossed his mind to wear a tie and suspenders made of matching fabric. A 1935 studio photo by Eugene Richee (right).

A moment that can range from the delicious to the terrible: choosing one's tie from the wardrobe. 1948 illustration published in *Adam* (below).

with black backgrounds. In 1951, Sydney D. Barney, the author of *Clothes and the Man: A Guide to Correct Dress for All Occasions*, recommended that company presidents own at least forty-eight ties, established professionals at least twenty-four, and young bachelors at least thirty-six.

Yet all of these figures fail to address the real question. The number of ties to own can vary, depending upon the rest of one's wardrobe. There is nothing more unfortunate than owning a shirt or suit and lacking a tie to wear with it. Therefore every shirt, suit, and jacket should have a coordinated tie. With white or light-blue shirts and solid, gray, or navy-blue suits, just about any tie will do. Problems arise with the more exuberant shirts and suits in bright colors, or with stripes, herringbone tweed, and so on. If one owns ten shirts and two suits or jackets in this more assertive mode, then one will need at least twelve carefully selected ties to accompany them. Obviously, wearing the same tie with the same shirt will eventually make you hate the shirt, the tie, and perhaps even life itself! Consequently, it is better to possess at least two ties for each shirt and suit. In principle, the second tie

should be chosen so that it completely changes the effect created by the ensemble. In this manner, buying a tie is almost like acquiring a new suit in your wardrobe.

COORDINATING

"It is by dint neither of study nor work that success will be achieved; a tie must be donned spontaneously, instinctively, under the sway of inspiration. A well-tied tie is one of those traits of genius that can be sensed and admired but not analyzed or taught. I assert with all the force of conviction that ties are essentially romantic —the day they succumb to general rules and fixed principles they will have ceased to exist." Appearing in the *Physiologie de la toilette* and attributed to Balzac, this profession of faith was meant to apply to the process of knotting. But is it not equally pertinent to the task of coordinating one's tie with a shirt and jacket? Many rule books and treatises have addressed this subject, and they are often in flagrant contradiction with one another. This is because elegance and charm are not subject to decree—they are by nature

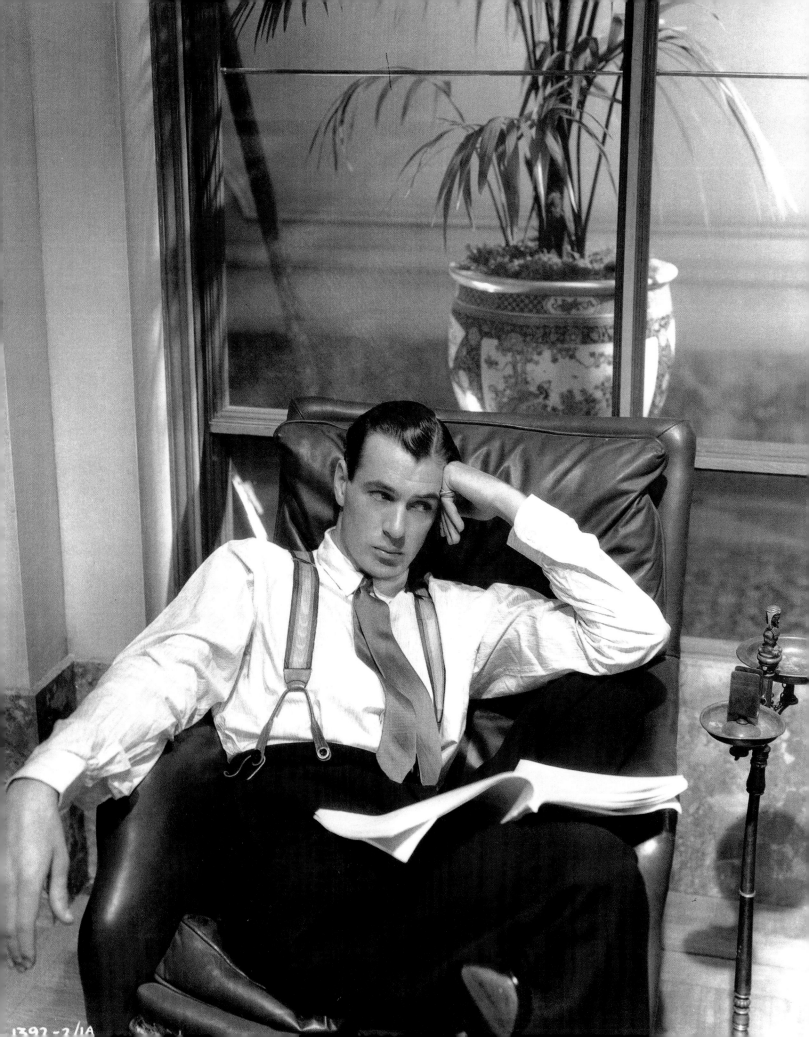

"One should
either be a work of art, or
wear a work of art."
(Oscar Wilde, "Phrases
and Philosophies for
the Use of the Young,"
published in the
Chameleon, December
1894).
Quel homme chic!
Illustration from
Monsieur magazine,
1921 (right).

ineffable and often thrive on subversion of "rules." This being the case, why bother to give advice about the coordinating process? First, because in the absence of guidelines most men tend to make decisions that are neither deeply repugnant nor truly seductive. They fall within a sartorial middle range: the slightest miscalculation or inspired touch can send this type of man's image careening off toward one or the other extreme. Second, because in one fundamental respect, the art of the wardrobe is like any other art: practice makes perfect. If you refuse to play your scales you will never become a virtuoso musician. In the realm of ties, scales consist of a few fundamental rules which must be mastered . . . if only to lay a foundation for breaking them in the future.

Colors. One day a salesman at Charvet was attending to an Indonesian customer who was taking advantage of his brief stay in Paris to satisfy a long-standing desire to buy a few ties that would match the color of his car. Photograph in hand, he showed the salesman a pinkish-lavender automobile. All efforts to find ties of that color in his own country had failed. Unable to make a match with any of his color samples, the salesman was tempted to suggest that the man buy a new car. In the end, however, a special order was made, and the ties were dispatched to Jakarta a few days later.

In the good old days of the four-in-hand,

problems of this kind never arose. The background color of men's ties was almost always black, navy blue, burgundy, or—more rarely—emerald green. Bright, lively colors were considered provocative. When the narrator of Proust's *A Remembrance of Things Past* first meets the baron de Charlus, he notes that ". . . there was an all but imperceptible touch of red on his

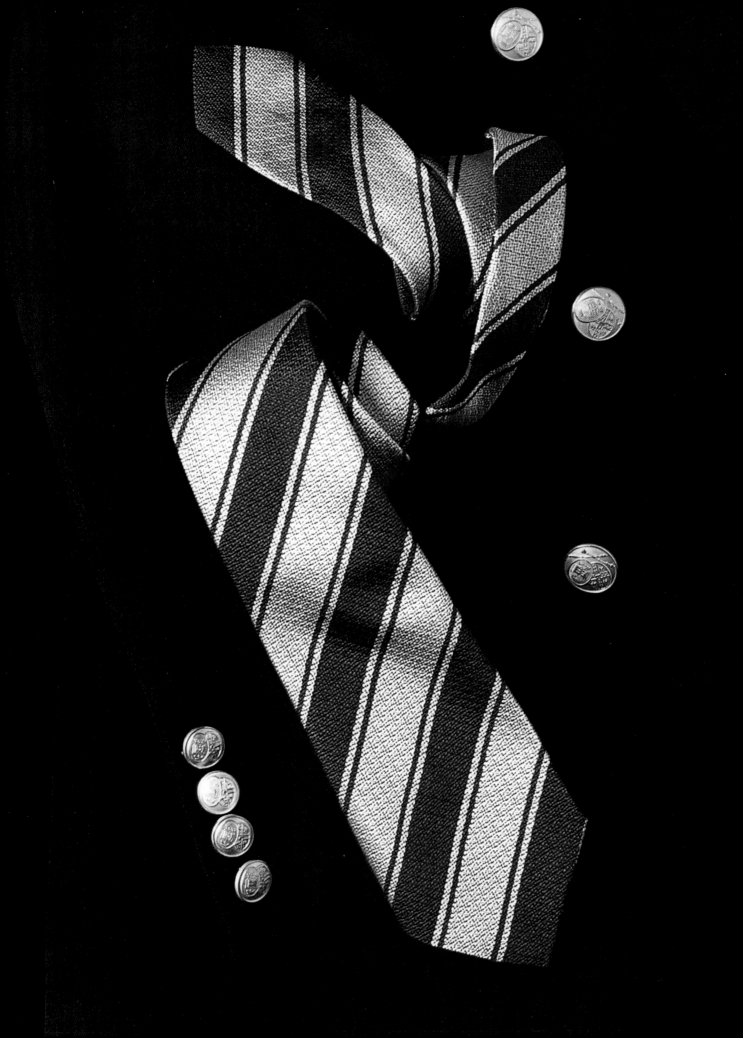

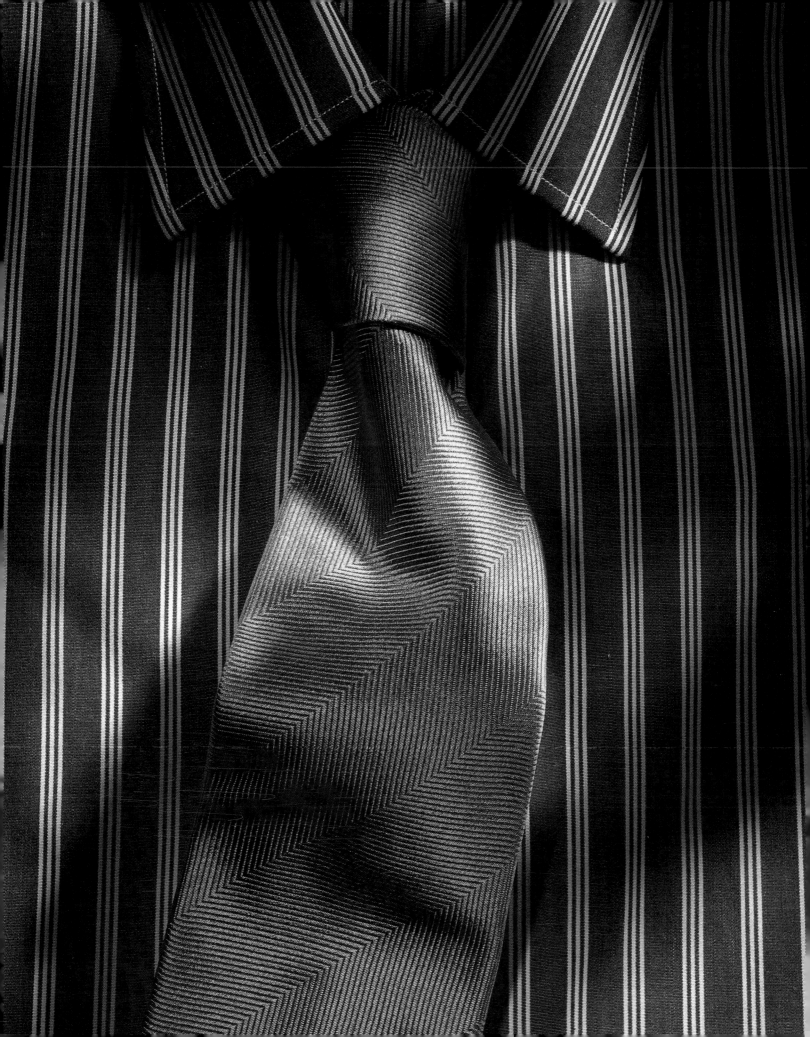

One of the key principles of the tie: the contrast of color between the tie and the shirt. Here, blue and golden yellow balance each other perfectly. The twill weave of the silk tie also echoes the triple stripes of the shirt (left).

tion of a tie, after all, is to be seen. (Those who disagree might consider purchasing one of Jean-Paul Gaultier's most recent creations, a tie sold with a matching shirt cut from the same linen. Yet if such discretion is to your taste, perhaps you should renounce ties altogether and wear, for example, the shirt by the Japanese designer Yohji Yamamoto, which has a collar with crossing flaps that precludes the wearing of a tie once and for all). Note, however, that the contrast can be subtle, say, between two dark colors.

The second pitfall, which errs in the direction of facility, consists of wearing different tones of the same elementary color —a red tie with a pink shirt, or a navy-blue tie with a sky-blue shirt, for instance. These combinations indicate a lack of imagination. Still, this bit of advice does not invalidate the tried-and-true method of emphasizing one of the colors on your jacket or shirt by repeating it in your tie. You can be sure of not making a blunder since you are essentially copying the color scheme chosen by the jacket's designer, who probably would not have become successful without a minimum of taste.

In short, your tie should always contrast to some degree with your shirt. The art of color coordination lies in making this contrast as harmonious as possible. A satisfactory result can be

A woven silk tie with small green and pink geometric patterns, in twill and satin, on a pink-striped shirt. The pink of the shirt echoes the pink of the tie, while the green, its complementary color, provides contrast. At the same time, the scale of the small geometric patterns is similar to that of the stripes (left).

cravat, like a liberty one dare not take." In the 1950s things brightened up considerably. One could see colors such as "pink champagne," "willow green," and "grapefruit yellow." In the 1980s Armani in Italy and Joseph Abboud in the United States made us love subtle, neutral and earth tones, especially browns, grays, and muted greens. These colors were all relatively easy to coordinate. More recently, the fashion has tended toward striking, multicolored ties, a trend that is perhaps linked to the darkening economic outlook, from which bright colors momentarily distract us. Many houses, including some of the more conservative English firms, now offer color combinations brighter than a florist's window display. While it sometimes seems that anything goes, care must be taken not to abuse shocking pink, apple green, and canary yellow, unless, of course, one wishes to make oneself conspicuous at any cost. Still, most errors result not from the colors themselves but from a failure to coordinate their use in tie, shirt, and jacket.

Common sense dictates that two pitfalls should be avoided. First, wearing a tie insufficiently contrasted with one's shirt will certainly cause you to be overlooked. The primary func-

An impression of harmony can be attained by the association of at least three colors. With a solid-color shirt it can be achieved by a three-color tie: one color evoking the hue of the shirt (here navy blue), and two others contrasting. Note that with a solid-color shirt all patterns are permitted. In this case the stripes are in three different reps (left).

obtained by juxtaposing two different but compatible hues, for example, two complementary colors—blue and orange, green and red, yellow and violet. Should doubts arise, a reliable rule to fall back on holds that a primary color should always be coordinated with a related secondary color—red with brown, blue with green, yellow with orange. It is also important to know that the most harmonious effects result when three different colors are coordinated. Ideally, a solid shirt should be worn with a tie of at least two colors. One should be in marked contrast with that of the shirt and should be the tie's dominant color, usually its background. The other color, often the motif, should echo the color of the shirt. If you are wearing a blue shirt, a tie featuring small indigo motifs against a red ground will work wonderfully.

This basic rule of contrast and echo can be applied in countless ways depending on the circumstances. In the case of patterned or striped shirts, it is often preferable to establish a contrast between motifs as opposed to colors, emphasizing the echo without repeating the colors tone for tone. Imagine a shirt with alternating navy blue and gray stripes against a white ground—a tie featuring more or less circular motifs in violet and light green will add the perfect touch.

Motifs. Quite a few rules regarding the proper use of motifs have been drawn up over the years and most of them tend toward a restrictive, classical dogma. For example, some will tell you that the size of motifs should not exceed one inch and that dots should measure no more than three millimeters. Regarding combinations, these same codes prohibit wearing stripes on both shirt and tie, or the presence of motifs on more than one of the three pieces of clothing worn above the belt.

Fortunately, most men of today ignore these clichés, as do many fashion houses with sterling reputations. The famous *toile de Jouy* motifs of Christian Dior—copied from the wallpaper in Dior's first shop, which was decorated by Christian Bérard—are both ample and gracious, while Charvet's basket weave ties have long been regarded as the height of elegance.

There are nevertheless a few basic, self-evident rules worth keeping in mind. For example, large comic motifs should be avoided unless one's primary goal that day is to make the children

Patterned shirts are naturally the most difficult to coordinate. With such shirts it is often preferable to let a tie play the role of echoing colors and opposing patterns. Three patterned shirts that are each well-coordinated to a tie with green worked background and red twill squares (left). A glen plaid shirt (bottom left) goes well with a Macclesfield tie. The colors are similar, and the patterns contrasting. The same is true for a blue shirt worn with a paisley print silk tie (bottom, right).

An image of the "soft man" as seen by Ermenegildo Zegna, in a harmony between fabrics, textures, patterns and colors: a tie and scarf in washed silk that looks like wool, worn with a wool jacket; a subtle interplay between ochre and burgundy, between squares and stripes (right).

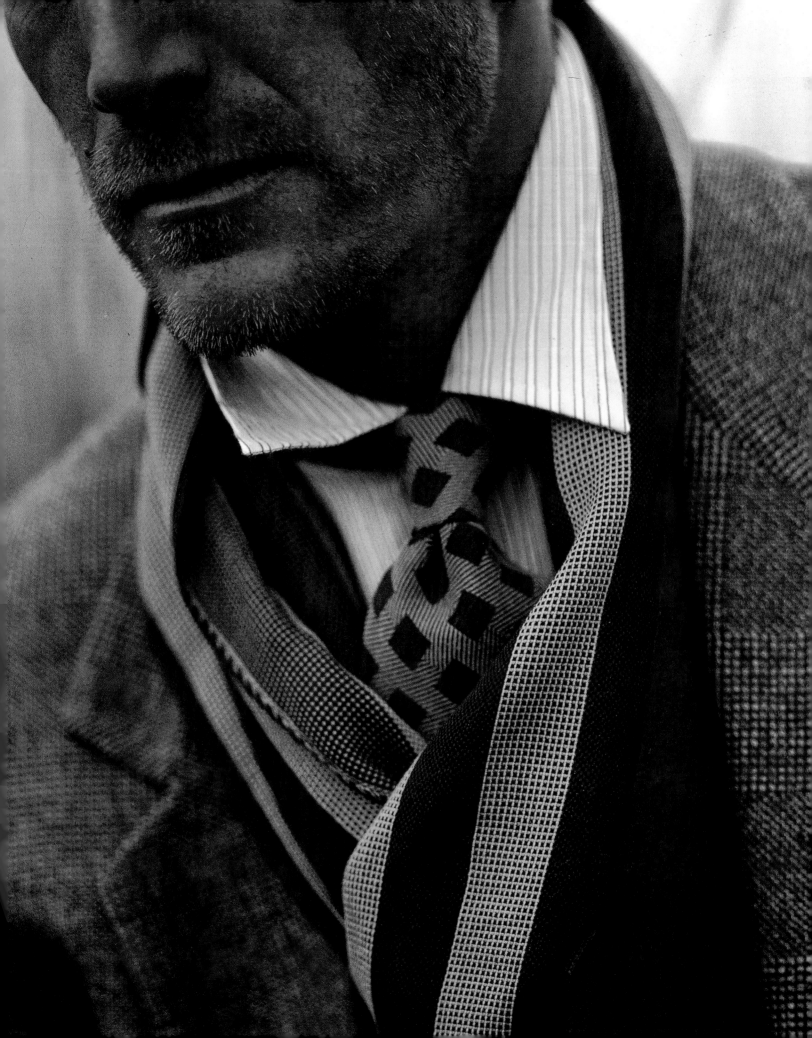

burst out in laughter. Generally speaking, the larger the motif, the more casual the effect created by the tie. But remember that beautiful weaving can compensate for the audacity of a large motif.

Regarding the combination of patterns, there is one basic rule which should be followed. In short, two motifs should not clash and contradict one another, nor should they be mutually indistinguishable. It follows from what has already been said that for proper contrast, motifs on a shirt and tie should not resemble one another too closely. Combinations of stripes are permissible, if daring, on the condition that they are of different sizes.

The first part of this rule calls for a minimum of sagacity. Motifs can clash in shape or size. Ocular sanity would be upset by the juxtaposition of complex or asymmetrical motifs with agitated stripe patterns. (One thing is certain about stripes: they always go well with solids). But there is no reason to avoid combining dots and stripes if you make sure that their sizes are in harmony with one another, for example, if the dots on your tie can fit into the spaces between the stripes on your shirt. As a general rule, motifs worn above the belt should have similar dimensions or their proportions should be coordinated as in the above case.

Motifs may be inappropriate because of the associations they evoke. A few examples will suffice to illustrate my point. A hunting tie sporting dogs or ducks should not be worn with a pin-striped business suit for the simple reason that wild game is not to be found in many offices. Likewise, a chic, ultra-classic satin tie with dots will always seem out of step with a checked tweed sports jacket. The avoidance of such choices is more a matter of common sense than evidence of sophisticated fashion sense. One simply cannot be both eccentric and staid, sporty and dressy, in the country and in the city, at the same time.

Finally, we must not forget that there are certain motifs, which should not be worn when visiting certain islands by just anybody—unless one wants to risk deeply offending their inhabitants. These islands are called England and Ireland. And while many of their shops freely sell authentic club, plaid, regimental, and old school ties, these should be worn only by those formally entitled to do so. Should you be sufficiently bold and inconsiderate to violate this rule by purchasing, say, a Cameron Highlanders tie, with its yellow and red stripes against a spinach-green ground, be advised that you had best wear it where you can be certain not to run into any British subjects. As for the principle itself, that is between you and your conscience.

Fabrics. The one-place-at-a-time rule also applies to materials. A climate cannot be simultaneously equatorial and polar, and it follows that there is no reason to wear a wool tie with a linen jacket, or vice versa. Special attention should be devoted to harmonizing different surface textures and weaves. A supple twill or silk sateen tie should not be paired with rough wool or stiff cotton. A useful rule holds that it is advisable to have a tie's weave echo that of the shirt or jacket. A serge suit is worn to best advantage with a tie made of finely textured fabric such as serge, twill, or rep. Likewise, a linen jacket will go perfectly with a shantung tie, as will a tweed

Any tie goes with a white shirt. As for button-down collars, they are particularly suitable for ties with imaginative figurative patterns. The Christian Dior *toile de Jouy* motifs, printed on Shantung silk, are a delicate version of this principle. But is it permissible to wear tie and vest made of the same printed fabric? Here opinions diverge (right).

Kenzo proposes two coordinating alternatives for his floral multicolored woven silk ties—an audacious one: vests that are equally outspoken (left and center)—and a more sober solution: a classic pin-striped vest (right). A choice to be determined by the occasion or the wearer's mood.

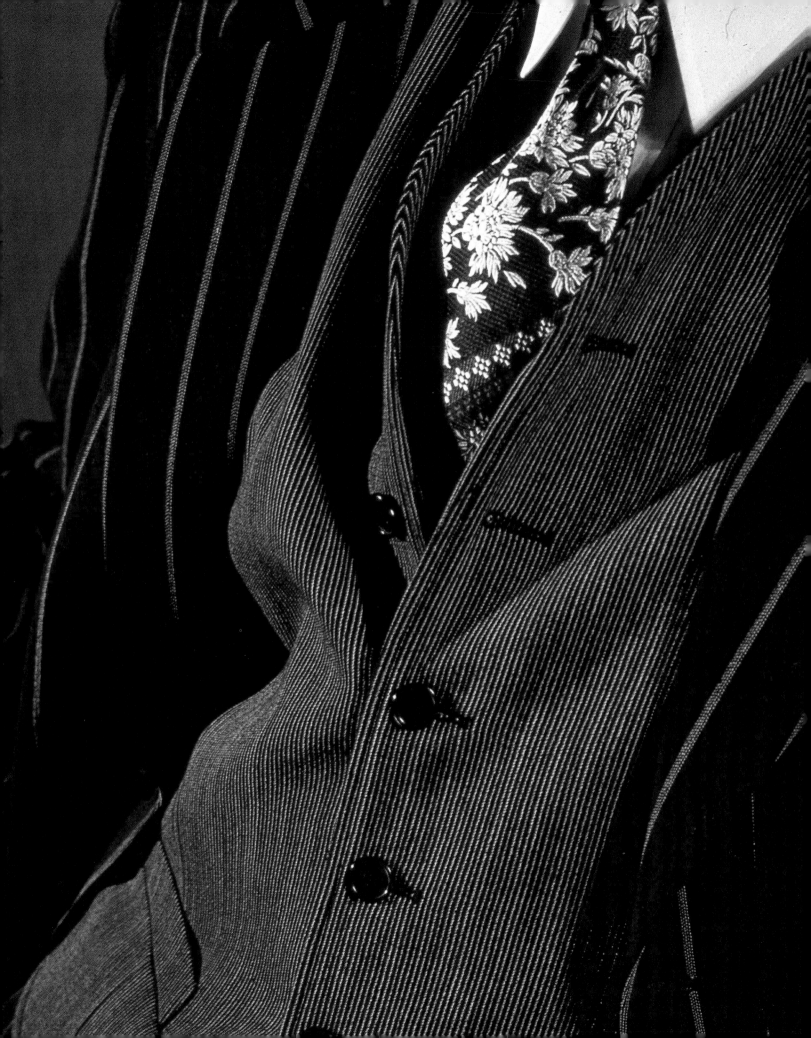

jacket with a wool tie or one whose basket weave is suggestive of carded wool. In any event, a tie's material should be suitable for the occasion. A richly woven silk tie is more appropriate with formal evening wear than with regular office attire, and the reverse holds for printed twill and cotton. Note also that one must be decidedly perverse to favor leather ties. First, because leather ties have been out of fashion for at least a decade—which (fortunately) makes them difficult to find—and second, because they do not seem at home with any fabric known to mankind.

Collars. Shirt collars also have a language of their own and a tie should know how to speak it. This goes for knots, which should comfortably occupy the space reserved for them, as well as for styles. Anything goes with a classic collar. Button-down collars, invented in 1900 by the American John Brooks of Brooks Brothers fame, go wonderfully well with sporty plaid, knit, and club ties. Collars with tabs designed to push the knot forward are unsuitable for use with large or bulky ties. Wide Italian spread collars are ill-adapted to thin discreet ties, unless a Windsor knot is used, and this is not a viable solution. Spread collars look best with woven silk models featuring assertive motifs or with knit ties.

THE OCCASION

Workdays, meetings with one's financial advisor, intimate dinners, friendly gatherings, birthdays, weekends in the country, and seasonal changes—any occasion can be viewed as an excuse to transform oneself by means of a tie. Elegance results from a successful negotiation of the conflicting demands made by originality and propriety. The art of wearing the right tie is being able to adjust the relative proportions of these two demands to suit the particular occasion. Here again, common sense lays down a few simple rules. Should you be lacking in this useful faculty, you are hereby informed that dark colors are both more severe and more modest than bright ones, that the fewer colors a tie has the more decorous it will seem, and that small motifs are dressier than large ones. And never forget the indisputable principle laid down by Marcel Proust: true elegance is never far from simplicity.

No one would sport a flowered tie at a funeral, and similar considerations preclude the wearing of formal ties, such as woven silk with severe dots, on relaxed occasions. It goes without saying that informal or gaudy neckwear should not be worn when strict adherence to the rules of etiquette is demanded.

Often, the occasion determines the tie fabric rather than the motif. Stripes and paisleys can be appropriate for the office or for a cocktail party, but they should be printed in the first instance and woven in the second. Wool ties are inconceivable except in the country where they are most suited for hunting trips, and only should be worn between late autumn and early spring. Linen and cotton are suitable for the rest of the year, but should be worn only with a linen or cotton jacket when the occasion is casual rather than formal. The existence of lightweight silks makes it difficult to justify wearing cotton ties after having outgrown short pants.

Other occasions have quite different implications where ties are concerned. A friend of mine compelled to undergo a detailed tax audit decided to wear the same modest tie each time he met with the tax inspector. Today he feels certain that this painful gesture paid off—the tax inspector was unusually indulgent.

It should be recalled here that some occasions allow for virtually no choice whatsoever. Bow ties in dark solid colors are the only option with a tuxedo, and the same goes for white bow ties with tails. Ascots, however, may be worn with the latter at English and French race courses and at certain high-society marriages.

MAINTENANCE

The proper treatment of ties does not stop at the art of selecting, coordinating, and wearing them appropriately—far from it. As with all other articles of clothing, and perhaps even more so, since they are the most prominently visible component of the male wardrobe, ties should be irreproachable. They should be properly knotted and suitable for the occasion, to be sure, but also impeccably clean and uncrumpled. Most ties are made of silk, and this delicate material requires that certain maintenance measures be taken.

The most widespread variety of tie abuse results from exhaustion. Often a man will return home after a long day at the office and carelessly remove his tie without unknotting it; he then abandons it in this contorted state. Sometimes this same tie will be left in this unfortunate position all night long and then put back on

Ideally ties shoud be hung to rid them of wrinkles. But certain men prefer to carefully roll their ties and store them in a drawer, as does Terence Conran in his London apartment (below).

In order to be truly elegant, the coordination of shirt and tie must take account of the fabrics, their texture and their "hand." Ermenegildo Zegna offers, in his customary "natural" range, an ideal combination of a linen shirt and a Jacquard tie in a blend of silk and linen. Perfect for summer (right).

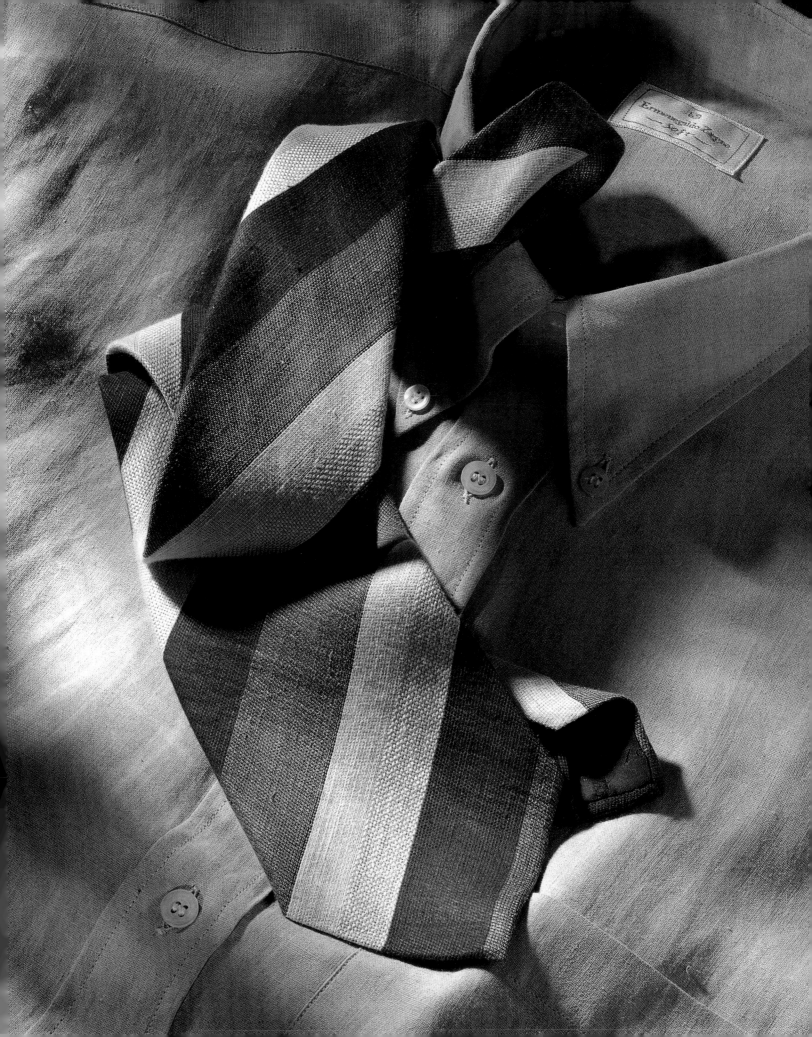

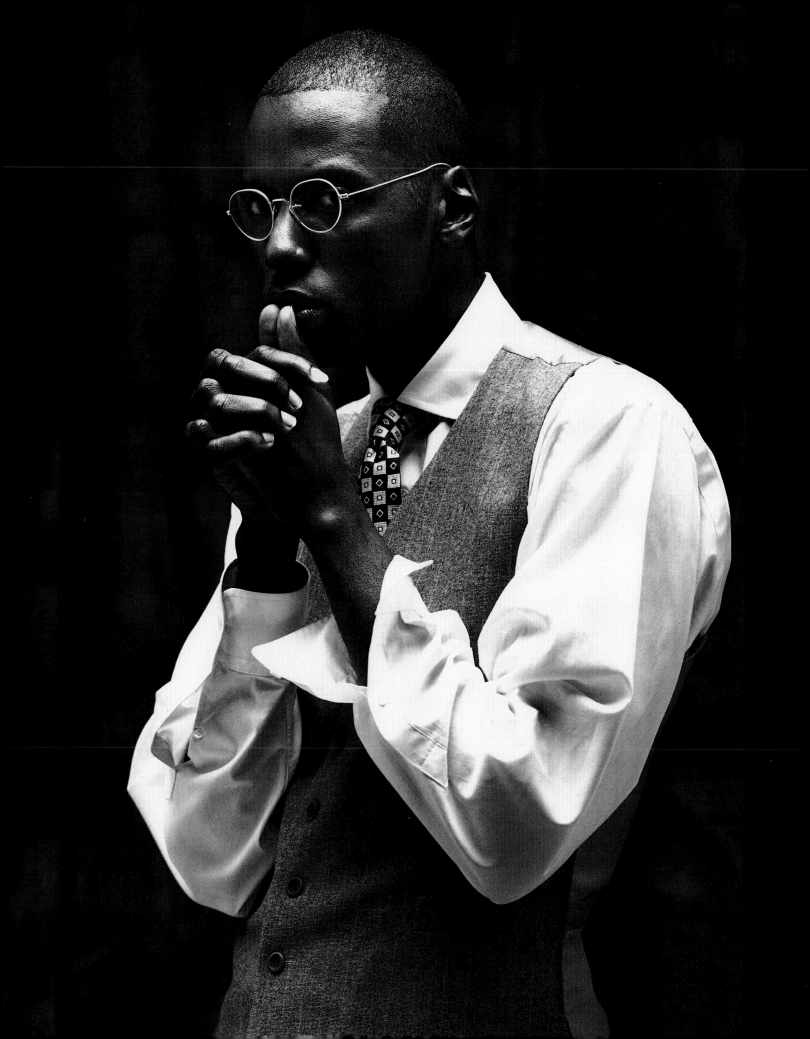

again the next morning as our careless individual makes do with readjusting the knot to its proper height. As victims of chronic abuse, these ties are not likely to last long. Fibers which have been ill-treated in this manner will deteriorate and the need for repeated ironing will wear out the material before its time. To guarantee a long life for your tie, knots should not be excessively tight and should be carefully untied after each wear. The tie should then be suspended—gravity will stretch the fibers and wipe away any wrinkles. The tie should also be given a rest—the same one should never be worn on two consecutive days.

Knit ties, whether of silk or wool, should not be suspended or they will lose their shape. They should be stored flat or rolled up in a drawer.

Ironing should be done as infrequently as possible—heat puts stress on the material, wearing it down and the fabric soon becomes shiny. There are, however, certain lightweight silk ties which tend to remain crumpled after use. A handy remedy for this problem is to suspend the tie in the bathroom during a shower to let the humidity stretch out the fibers. Afterwards lay the tie out flat to dry. If the sauna method fails, then ironing will be necessary—remember to avoid direct contact between the iron and the silk by covering the tie with a cotton pressing cloth. It is perhaps worth pointing out that small electric tie presses designed for home use are on the market, but they are no real improvement over the conventional iron, because any combination of heat and pressure will damage the silk.

Stains are the second most frequent form of damage to ties. Is there a need to specify that ties cannot be washed in water? Their envelopes, linings, and interlinings, being made from different fabrics, will not shrink to the same extent, resulting in irreparable damage. Ties should be dry cleaned, preferably by a high-quality professional dry cleaner. The correct method involves disassembling the tie, cleaning its parts separately, and

then reassembling it—an exacting procedure which few dry cleaners are prepared to perform. Commercial stain removers are another option, but we all know from personal experience that these products often leave rings. Catherine Simon, who lovingly manages the Hermès tie department in the Paris boutique, recommends the following method for getting rid of these rings: place the tie in an empty jar, fill the jar with liquid stain remover, close the lid, and shake it for a moment; then remove the tie and hang it up for a few minutes to dry. Sometimes the damage can be minimized without resorting to such radical measures. In some cases one can act before a stain has penetrated the fabric, and lightly dab it with a piece of absorbent material, taking care not to rub.

If circumstances should preclude using the services of a professional dry cleaner, note that chocolate, coffee, and tea stains can be minimized with a bit of soapy water, and fruit and wine stains can be made much less apparent with a dab of cold water. But the tie might also change color slightly at the same time. As for ink and lipstick stains, only a professional dry cleaner can get rid of them.

Over time, light will fade a tie's colors. It is a good idea to store them in the dark, either in a drawer large enough to accommodate them without folding or, best of all, in a closet where they can be suspended from a tie hanger. Any of the widely available models will do.

To end this section, here are a few suggestions for dealing with ties while traveling—tightly packed suitcases are not exactly tie-friendly environments. The best solution to avoid crumpling is to use a tie case, preferably in leather. Another, more primitive solution is to loosely roll up the ties and place them inside a pair of socks. A third possibility, which at first sight seems more appealing, but which in the end is less reliable, is to fold the ties once in the middle and slip them into a thick article of clothing.

A scenario of classical elegance: the dancer Stephen Galloway. His woven silk tie features a perennial motif—small geometric designs. A lesson in simplicity, a lesson in beauty. Photo published by courtesy of Windsor GmbH, Bielefeld (left).

"I am against systems; the most acceptable of systems is never to have one." So declared Tristan Tzara (1896–1963) in 1918, in a manifesto of the Dada movement, of which he was one of the founders. Nevertheless there was one system that he did respect—that of evening dress demanding a black bow tie. Tristan Tzara photographed by Man Ray circa 1925 (left).

Ties are fragile; they do not like sun and light; they should be cleaned and ironed as infrequently as possible. Tie cases are one way of protecting them. A tie case decorated with a paisley motif, as sold by Lubin in the 1960s (below).

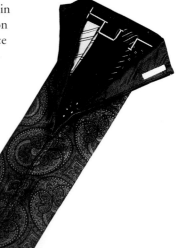

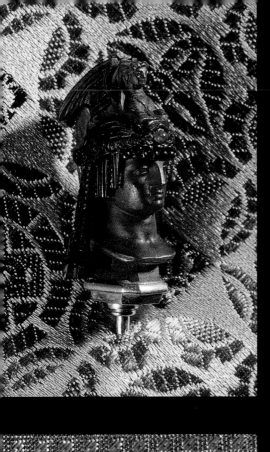
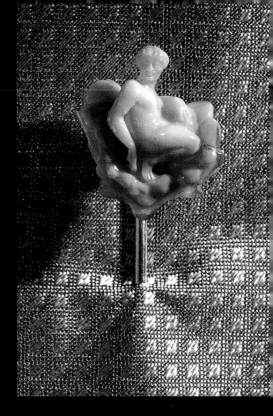
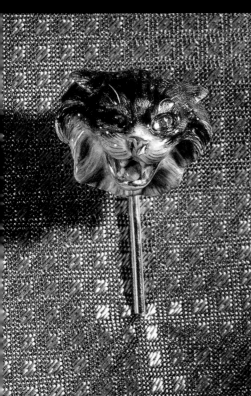
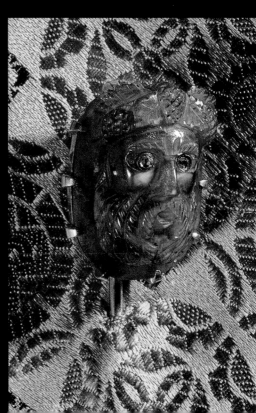

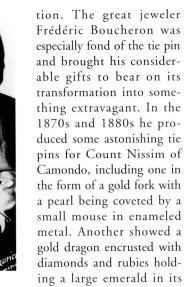

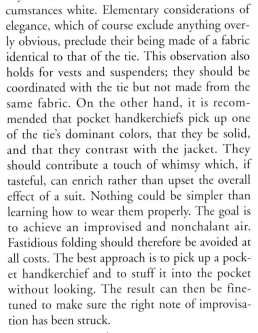

At the end of the nineteenth century, the jeweller Frédéric Boucheron and his collaborators designed a set of extraordinary tie pins for Count Nissim of Camondo (left): a head of Minerva in gold and semi-precious stones; a naked woman in a shell, in gold and opal; a head of an angry cat in enameled gold and emeralds; the head of a Frankish warrior in gold and sardonyx. Today, the accepted practice for an ascot is to wear a simple pearl tie pin.

Rather than tie clips, the British prefer to wear a simple gold pin. An Armour & Winston gold pin (above) on a unique tie produced by Thresher & Glenny for the royal house of Greece, woven with the monogram K (Konstantinos) and AM (Anne-Marie).

THE POCKET HANDKERCHIEF

Pocket handkerchiefs —exclusively white ones— became such an obligatory suit accessory in the fifties and sixties that a few wags parodied the new practice by wearing white cardboard in their pockets! Just as suddenly and mysteriously pocket handkerchiefs disappeared from the scene altogether in the seventies, only to make their return in the eighties. Today they can be any color, but under no circumstances white. Elementary considerations of elegance, which of course exclude anything overly obvious, preclude their being made of a fabric identical to that of the tie. This observation also holds for vests and suspenders; they should be coordinated with the tie but not made from the same fabric. On the other hand, it is recommended that pocket handkerchiefs pick up one of the tie's dominant colors, that they be solid, and that they contrast with the jacket. They should contribute a touch of whimsy which, if tasteful, can enrich rather than upset the overall effect of a suit. Nothing could be simpler than learning how to wear them properly. The goal is to achieve an improvised and nonchalant air. Fastidious folding should therefore be avoided at all costs. The best approach is to pick up a pocket handkerchief and to stuff it into the pocket without looking. The result can then be fine-tuned to make sure the right note of improvisation has been struck.

PINS AND CLIPS

Tie pins entered widespread use at the beginning of the nineteenth century when one of the remarkably diverse options in neckwear was the ascot tied with a "Gordian knot." The ends of the ascot were worn crossed one over the other and secured by a pin. Initially this tiny accessory was subdued, discreetly decorated with a cameo, a pearl, or a precious stone such as a ruby, an emerald, or an amethyst. Gradually, imaginative jewelers, encouraged by the proclivities of contemporary dandies, metamorphosed the simple tie pin into an ornament of unusual sophistica-

tion. The great jeweler Frédéric Boucheron was especially fond of the tie pin and brought his considerable gifts to bear on its transformation into something extravagant. In the 1870s and 1880s he produced some astonishing tie pins for Count Nissim of Camondo, including one in the form of a gold fork with a pearl being coveted by a small mouse in enameled metal. Another showed a gold dragon encrusted with diamonds and rubies holding a large emerald in its claws. But the advent of the four-in-hand tie signaled the decline of the tie pin, which reverted to its original sobriety and came to be used only with dress coat and ascot, a rigorous form of attire precluding ostentation. And so it is worn today, although rarely, decorated with a single pearl, ideally a real one.

The tie clip appeared with the four-in-hand and was fashionable in the years following the Second World War, especially in the United States where it had become perfectly acceptable to show oneself in public without a jacket. This change made it seem prudent to secure the tie to the shirt. In addition to sober models in metal, precious or otherwise, American designers came up with exuberant variations featuring every creature imaginable: comic-book characters, cowboys, movie stars, you name it. A wide range of tie clips can still be found today. In principle, they should be worn low enough to be hidden if worn with a jacket, and of course their color, shape, material, and motif must harmonize with their surroundings. However, there are those who judiciously maintain that tie clips are impossibly vulgar and should not be worn at all—notably the British, for whom this is an article of faith. On the rare occasions when they don such accessories, they are likely to resemble large safety pins and be made of gold.

Such are the guidelines, but they should never be allowed to compromise the tie as the most liberated, varied, expressive, and therefore the most seductive element in male dress. Questions of elegance aside, and despite their seeming uselessness, ties are quite indispensable to men, for

A very jazzy tie clip, worn by Duke Ellington in 1931. It is positioned at the appropriate height (left).

In the days when people used to travel with large amounts of luggage, the storage of ties was not a problem. In today's suitcases other procedures are necessary, including the tie case. An illustration from The Tie: a Breviary of Good Taste, 1912 (below).

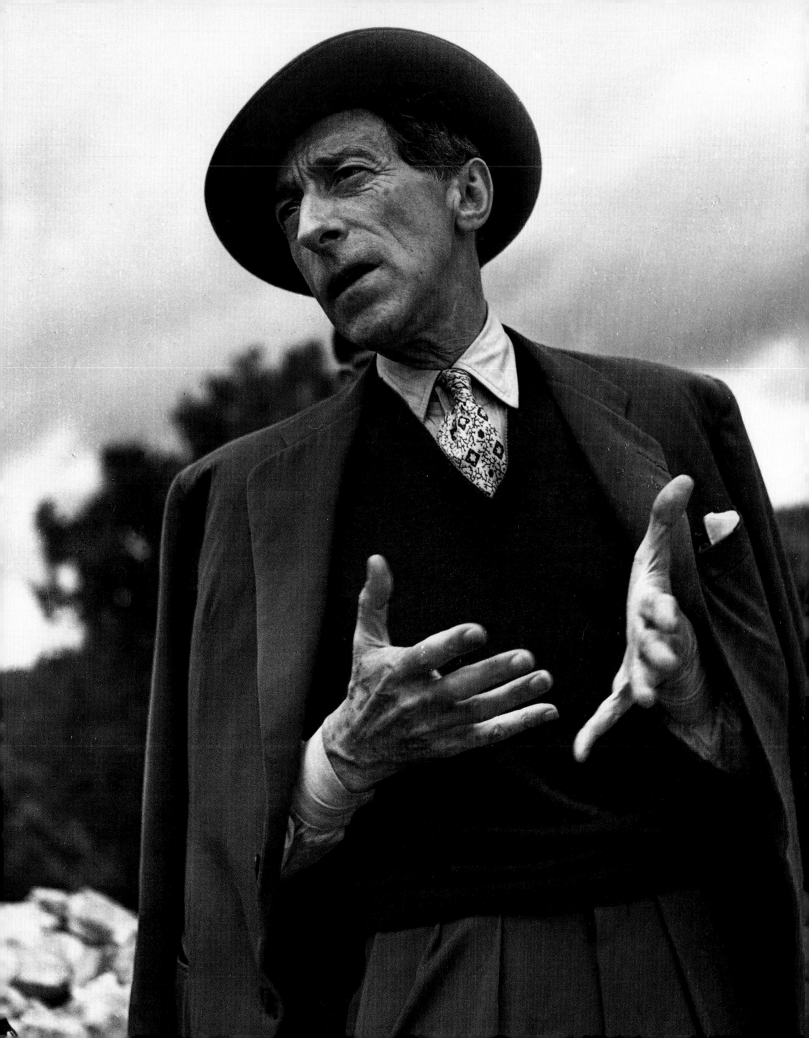

Poet, playwright, novelist, painter and film-maker—the multifaceted Jean Cocteau was endlessly inventive. He was equally inventive in his dandyism, taking care to coordinate the patterns of his clothing, and he had a habit of rolling up the forearms of his jackets, which were designed specially for this effect. But Cocteau knew that there were some limits that could not be transgressed, and once stated a principle which was absolutely correct: "Elegance ceases when it becomes noticeable." Jean Cocteau, photographed by Robert Doisneau in 1949. He is wearing a brilliantly patterned tie against a dark suit, as if evoking a symbolic fetish: a star in the night (left).

talented designers invest them with everything that is otherwise absent from the male wardrobe: a patch of light, a smile, a touch of poetry. At the same time, and this is the paradox from which they derive their potency, ties answer a profound need felt by men to forget or dissimulate their fragility. In a compelling analysis of men's fashion magazines recently published by the French newspaper *Le Monde*, Philippe Boggio stresses the astonishing contrast between the fictional universe of passing fashion and the real world. On the one hand we find the conceit of the "new man"—tie-less and a bit disheveled, "who tries to disguise his chronic depression by affecting the look of a wary pirate." On the other hand is an elusive yet persistent reality: "As soon

as we leave the realms of advertising and fashion, as soon as these are replaced by information, say, in a television profile or travel documentary, man remains classic, deaf to the dangers of the day, a prisoner of his education and his background, inclined to honor the mode of life embraced by his grandparents." Even at cocktail parties organized by famous clothing designers, Boggio notes that, "these gentlemen, who ought to count for something in the precarious alchemy of the new man, are all wearing ties." It would be pointless to seek out other reasons for their continued survival in the face of sustained attacks and challenges. Ties make light of fashion, however radical it may seem, and nothing will ever prevent us from loving them.

The gracefulness of a bow tie worn by a man of solid appearance, who has been matured by experience and has come back to tell the tale—is this not a more or less willing expression of his latent frailty?
A charming adventurer: Humphrey Bogart, photographed by Robert Coburn in 1949. Note the irreproachable pocket handkerchief (left).

A tie looks good when it respects the rules, but it also looks good when it's given freedom.
It is the opposite of a constraint: an ornament which can be used as one wishes, to signal to the world one's individuality. Pierre Cardin in 1969 (below). Karl Lagerfeld, photographed by Helmut Newton in 1976 (following page).

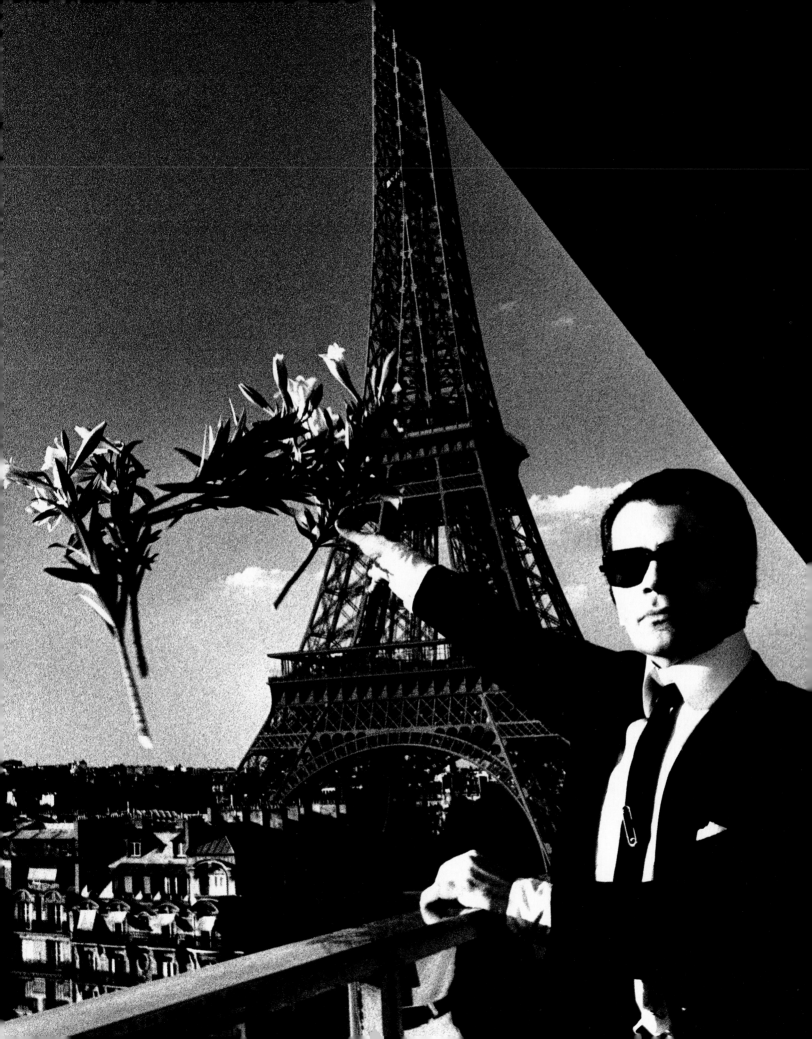

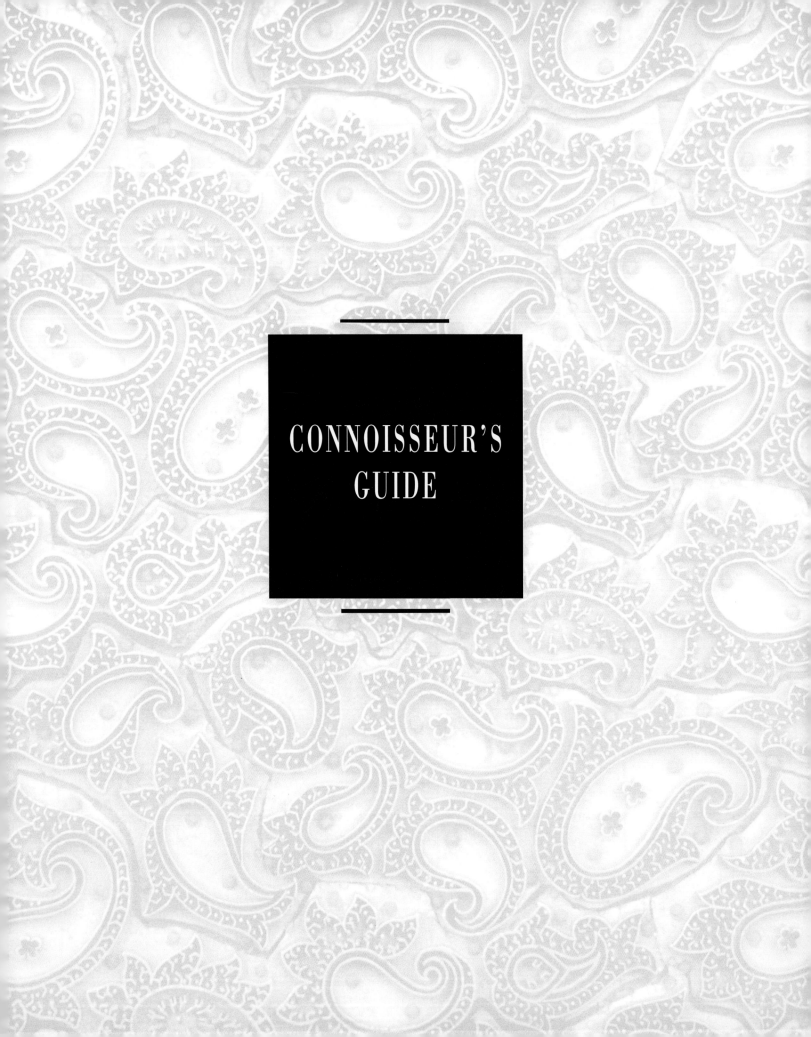

CONNOISSEUR'S GUIDE

DISTINGUISHED ADDRESSES

Where can you find a beautiful tie? An unusual tie? A custom-made tie? Fortunately, fine ties are available in so many shops and department stores that not all of them can be mentioned here. We have listed just a few of the best, chosen to cover a wide range of tastes. Our selection is limited to stores in major cities that are overwhelmingly popular with tie aficionados. We have also included addresses, grouped by country, of those manufacturers mentioned in this book who do not have their own shops. Some of them will gladly fill special orders for ties with sporting club or company emblems.

FRANCE

Paris must offer the most astounding array of ties of any city in the world, especially at the upper end of the market. Ties by prestigious French designers, as well as nearly all the world's finest labels, can be found there. Unfortunately, ties, as a rule, are more expensive in Paris than in other cities. The most beautiful sell for around $100. Some customers prefer taking advantage of a trip to London or Milan, where ties are generally 25% less expensive, to freshen up their wardrobes. But Paris offers something other cities do not, a wonderful "tie district" where a marvelous stroll takes you from the Opéra to the Left Bank of the Seine, by way of the Madeleine, rue de la Paix, Place Vendôme, rue de Rivoli, and the Louvre.

THE BIG BEN CLUB
28 rue Rambuteau, 75003 Paris
Tel.: (1) 42-72-88-00
This small firm deserves notice for its novelty ties. Enemies of the serious can browse through a delightful selection of patterns including jungle motifs, vineyards, a menangerie of animals, Mozart and Picasso—if they are still available. In fact, the store is constantly changing themes. The Big Ben Club also carries women's ties, which are shorter and wider than those for men. In solid colors and thus more sober than their male counterparts, they are still of the same infallible quality. Another Paris store is located at 119, rue de Rennes.

LE BON MARCHÉ
5, rue de Babylone, 75007 Paris
Tel.: (1) 44-39-80-00
This traditional department store at the corner of the rue de Bac and the rue de Babylone has a magnificent, recently renovated tie department on the ground floor. The some ten thousand ties displayed on the long, dark wooden tables feature most of the French *haute couture* labels, including Kenzo, Yves Saint Laurent, Montana, Givenchy, and Dior. Among other models to be found are Zegna, Armani, Fornasetti, Michelsons, Michael Drake, Gianfranco Ferre and Balthazar, which is both the label of Le Bon Marché's tie line and the name of their new men's department. You will find some astonishingly rare items, such as Japanese crinkled silk ties, along with traditional old stand-bys. Le Bon Marché pampers its clients with a currency exchange service, a newspaper stand, and a fax machine in the middle of the best tie department of all the major Parisian department stores.

BRUMMELL
61, rue Caumartin, 75009 Paris
Tel.: (1) 42-82-50-50
Brummell, the men's clothing section of the Printemps department store, has an immense tie department offering one of the widest selections in Paris. The connoisseur will find ties by major French designers such as Kenzo, Nina Ricci, Louis Féraud, Givenchy, Courrèges, Christian Dior, Sonia Rykiel and Claude Montana. But Brummell also has its own label and presents two collections every year.

CARROUSEL DU LOUVRE
99, rue de Rivoli, 75001 Paris
Tel.: (1) 46-92-47-47
Since ties are an art, finding them at the Louvre should come as no surprise. They are not actually in the museum itself, but in the Carrousel shopping gallery under the Pyramid, which opened in November 1993. This is tie heaven. Two dynamic tie-store chains have shops in the gallery, while two other boutiques feature more exceptional ties.

The Italian **Cravatterie Nazionali** has opened its third Paris store in the Carrousel du Louvre shopping gallery. The space is small but the warm welcome comes in several languages. One of the two salesmen was born in Singapore and speaks French, English, Chinese, and Japanese. "I'd better," he points out, "because French clients come in only on the weekends." There are more than one thousand models by French and Italian designers available, all in silk. Prices range from 20 to 120 dollars, the most expensive being Léonard printed silk ties. These are the world's most costly ties because they are the most richly colored. Cravatterie Nazionali accents the contemporary, offering the boldest designs by Versace, Gianfranco Ferre, Montana, Moschino, Missoni, Kenzo, Valentino, Dior, Givenchy and Yves Saint Laurent. The shopper's choice is packaged in a beautiful black-and-gold round metal box that can later serve as an ideal tea tin. For a list of Cravatterie Nazionali stores around the world, call or fax the head office in Italy.
Tel.: (2) 48-00-72-13 / Fax: (2) 469-0120.

A gleaming, impeccably British **Tie Rack** shop called **The Art of Silk** has just opened a few steps away, near I. M. Pei's pyramid. The British chain has 305 stores throughout the world, including 28 in France. All the ties are made in Italy for the store's own label and most are of printed silk. Nearly every style is available, from solids and stripes to polka dots, paisleys, and small animal patterns. Disney ties are especially popular with Japanese tourists. The huge chain buys in mass quantities from manufacturers, so the quality/price ratio is excellent. Expect to pay from 20 to 35 dollars. Granted, the ties are not top of the line, but they are well-crafted and made of silk. Another advantage of the Tie Rack is the wide choice of tie clips, travel cases, tie racks and pocket handkerchiefs, all at very low prices. A full list of Tie Rack stores around the world is available from their head office in Great Britain.
Tel.: (71) 995-1344 / Fax: (71) 995-0352.

A trip to the **Flammarion 4** Louvre store may be the best way to satisfy a love of ties and art at the same time. The Flammarion 4 boutique, which offers a line of products directly inspired by art works, is located on the way to the museum's ticket desk beneath the pyramid. The magnificent ties are knit or printed by the distinguished Ratti firm. There are ties with a feather design by Cocteau, an alphabet pattern by Sonia Delaunay, and illustrations drawn by Dufy for the Lyons silk-manufacturer Bianchini-Férier. Flammarion's own ties feature designs based on works by Monet, Van Gogh, and Magritte. Flammarion 4 also sells ties with a motif—tiny tubes of paint—that was specially designed by the French contemporary artist Arman.

Tie enthusiasts who are still up for more should keep walking until they reach the museum's large, official store run by the Réunion des Musées Nationaux. They can leaf through the books in the ground-floor store before going upstairs to where a small

THE CLASSIC TIE KNOTS

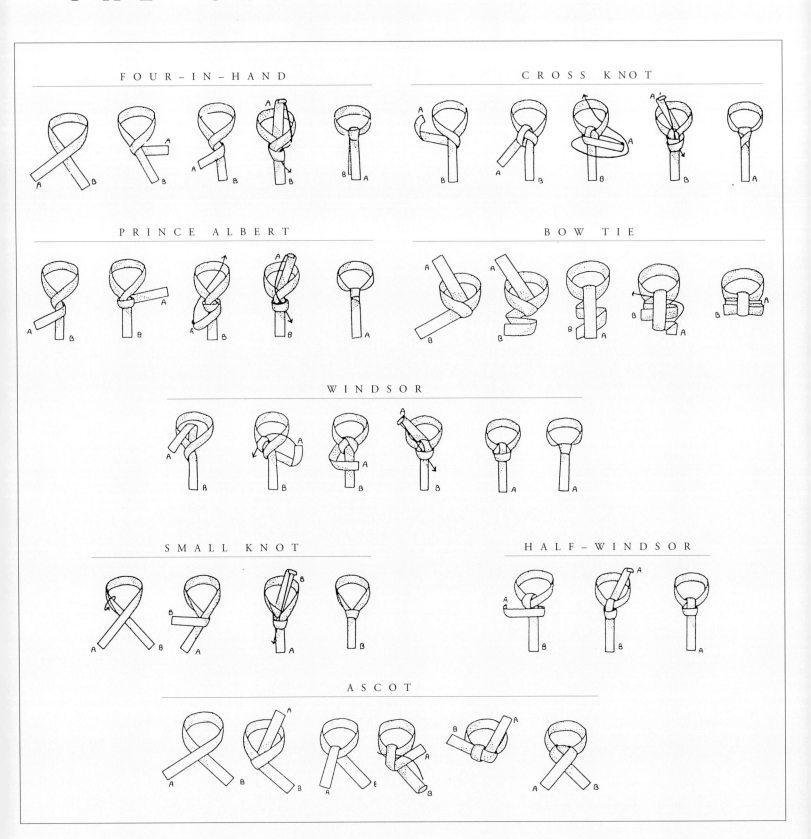

FOUR-IN-HAND

CROSS KNOT

PRINCE ALBERT

BOW TIE

WINDSOR

SMALL KNOT

HALF-WINDSOR

ASCOT

selection of silk ties in several colors can be found among reproductions of ancient Greek and Roman statues and various other art works. One such tie, featuring Toulouse-Lautrec's monogram, was issued simultaneously with the Louvre's blockbuster show of the painter's works. Another is a copy of a pleated silk tie designed by Fortuny. There are also printed silk ties, decorated with a motif of antique draughtsman's tools, by Jean-Michel Wilmotte, the architect of the new rooms in the Louvre's Richelieu wing.

CHARVET

28, Place Vendôme, 75001 Paris
Tel.: (1) 42-60-30-70

The magnificent Charvet shop on the Place Vendôme is worth a visit just to see the Louis XV furniture, antique Chinese tables, light oak paneling and gorgeous carpets. Charvet offers the world's widest selection of silk ties. The quality is unsurpassed and highly professional salesmen offer excellent advice. For just ten percent more (around $100) you can have a custom-made tie. The store features Jacquard silk, classic print, grenadine, silk knit and "seven-fold" ties. Charvet bow ties are knotted, but not sewn, and come in three sizes. Besides the Place Vendôme store, Charvet ties are available only in New York at Bergdorf Goodman and Saks Fifth Avenue, in Chicago at Marshall Field's and Ultimo, in San Francisco at Wilkes Bashford, in Munich at Theresa, in Hanover at Möller and in Japan at Mitsukoshi and Yanase.

CRAVATTERIE NAZIONALI

(see "Carrousel du Louvre")

CHRISTIAN DIOR MONSIEUR

30, avenue Montaigne, 75008 Paris
Tel.: (1) 40-73-54-44

Thanks to its worldwide fame, the Christian Dior house sells 2.5 million ties a year. Yet quality also plays a part in such enormous sales figures. The ties, one hundred percent silk, are printed or woven, and hand-sewn. The motifs, often fancy, are inspired by the insignia of Patrick Lavoix's men's collection, which were themselves drawn from the interior design patterns created by Christian Dior himself for his first boutique: canework, *toile de Jouy*, hounds tooth check, ovals, and wrought iron. Some of the more recent collections were inspired by, among other things, the city of Venice and the graphic work of Jean Cocteau. Christian Dior ties are also available in department stores and a large number of specialty shops. This internationally acclaimed fashion house has some thirty or more Christian Dior Monsieur boutiques scattered across the world: Monte Carlo, Barcelona, New York, Tokyo, Singapore, and Hong Kong to name only a few.

FAÇONNABLE

9, rue du Faubourg Saint-Honoré
75008 Paris
Tel.: (1) 47-42-72-60

This sprawling, warmly decorated boutique symbolizes the success of the house Albert Goldberg founded thirty years ago. A wide selection of extremely well-made ties by Thiercelin is available here. The craftsmanship is outstanding and the style thoroughly contemporary. Façonnable ties can also be found in France, Belgium, Spain, Portugal, Germany, Switzerland, the United States (in Nordstrom stores) and Japan.

SALVATORE FERRAGAMO

(see Italy, Florence)

FLAMMARION 4

(see "Carrousel du Louvre")

GENTLEMAN GIVENCHY

51, rue François-1er, 75008 Paris
Tel.: (1) 40-76-00-21

Since 1988 Givenchy has presented a "Selection Couture" collection of magnificent silk ties in a numbered, limited series. Designed in-house, they are woven, printed, and assembled in the Como region, under the direction of Orsini, one of today's finest tie manufacturers. Their fancy motifs are inspired by themes of famous Givenchy prints, such as Impressionism, Van Gogh, Etruscan Art, or the Lascaux caves. But also to be found are classic motifs such as dots, stripes, paisley, and geometric patterns. Givenchy ties are also available in their Paris boutique located at 21, boulevard de la Madeleine, as well as at Galeries Lafayette and Printemps. They are sold by the Italian chain Cravatterie Nazionali in New York, Milan, Monte Carlo, and Mexico; in Rome at Bictoria Cravatte; in Madrid at Yusl, in Munich at Ludwig Am Dom; in Frankfurt at Best; and in Tokyo at l'Hotel Imperial.

HERMÈS

24, rue du Faubourg Saint-Honoré
75008 Paris
Tel.: (1) 40-17-47-17

Hermès' Faubourg-Saint-Honoré store resembles both a bee hive, with customers buzzing about sought-after salesclerks, and a museum, where the leather, silk and precious metal works of art are displayed in the windows or hung on the walls. The tie department is one of the boutique's liveliest. Besides the Paris flagship boutique, Hermès also has two hundred shops, most of them under the Hermès name, in seven other countries on every continent. The soft silk ties are always displayed on a stirrup-shaped rack, which is a nice touch but not very practical because they keep slipping onto each other. All of the printed ties have a code number on the back of the narrow end that indicates the tie's model number as well as when and where it was made. The boutique also offers a wide array of bow ties. It is possible for clubs and companies to have ties made with personalized emblems or logos. Paris: 24, rue du Faubourg Saint-Honoré; Lyon: 95 rue du Président Herriot; London: three Hermès stores and at Harrods; Rome: Via Condotti 60; Milan: Via Sant'Andrea 21; Geneva: 43 rue du Rhône; Madrid: Jose Ortega y Gasset 12; Munich: Maximilianstrasse 13; New York: 11 East 57th Street and at Barney's and Neiman Marcus; Tokyo: Hermès Marunouchi and Seibu.

PATRICK HOLLINGTON

9, rue Racine, 75006 Paris
Tel.: (1) 43-25-54-79

Fashion designer Patrick Hollington draws his inspiration from work clothes. Most of his Irish tweed ties are made of suit jacket remnants and come from Connemara. He also sells a few models of a vanishing breed: knit silk ties made with yarn that is woven in the Cévennes region of France.

LANVIN

15, rue du Faubourg Saint-Honoré
75008 Paris
Tel.: (1) 44-71-33-33

In 1992 the architect Terence Conran completely redecorated all seven floors of the men's boutique. Everything has been designed to recall the store's founder, Jeanne Lanvin. Her favorite color, the famous blue she discovered in a Fra Angelico painting, sets the overriding tone and is beautifully highlighted by light oak woodwork and sand-colored walls. Madame Lanvin's favorite symbols, which were designed for her by the decorator Armand-Albert Rateau, are everywhere. For example, his wave design adorns both furniture and carpet. On the ground floor, several hundred ties are splendidly displayed horizontally on tables or fanned out on special display cases. Lanvin ties are dreamed up by the house designer, Dominique Morlotti, in conjunction with the renowned tie manufacturer Anthime Mouley. They have a style all their own. Bravado and luxury come together in intricate weaves, heavy, very shiny silk, large figurative patterns (particularly flowers) and abstract designs—all with a preponderance of blue. The great classics are here as well, such as the solid navy blue, white dot, and club stripe ties Jeanne Lanvin designed for her

first collection in 1926. They will never go out of style. The fifth-floor custom-made department is another world. You walk past a boot- and a hat-maker at work and through the shirt and suit department on the way to the ties. A tailor shows you sixty rolls of shimmering silk, most of them woven with small geometric or dot patterns. He then takes your measurements and asks whether you prefer a four-in-hand or a Windsor knot, (the fabric is longer for the latter) and a straight or a bottle-shaped cut. A tailor-made tie costs around $200. The price is reasonable, for the tie will be made without an interlining, of a single piece of silk folded in on itself—almost a "seven-fold" tie. The lining is made of the same material as the envelope, the height of luxury. Afterwards, satisfied shoppers can relish their experience in the "Café Bleu" located beneath the store's ground floor. The bar is shaped like a wave, the decoration is summery, the wood is light-colored, the chairs are wicker and the Hédiard hot chocolate and tea are delicious.

LÉONARD
48, rue du Faubourg-Saint-Honoré
75008 Paris
Tel.: (1) 2-65-53-53
Léonard ties are designed by in-house designers and manufactured by the excellent Italian tie-maker Orsini. Owing in part to their large figurative prints and supersaturated color schemes, Léonard ties are noticed from a distance and recognized at a glance. One either likes or dislikes the large birds with their multicolored plumage, or the garish evocations of Carnival in Venice. It is the quality of the impression which is extraordinary, justifying the mind-boggling prices. These ties are for those who do not like to pass unnoticed. Léonard ties are sold in the firm's Paris boutique, at Cravatterie Nazionali and Léocadia, in Montreal at Brisson & Brisson, in New York at Napoléon, in London at Harrods, in Rome at Roland's and Davide Cenci, in Milan at Avolio, in Frankfurt at Italian Fashion, and in Hamburg at Braun.

MADELIOS
23, boulevard de la Madeleine, 75001 Paris
Tel.: (1) 42-60-39-30
A true connoisseur, Manuel Roman, does a splendid job managing Madelios's superb tie department. The store sells its own as well as a wide range of *haute couture* labels. In either case the quality is impeccable. The wonderful selection includes ties made of grenadine, faille, cashmere wool, Irish poplin (a silk and wool blend) from Atkinson's, and real madder from David Evans. Madelios is strictly upmarket; there are no polyester or cotton ties to be found in the store.

CLAUDE MONTANA
31, rue Saint-Denis, 75001 Paris
Tel.: (1) 44-76-87-00
Claude Montana is one of the few French designers genuinely interested in making the ties that bear their labels. His inspired designs have taste, imagination and a thoroughly enjoyable sense of humor. The boutique features wonderful creased, crinkled and flocked silk ties and astonishing trompe-l'oeil patterns. A new Claude Montana collection comes out twice each year.

THIERRY MUGLER
4-6, rue aux Ours, 75003 Paris
Tel.: (1) 44-78-78-44
As for all of his other creations, Thierry Mugler proves himself to have an equally remarkable sense of inventiveness in the domain of ties. The majority are in woven silk (silk sateen or moiré silk) or inlaid with engineered geometric motifs, such as a single diagonal or vertical stripe, and, in addition, they are reversible. But it is their tips, above all, which distinguish them from classic ties: extremely tapered, or cut obliquely, they give new life to the traditional image of the tie. For all those enemies of conventional dress who must wear a tie, Thierry Mugler's are available in New York at Saks Fifth Avenue, in Toronto at Giorgio, in Tokyo at Takasimaya, in London at Linea, in Barcelona at Sergu, in Geneva at Thierry Mugler and even in Moscow at the Salon Charme Kovsag.

OLD ENGLAND
12, boulevard des Capucines, 75009 Paris
Tel.: (1) 47-48-81-99
Never mind the name and traditional English decor. This store is thoroughly French. Madame Muet manages the tie department with a subtle touch. Old England features smashing madders as well as Charles Hill ties, which bear either his or the Turnbull & Asser label.

RÉUNION DES MUSÉES NATIONAUX
(see "Carrousel du Louvre")

SULKA
2, rue de Castiglione, 75002 Paris
Tel.: (1) 42-60-38-80
Sulka was founded in New York in 1895 and the Paris store has enjoyed a prestigious reputation since it opened in 1911. This double identity gives the store a unique character that the manager, Monsieur Beaussard, sums up as: "Neither American, nor French, nor English, but international." The ties sold on rue de Castiglione are designed by the Sulka company in New York. The fabrics come from the best Italian suppliers, including Ratti, Campi, Mantero, and Fermo Fossati.

And the manufacturing is carried out by Thiercelin in France, using a special procedure in which the neck band is topstitched for reinforcement. These combined efforts create sober, classic, superior quality ties, most of which are made of woven silk. The store has every reason to be proud of its four specialities: solid-color silk sateen, grenadine, hounds tooth motifs and custom-made ties. For around 120 dollars customers can choose their own fabric from an incredibly wide range of samples, have a unique motif embroidered if they wish, and receive their personalized, made-to-measure tie within four to six weeks.

TIE RACK
(see "Carrousel du Louvre")

Yves Saint Laurent
32, rue du Faubourg-Saint-Honoré
75008 Paris
Tel.: (1) 42-65-01-15
In absolutely French tradition, Yves Saint Laurent offers a selection of classic ties mixed with a bit of avant garde through the use of strong colors in sometimes unusual combinations. You will also find the fetish of the master, a small heart in a repeating pattern that covers the exquisite silk. In addition to the accessories boutique within the Faubourg-Saint-Honoré store, a large selection of ties is to be found in Paris at Yves Saint Laurent Rive Gauche, place Saint-Suplice; in Italy at Cravatterie Nazionali; in Great Britain at Harrods; in the United States at Yves Saint Laurent in New York and Beverly Hills; and in Japan at Yves Saint Laurent Rive Gauche in Tokyo's Prince Hotel.

ITALY

ROME. Milan may be the Italian fashion capital, but Rome is the capital of tailors. Finding one to make a tie is no problem. Otherwise, of course it's easy to find a wide array of often stunning Italian-made ties cut from gorgeous silk, often in spectacular weaves. Long lines of Japanese visitors in front of the via Condotti's famous fine leather goods shops may make the street look like a tourist trap, but don't let that discourage you. This is where Rome's most beautiful ties can be found, and at very reasonable prices.

BATTISTONI
Via Condotti, 57 and 61 A
Tel.: (6) 678-6241
The boutique at No. 57 opens out on to the street, but the choice is rather limited. Shoppers are better off entering at No. 61a. At the end of two courtyards, graced by fountains and lush plants, they will discover Battistoni's

wonderful store, an inner sanctum of authentic Roman chic. The style is classic: superb silk ties, most of which are woven rather than printed (demand for Jacquard silk ties is booming in Italy), exhibit all the traditional patterns. The ones with the cute little animals on them are reminiscent of Hermès. The very fine ties made of mogadore, a silk and cotton blend, and knit chiné cashmere are much more original. New models created by house designers come out every three or four months. Battistoni also offers custom-made ties.

EDDY MONETTI
Via Condotti, 63
Tel.: (6) 678-3794

Battistoni's neighbor is heir to a long family tradition. The Monettis have been a leading name in elegant men's fashions since 1867. Originally the house specialized in hats as well as ties, but the latter is what made them famous. Not every customer is lucky enough to be received by Signor Monetti himself, but the thoroughly knowledgeable salesmen are a paragon of courtesy. Shoppers can choose from hundreds of woven or printed silk ties, often lined with the same fabric as the envelope. The store has so many dot and stripe designs that choosing one is a daunting challenge. The paisley patterns printed in England are amazingly detailed. Clients who would like to order an entirely hand-sewn, custom-made tie have shimmering sheaves of silk unrolled right before their eyes. The lining is made of the same material and the price is around $100. Other stores are in Milan at Piazza San Babile, 4 and in Naples at via dei Mille, 45.

CRAVATTERIE NAZIONALI
Via Vittoria, 62
Tel.: (6) 321-7085

The famous tie store chain amazingly manages to offer more than 5,000 models in this tiny shop tucked away on a small, snazzy street parallel to the via Condotti. Nearly all the world's greatest tie names can be found here, in addition to their own label. The sales staff is friendly, knowledgeable, and multilingual. Cravatterie Nazionali also has stores in Milan, Monte Carlo, Paris, and New York.

DAVIDE CENCI
Via Campo Marzio, 1–7
Tel.: (6) 678-4537

Davide Cenci's fashion boutiques take up a good part of via Campo Marzio between the Spanish Steps and the Pantheon. A wide variety of creations by house designers, exclusive models from Brooks Brothers, and ties by Holliday & Brown, one of England's greatest tie makers, are available here. Davide

Cenci also has stores in New York and at via Manzoni 7 in Milan.

EZIO PELLICANO—MADE-TO-MEASURE TIES
Via del Seminario, 93
Tel.: (6) 994-2199

Ezio Pellicano's small boutique is probably the only one in the world that offers nothing but made-to-measure ties. On the ground floor an enormous trunk is opened to reveal a treasure of some hundred or so rolls of gorgeous silk. But Ezio Pellicano also offers a wide range of other fabrics, in addition to a broad array of patterns and colors. On the loggia, skilled tailors cut the fabric of your choice to match your size. Regular clients have their names woven on the label which is stitched to the back of the tie's wide end. Prices range from around 80 to 100 dollars.

MILAN. No tie lover should pass up a visit to Como, a small, magnificent northern Italian town and the world's tie silk capital. An hour away is Milan, where the best-dressed men in search of variety will be overwhelmed by the astounding array of choices. Most of the top Italian designers, including Armani, Ferragamo and Gucci, as well as the leading international fashion houses have shops in the classic via Montenapoleone and the surrounding neighborhood. Gucci has just completed a lavish store renovation. Etro and Mila Schön, two lesser known, but equally exciting houses also have boutiques on via Montenapoleone.

ARMANI
Via Sant'Andrea, 9
Tel.: (2) 76-00-32-34

Giorgio Armani and his design team are on the cutting edge of tie fashion. This shop features a stunning array of silk ties that are embossed, pleated, or made to resemble wool, as well as more conventional models. Armani ties are still famous for their subdued beige, brown and ochre tones. The house was one of the first to offer printed silk ties, which continue to be one of its specialties. The store offers two different lines. The red labels are for mass-produced models, the black for limited series. Armani has beautiful stores in Paris at 6, Place Vendôme, in Rome at via Condotti, 77, as well as boutiques in London at 178 Sloane Street, in New York at 815 Madison Avenue, in Madrid at Jose Ortega y Gasset, 17, in Munich at Maximilienstrasse 32 and in some thirty of the world's other major cities.

BYBLOS
Via della Spiga, 42
Tel.: (2) 79-90-74

Founded in 1973, Byblos has been involved

in men's fashion since 1983, shortly after the arrival of Keith Varty and Alan Cleaver, two young English designers from the Royal College of Art in London. Byblos ties are all manufactured in Como after the designs of Varty and Cleaver. The Anglo-Italian combination gives a surprising result: brightly colored, extremely audacious motifs that mix together flowers, ethnic patterns, and hyper-realistic scenes of themes such as "shipwrecked" or the "swimming pool." Byblos ties are also available at Michel Axel and Théofil in Paris, Harrods and Selfridges in London, Mailander Fenster in Dusseldorf, Robbert Max in Madrid, Holt Renfrew in Toronto, Mark James in Vancouver, Giatur and Simona in Rome.

ETRO
Via Montenapoleone, 5
Tel.: (2) 78-11-90

Etro opened this purely Victorian-style store in the heart of Milan's fashion district in 1988. Paneling, silver sports trophies, and equestrian paintings provide an English setting for very elegant ties, half of which are created by house designers. All are entirely hand-sewn. Gimmo Etro is especially fond of paisley patterns, club ties, and complex zigzag and wavy stripes. In winter the house offers a wide range of wool and cashmere ties. Whatever the season, they are beautifully displayed in tabletop rosettes or tied to horizontal bars, which gives a better idea of what they will look like once they are knotted around the wearer's neck.

GUCCI
Via Montenapoleone, 5
Tel.: (2) 76-01-30-50

The via Montenapoleone store has just been redecorated. Light-colored paneling with an old-looking patina, eighteenth- and nineteenth-century furniture, Empire tables and period paintings all make it seem as though you have just stepped into a patrician manor house. A serious-looking, terribly polite salesman welcomes clients to the tie department. Gucci also has two stores in Paris, at 2, rue du Faubourg Saint-Honoré and 350, rue Saint-Honoré. Their ties can be found in all the world's major cities, including Rome at via Condotti, 8; London at 16–17, Sloane Street and 32–33, Old Bond Street; New York at 685 Fifth Avenue; and Beverly Hills at 347 North Rodeo Drive.

PROCHOWNICK
Head Office:
Via Matteo Bandello, 14
Tel.: (2) 48-00-86-66

Prochownick is rightly considered to be one of Italy's finest makers of printed and woven

silk ties but does not have a store of its own. The success of this firm, which also makes smashing wool ties, is based on a solid foundation of creativity and flawless workmanship. Prochownick ties are available in twenty or so men's stores in Paris at Jack Romoli, Michel Axel, Madelios, and Hubert H.; in London at Liberty, Harrods, and Selfridges; in Los Angeles at Sami Dinar's; in Chicago at Ultimo; and, of course, in many boutiques throughout Italy.

MILA SCHÖN
Via Montenapoleone, 2
Tel.: (2) 76-00-18
At Mila Schön the accent is on originality. The designer's two specialties, silk and wool reversible ties and ties edged with strips in contrasting colors, can be found on this ultra-modern store's lower ground floor. Mila Schön also has boutiques at via Condotti, 64 in Rome as well as in Florence, Bari, and Monte Carlo.

ERMENEGILDO ZEGNA
Via P. Verri, 3
Tel.: (2) 76-00-64-37
It's hard to find more beautiful fabrics than those offered by Ermenegildo Zegna, who specializes in all kinds of wool and silk ties. Zegna has many boutiques throughout the world but of course the one in Milan has the widest choice of ties. Other major stores are in Paris at 10, rue de la Paix; London at 37, New Bond Street; Berlin at Bleibtreustrasse, 24; Madrid at calle Serrano, 21; New York at 743 Fifth Avenue; and Tokyo at Aoyama Twin East 2F.

FLORENCE. It is no longer possible to pass through Florence simply for its museums and churches. This resplendent city must also be visited for the magnificence of its ties, particularly those bearing the Ferragamo label.

SALVATORE FERRAGAMO
Piazza S. Trinita
Tel.: (55) 43-951
All of Ferragamo's thirty or so worldwide stores are, like his ties, the height of elegance. The main ones are in Florence, with both head offices and boutique on the Piazza Trinita; Milan on via Montenapoleone, 20/5; London at 24, Old Bond Street; New York at 730 Fifth Avenue; and Tokyo on Minami-Aoyama 5-Chome. In July 1993 Ferragamo inaugurated a second superb Paris store at 45, avenue Montaigne (the first one, on rue des Saint-Pères, is exclusively a women's boutique). Lacquered beige walls, leather and ivory sofas, and an ecru and grey pearl wool rug on a grey and pink granite floor, provide a magnificent setting for the world's most

subtle printed ties. Ferragamo also has stores in Bordeaux, Deauville and Lyon.

GREAT BRITAIN

Many people, including tie lovers, cross the English Channel to freshen up their wardrobes in London. Prices are much lower than in France, and British tradition is still at the forefront of tie fashion. The elegance of British ties owes much to their sobriety, to their classic patterns, which are over a hundred years old, and to the good taste comprised of almost imperceptible details, that were exemplified by "Beau" Brummell. But London is also home to more daring designers who use lively colors and invent new patterns while respecting old-fashioned workmanship and the quality of fabrics. Except for a few stores in the western part of the city and Covent Garden, the most smashing ties in London can be found between Piccadilly Circus and Oxford Street.

AUSTIN REED
103–113 Regent Street, London W1A 2AJ
Tel.: (71) 734-6789
This small department store offers an intelligent choice of grenadine, very popular in London, and Atkinson's Royal Irish Poplin (a silk and wool blend). Austin Reed also sells ties by Lanvin, Hugo Boss, and other designer labels. The elegant hanging tie case on sale here is an ideal way to store your purchases or take them along on trips. By the way, a staircase in the middle of the tie department leads to one of London's most beautiful Art Deco interiors, a barber shop with its original chairs, sinks, and folding screens.

S. CONWAY
10 Princes Arcade, Jermyn Street
London SW1
Tel.: (71) 439-4471
S. Conway specializes in custom-made shirts, but the small store also offers a fabulous choice of woven and printed ties. They are often decorated with the shop's favorite animal: the elephant, depicted in a wide range of colors. S. Conway is proud of the fact that Princess Diana is quite fond of their ties.

DRAKE'S
Carrington Hull Associates Ltd.
Leo Yard, 122a St. John Street, London
Tel.: (71) 608-0321 / Fax: (71) 251-3820
This firm does not have a store under its own name but the label is sold through Carrington Hull Associates. Michael Drake is one of the stylists who knows how to give a kick to British tradition, by breathing new life into classic motifs through the use of adventurous colors. Drake's ties are also distinguished by

the quality of their silk and perfect craftsmanship, sewn entirely by hand. The authentic madders are made with particularly heavy silk prints, from 22 to 40 ounces, and the other silks are woven of thick thread which gives them an exquisite "hand." The interlinings are of primarily pure wool and the linings are of pure silk. Not all of the ties made by the firm carry the Drake label. These are distributed in London at 77, Fulham Road; in Paris at Cairns, Darel, and Renoma; in Milan at the Biffi Boutique; in Rome at FF; in Munich at Ludwig Beck and Eckerle; in Frankfurt at Grey Flannel; in Madrid at Denis and Yusti; in New York at Barney's and New Republic; and in San Francisco at Wilkes Bashford.

DUNHILL
30 Duke Street, Saint James's
London SW1 Y6DL
Tel.: (71) 499-9566
This store at the corner of Jermyn Street and Duke Street, which offers fine cigars, beautiful pipes and stylish ties, is the pinnacle of masculine elegance. This is especially true for the wide variety of designs in The Royal Collection of ties. Dunhill likes to point out that its ties are woven in Italy on the same looms that are used to make the Vatican's sacerdotal vestments.

GIEVES & HAWKES
1 Savile Row, London W1
Tel.: (71) 434-2001
One of the most highly esteemed houses on London's prestigious Savile Row, Gieves & Hawkes are the official purveyors to the Queen, the Duke of Edinburgh, and the Prince of Wales. Their very traditional ties made of exquisite silk come in dots, stripes, and plaids. Gieves & Hawkes also sells regimental ties, but exclusively to those with the right to wear them. Only ties of regiments that were created during the First World War, but have since disappeared, are available to everyone. The house designed and still sells one of the items most sought-after by the world's collectors—the "Battle of England" tie, which can be worn only by the brave RAF airmen who defended Great Britain in 1940. It is woven with a motif of the rose of England and the British isles in a repeating pattern on a navy blue background.

HARRODS
87–135 Brompton Road
Knightsbridge, London SW1X 7XL
Tel.: (71) 730-1234
Even the most demanding tie lovers will be delighted with England's greatest department store, Harrods, which was built in high Edwardian style at the turn of the century. A

stunning array of ties can be found next to the famous food hall. The world's finest labels—Atkinson, Charles Hill, Lanvin, Joseph Abboud, Gene Meyer, Byblos, Christian Lacroix, Paul Smith, Michelsons, Armani, Ferragamo, Ascot, Prochownick, Holliday & Brown, Valentino, Léonard and even Hermès—rarely found outside stores bearing its name—are lined up within hand's reach in dark wooden chests. Harrods undoubtedly has the widest selection of ties in all of London.

HILDITCH & KEY
73 Jermyn Street, London SW1
Tel.: (71) 734-4707

Jermyn Street is the thoroughfare of London's shirtmakers. All of them also sell ties, and Hilditch & Key is undeniably one of the most well-known. Founded in 1899, the establishment has become an institution, where members of the royal family do their shopping. Lord Lichfield, the Queen's cousin, is a regular customer. The venerable store's small wood and glass door opens into a softly-lit temple built to the glory of shirts and ties. Seriousness and superior quality are guaranteed, and tradition is at the peak of perfection here. Hilditch & Key offers twill, gumtwill, heavy woven silk (14 to 22 ounces), striped and dotted ties, ties with geometric patterns, and very handsome madders. All of them are made by Hilditch & Key, and they all share a unique feature: the wide end is slightly broader than usual under the knot, providing the tie's most visible part with greater fullness. Hilditch & Key opened a second store at 37 Jermyn Street in 1978. The firm also has a store at 252, rue de Rivoli in Paris, but with a more limited selection.

CHARLES HILL
Head Office:
Linton House, 164–180 Union Street
London SE1 OHL
Tel.: (71) 928-5785 / Fax.: (71) 928-8673

Charles Hill does not have a store of their own, but their ties—the quintessence of British style—are sold at men's haberdashers worldwide. In Great Britain they can be found at the in-store boutique "Charles Hill for Harrods." Charles Hill has a similar arrangement with Barney's in New York and in Tokyo. Ties designed and made by Charles Hill under the "Turnbull & Asser" label can be found at Turnbull & Asser in London, Bardelli in Milan, Old England in Paris, Aquascutum in London and New York, Burberry's in London and New York, Bullock & Jones in San Francisco and Mitsumine in Tokyo. Whatever the name on the label, Charles Hill ties also bear the initials "CH" on the small tag indicating the fabric

and country of origin, which is found on the back of the tie's narrow end.

HOLLIDAY & BROWN
Head Office:
16 Savile Row, London W1
Tel.: (71) 734-1743

Holliday & Brown is another venerable British institution whose name is associated with painstaking attention to detail and impeccable quality. The house does no retail business and does not have a store. Holliday & Brown is famous for its personalized, made-to-order ties as well as ready-to-wear printed and woven models. Madders and rep weave stripes are a specialty. The house has always been a purveyor to regiments and clubs, and on request will design original motifs—such as those inspired by antiquity, or Turkish and Persian themes.

RICHARD JAMES
37a Savile Row, London W1
Tel.: (71) 434-0605

Richard James can be a welcome change of pace from the stuffy elegance of Savile Row. There is nothing Edwardian about his store's pure lines, austere, bright spaces, white walls and ceilings, or the large imposing painting of an aged Indian wearing an impressive turban. "I'm a bridge between today's fashions and the old tradition of quality tailors," says the young designer, who opened this store in 1992. Richard James offers an exciting combination of bold fabrics and traditional cuts for his custom-made and ready-to-wear shirts and suits. He designs the bold, bright, colorful ties himself and has them woven from heavy silk in England. They certainly achieve his goal of reconciling tradition with innovation. On the simple white display tables, splendid weaves and classic patterns, such as basket weaves and stripes, harmonize with shirts the colors of fresh fruit. Not to be missed are the extra-wide stripes that are rarely seen today. Richard James is a breath of fresh air on Savile Row.

LEWIN & SONS
106 Jermyn Street, London SW1
Tel.: (71) 930-4291

This venerable house founded by Thomas Lewin in 1888 specializes in making and selling regimental, school, and university ties—which can, of course, be worn only by members. Some of these models are quite rare. None can be seen in the store; they are carefully stashed away in the basement. The ties on display are meticulously lined up at eye level between the shirt displays. All are handmade in the Lewin workshop. Printed or woven in exquisite silk, they are outstanding examples of British tradition and quality.

By the way, Astley's, the superb Art Deco store next door at 108, Jermyn Street, sells the most handsome pipes in London.

LIBERTY
210–220 Regent Street, London W1
Tel.: (71) 734-1234

This well-known store, located in a magnificent Tudor-style building dating back to 1924, features cotton and silk ties printed with Liberty patterns. The "Tana Lawn" cotton from Sudan is of especially fine quality. Liberty's ground floor features an exciting selection of ties by Atkinson, Paul Smith, Armani, Richard James, Versace, Jean-Paul Gaultier and others. There is also a collection of "Tintin ties" straight out of the famous comic books. Liberty ties can be found in Paris at 3, rue Jacob.

LORD'S
66–70 Burlington Arcade, London W1
Tel.: (71) 493-5808

The stunning windows of Lord's, shirtmakers for centuries, are on the Piccadilly Circus side of the entrance to this very attractive arcade. Some shoppers have been coming here to buy the same tie for twenty years. The highly knowledgeable sales staff gladly shows the head-spinning array of grenadines, madders, paisleys, macclesfields, and other unmistakably British specialties, such as the unique Shepherd's check pattern, which at first glance looks like a solid color. Lord's also sells regimental and club ties. The very handsome MCC (Marylebone Cricket Club) tie, of dark blue background with rhubarb and custard motifs, is displayed in the window, but of course it is reserved for club members only.

MICHELSONS OF LONDON
Head Office:
9 Clifford Street, London W1
Tel.: (71) 408-2466

Michelsons, the least British of English haberdashers, has been making ties since 1937. The house specialty is still novelty patterns such as little animals, flowers, and geometric shapes from the fifties. Most of the ties are made of printed silk. Michelsons is famous for high quality craftsmanship and makes ties for world-famous labels such as Yves Saint Laurent, Missoni, and Liberty. A German engineer designed the "liba", a machine that was to revolutionize tie-making in the seventies, while working in Michelsons Rayleigh mill near Southend. Michelsons was the first firm to import the machine, which was developed and manufactured in Germany. More than three thousand retailers all over the world now offer Michelsons ties, which are sold in London at Austin Reed, Aquascutum, Fortnum & Mason, Hardy Amies (the

Queen's fashion designer), Harrods and Liberty; in New York at Saks Fifth Avenue and Bloomingdale's; in France at Printemps and Le Bon Marché; in Spain at El Corte Inglés; and in Australia at David Jones.

NEW & LINGWOOD—BOWRING ARUNDEL
53 Jermyn Street, London SW1
Tel.: (71) 493-9621

New & Lingwood still has a boutique in Eton, where it was founded in 1865. The London store, at the corner of Jermyn Street and Piccadilly Arcade, sells shirts, hats, and shoes. Students and gentlemen from the City are regular customers, just as their fathers and grandfathers were. New & Lingwood's famous affiliated store, Bowring Arundel, has left Savile Row and moved across the street. It is still too soon to tell whether the label will survive, but the quality is as high as ever. The traditional woven and printed English ties always come in the same size, three and one-half inches wide and 54 or 55 inches long. But the house also takes orders for custom-made ties, with a minimum of two per model. Prices are reasonable. New & Lingwood also sells regimental and club ties, including the famous rhubarb and custard MCC (Marylebone Cricket Club) tie.

THOMAS PINK
85 Jermyn Street, London SW1
Tel.: (71) 930-6364

This shirtmaker has many boutiques in London, especially in the City. Classic yet lively, Thomas Pink fashions are highly popular with young executives as well as office and bank employees. Woven and printed silk ties are arranged at eye level in shimmering, well-designed rainbow patterns.

SELFRIDGES
400 Oxford Street, London W1A 1AB
Tel.: (71) 629-1234

Selfridges' huge department store, located on one of London's busiest shopping streets, is the city's earliest exposed steel beam structure. The first-floor tie department spoils wool-lovers with a wide array of wool jersey, wool knit, lambs wool, and Atkinson's Royal Irish poplin. But the overall choice is eclectic, ranging from the subdued tones of Calvin Klein, Joseph Abboud and Armani to the bright colors of Richard James, Valentino, and Memphis. Very fine prints from Ferragamo and lavish fabrics from Zegna round out the selection. It is evident that Selfridges' tie department manager is a real connoisseur.

PAUL SMITH
40–44 Floral Street
Covent Garden, London WC2E 9DJ
Tel.: (71) 836-7828

Paul Smith is a trendy young designer who has created his own elegant, tasteful and magic world on quiet Floral Street, a stone's throw from bustling Covent Garden. Smith had the interior of an old brick warehouse converted into a group of boutiques. The beautiful antique mahogany counters and windows come from former dentists' offices and were bought at auction. So was the huge, remarkable copper-topped table (it weighs a ton!) on the basement level, where the ties are displayed flat in the form of nooses fastened by little plaid ribbons. The silk and wool are of superior quality, and the ties are classic or decorated with large motifs in dazzling colors. Paul Smith also offers rare items such as hand-painted, re-embroidered pure linen ties to go with linen suits. They are displayed knotted on shirts, accompanied by matching suits.

THRESHER & GLENNY
Lancaster Place, Strand, London WC2
Tel.: (71) 836-4608

Established in 1755, this venerable London retailer has been furnishing the royal family for over two centuries. But Thresher & Glenny also specializes in personalized ties for clubs and businesses. Although an institution's existing logo can be used, they are willing to design an original insignia based on information about the client's history and activity. Thresher & Glenny also produce county ties—each county having its own motif—and they single themselves out by a tie of their own invention, the "oneholer." It can only be worn by golfers who have accomplished a hole in one. The oneholer is a small woven repeating pattern of a golf ball, a golf club, a flag, and the number one. All of their personalized ties are in woven silk and, once again, the client can choose between rep, ottoman, silk sateen, and more. Always concerned with customer demands, the shop offers polyester as well. Thresher & Glenny has numerous boutiques in London, offering traditional British models, along with their special order ties.

TURNBULL & ASSER
71–72 Jermyn Street, London SW1
Tel.: (71) 930-0502

Turnbull & Asser is another hallowed British institution. Charles Hill designs and makes all the ties carrying the house label, which are displayed in this old-fashioned store's famous window. Most of them are made of woven silk. Many are quite bold and colorful.

UNITED STATES

Department stores are the best places to go tie shopping in New York for two reasons. First, the city is not really conducive to long shopping trips by foot—the distance from one shop to another can be prohibitive. And second, New York City department stores offer shoppers everything they dream of—very friendly, highly knowledgeable service, a wonderfully comfortable setting and an elegant atmosphere.

JOSEPH ABBOUD
Head Office:
650 Fifth Avenue, New York, NY 10019
Tel.: (212) 586-9140

Joseph Abboud creates America's most elegant ties. This designer's very subtle neckwear can be found in his shops in Boston, and Seattle, and in New York at Bloomingdale's, Bergdorf Goodman and Saks Fifth Avenue. Unfortunately, his ties are not distributed in Europe, except for Great Britain (at Harrods, Selfridges, and Harvey Nichols in London). Joseph Abboud ties are also sold in Japan, Canada, Australia, and Mexico.

BARNEY'S NEW YORK
62nd Street and Madison Avenue,
Tel.: (212) 826 8900

In a store that spans an entire city block, Barney's new location on Madison Avenue is one of the hippest clothing stores in New York, offering the finest in contemporary men's and women's fashion. Their array of ties is impressive, and some twenty international designers—Donna Karan, Calvin Klein, Garrick Anderson, Dunhill, and Farragamo. Ties are available on the first and fourth floors, the less expensive ties on the first and the more highly priced upstairs. The materials include silk, wool, and cotton and the patterns are highly stylish and contemporary. The sales staff is knowledgeable and extremely helpful.

BERGDORF GOODMAN
745 Fifth Avenue, New York, NY 10019
Tel.: (212) 753-7300

This recently opened, lavishly appointed Fifth Avenue department store is a dream. Decorators scoured the city looking for the finest French and English antiques and designed corners that look like little boutiques while respecting brand identities and the store's overall harmony. The customer is king at Bergdorf Goodman. Portable phones are scattered throughout the store, so clients can carry on with their business while they shop. With the store's personal shopping service customer's can even have articles shown to them in the quiet comfort of their own homes or hotel rooms. Some of the world's most beautiful ties can be found at Bergdorf Goodman, which features labels such as Armani, Joseph Abboud, Hugo Boss, Charvet, Hermès, Ferragamo, Gene Meyer,

Stefano Ricci, Robert Talbott, and Turnbull & Asser. A superb selection.

BROOKS BROTHERS
346 Madison Avenue, New York, NY 10017
Tel.: (212) 682-8800
Founded in 1818 by Henry Sands Brooks in New York City, today Brooks Brothers is a by-word in the United States for fine men's and boy's apparel and, more recently, fine women's wear. On the ground floor of the four-storey flagship store on Madison Avenue is an abundant selection of ties, all Brooks Brothers original designs. The ties are arranged by price, ranging from around 18 to 78 dollars. There are the usual classic designs—paisley, old school stripes, dots, equestrian motifs—as well as more fanciful motifs such as flowers, squares, circles, and triangles. A helpful staff will assist shoppers in selecting ties to accompany a particular suit or jacket, or that are appropriate for any given occasion. Brooks Brothers has three other locations in the greater New York area, as well as stores in twenty-six other states and a mail order catalogue serving the entire United States and overseas customers.

COUNTESS MARA
445 Park Avenue, New York, NY 10022
Tel.: (212) 688-3050
This firm holds the name of its founder, the Countess Mara, and has existed for 60 years. She built her reputation on the creation of ties which are among the most original and the most refined in America. The silk, woven by the best manufacturers in Como, Italy, England, and Switzerland, is still the fabric of preference for the finest ties. The motifs, in splendid dichotomy, are as much a representation of classical elegance as of modern trends at their best. Other Countess Mara boutiques are located in Los Angeles and her ties can be found in the finest retail shops worldwide.

CRAVATTERIE NAZIONALI
4 West 57th Street, New York, NY 10019
Tel.: (212) 957-3016
The New York outlet of the Italian Cravatterie Nazionali, just off of 6th Avenue, is a delightful and deceptively small boutique devoted exclusively to neckwear. In the small space, over twenty international designers are represented. Americans such as Calvin Klein, Donna Karan, and Bill Blass; French designers such as Givenchy and Yves Saint Laurent; the Italians Zegna, Ferragamo and others; as well as the Cravatterie Nazionali's own label. The sales staff is welcoming and informative and will spend great amounts of time with customers to help them make their selection. And if the tie you are buying is a gift, it will

be wrapped in an unusual square package reflecting the originality and refinement of the store itself.

CALVIN KLEIN
205 West 39th Street, New York, NY 10018
Tel.: (212) 719-2600
One of America's favorite designers, Calvin Klein made his mark on American fashion in the 1980s by designing body-conscious and easy-to-wear fashion in natural fibers and neutral colors. While Calvin Klein clothing is sold in fine department stores throughout the United States, the Calvin Klein Corporation does not possess any shops under its own name. Calvin Klein ties—in natural fibers and in a unique array of subtle, modern patterns designed to mix and match with Calvin Klein menswear—are some of the most original American ties available, and can be purchased in most better men's clothing stores around the world.

NICOLE MILLER
780 Madison Avenue, New York, NY 10021
Tel.: (212) 288-9779
Nicole Miller's daring, rainbow-colored ties can be found in approximately one thousand points of sale all over the United States and Canada, including fourteen of her own boutiques in North America's major cities. Her creations are updated versions of American ties from the 1940s. Nicole Miller also has stores in Madrid, Seville, and Frankfurt.

MODULES
Nasett International Corp
242 West 38th Street, New York, NY 10018
Tel.: (212) 764-7827
Based in New York now for some fifteen years, the Japanese designer Toshiya Takahashi launched his own Modules label in 1987, inspired by the 1940s "bold look," but interpreted in his own manner: smaller "conversation starter" motifs and more contemporary colors—including a frequent use of black. The ties are made of figured printed silk, which is woven with traditional Japanese techniques. The crafting is luxurious, employing pure wool interlinings, linings cut from the same silk as that of the envelope, and a semi-bottle shape. The result is spectacular. Modules ties are available in New York at Barney's and Charivari, in Paris at Alain Martiniè, Réversible, and the Bon Marché; in London at Liberty and Harvey Nichols; in Stuttgart at Holys, in Hamburg at Herrenhaus; and in Toronto at Holt Renfrew and Harry Rosen.

POLO/RALPH LAUREN
650 Madison Avenue, New York, NY 10022
Tel.: (212) 753-4000

Ralph Lauren began his career as a tie designer before founding his own menswear company in 1968 and starting the trend for wide ties (almost five inches across) in the United States. Ralph Lauren's tie designs reflect a lifestyle of tradition and refinement. Polo/Ralph Lauren ties are available in finer department stores, but the best source continues to be his magnificent store located at 72nd Street and Madison Avenue, in the former Rhinelander Mansion. In an atmosphere that recalls an exclusive British men's club, four floors of Ralph Lauren designs—from three-piece suits to bed linen—are on display. An enormous array of ties, exclusively Polo/Ralph Lauren, are available on the first floor. They are fashioned from silk, wool, and cotton, in updated classic patterns. A helpful sales staff is there to assist you in selecting ties to coordinate with other Polo/Ralph Lauren clothing. There are 140 Ralph Lauren stores worldwide, including shops at place de la Madeleine in Paris, and on New Bond Street in London.

SAKS FIFTH AVENUE
611 Fifth Avenue, New York, NY 10022
Tel.: (212) 753-4000
The design of Saks Fifth Avenue's beautiful stone building across the street from Rockefeller Center has a more traditional feel than Bergdorf Goodman's. Surprisingly large spaces bring to mind the department stores of bygone days. Ties are on the ground and sixth floors. Most of them are grouped by label and displayed on counters, but Charvet and Hilditch & Key have their own in-store boutiques on the ground floor. Saks Fifth Avenue carries twenty tie labels, including Nicole Miller, Ralph Lauren, Ermenegildo Zegna, Versace, Chanel, the Metropolitan Museum of Art, and its own Saks Fifth Avenue label, designed in Italy and featuring the full range of traditional patterns.

PAUL STUART
Madison Avenue at 45th Street
New York, NY 10017
Tel.: (212) 682-0320
Haberdasher Paul Stuart offers a change of pace from New York's department stores. This shop has all the plush coziness of a family business that has been making suits, shirts, and ties since 1938. A bust of "Beau" Brummell at the entrance seems to urge those looking for the latest fashions to turn around and go elsewhere. The rather spacious store's airy, modern decoration is a radical departure from the atmosphere found in British shops, but most of the articles here are the height of traditional elegance. A splendid collection of old canes is on the staircase. Hundreds of models of ties created

by house designers can be found on the first floor. Stripes, dots, geometric and club patterns, paisleys and a smattering of novelty designs blossom on gorgeous printed and woven silk. All the models are exclusive—they cannot be found anywhere else. Paul Stuart also offers a custom-made tie service.

ROBERT TALBOTT

Carmel Valley, California 93924-0996
Tel.: (408) 649-6000
This great American classic is highly popular with the traditional urban elite. Robert Talbott ties and bow ties are distributed in three charming California shops—two in Carmel and one in Pebble Beach—in their New York shop at 680 Madison Avenue, and in several hundred menswear stores in the United States, Canada, and Asia. Robert Talbott also makes personalized ties for clubs and companies. Unfortunately, Talbott ties are not distributed in Europe.

GERMANY

Certain German tie makers have no reason to envy their more famous counterparts in other European countries. Germany may not offer the boldest fashions, but lovers of beautiful ties will be impressed by the flawless quality, innovative fabrics, and a German specialty—knits.

ASCOT

Head Office:
Hulserstrasse 335, 4150, Krefeld 1
Tel.: (2151) 75-00-25
This house does not have a store of its own, but wonderful Ascot ties, crafted with rich luscious fabrics and entirely hand-sewn, can be found at Ladage & Oelke in Hamburg and at Sauer's in Cologne. In Paris they are available at Roland Eveline (167, rue Saint Honoré), Jean-Pierre Mortimer (30, avenue Franklin Roosevelt), Jack Romoli (187, boulevard Saint Germain) and Vernet (116, avenue des Champs Elysées). They are also distributed in Lyon (Graphiti), Toulouse (Cartouche), London (Harrods, Herbie Frogg, Liberty, and Austin Reed), Zurich (Grieder), Vienna (Knize), Milan (Effebieffe), Rome (Tebro) and Copenhagen (Brodrene Andersen). In the United States they can be found at Paul Stuart and Peter Elliot in New York, and Bullock & Jones in San Francisco.

HUGO BOSS

Head Office:
Dieselstrasse 12, 7430 Metzinger
Tel.: (7123) 16-00 / Fax: (7123) 16-06-66
Created in 1923 in Metzinger by Hugo Boss, the firm originally specialized in work clothes and rain coats. Now it has become one of the largest fashion houses in Germany and has

been an unmitigated success with yuppies around the world. The first Hugo Boss tie collection was launched in 1982 in response to the demand for ties which would coordinate perfectly with the Hugo Boss clothing line. The ties are of printed or woven silk, in both classic and fancy motifs. They are available in Germany at Peek & Cloppenburg, Dusseldorf; in the United States at Saks Fifth Avenue, New York; in the United Kingdom at Moss Bros Group, London; and in better retail stores worldwide.

LACO

Stahltwitestrasse 22, 22761, Hamburg
Tel.: (40) 85-70-85
This honorable establishment was founded in 1838 by a Londoner, Charles Havy, but it did not definitively take the name "Laco—Ties and Scarves" until after the Second World War. Since they have always specialized in the creation of ties—hand-sewn of course—Laco offers an incredible choice of magnificent silks woven in Italy, Switzerland, and Lyons. The designs are both classical (paisleys, small animals, heraldic motifs) and novel (exotic scenes, Far Eastern themes, fruits and vegetables) and are rendered in countless colors. Laco has only one house rule: Quality! Their ties are sold around the world in the finest retail stores: Brooks Brothers, Saks Fifth Avenue and Bloomingdale's in New York; Waco in Tokyo; E. Braun & Co. in Berlin; van Hees in Munich; and Myer in Melbourne.

THE NETHERLANDS

CHAPON & HAAR
Head Office:
Berghaus Plaza 2P, K. Wilhelminaplein 2–4
1062 HK Amsterdam
Tel.: (20) 614-2526
The Chapon & Haar designer, Jack Chapon, has created an astonishing item called the Fourtie. Two reversible ends of equal width showing four different designs actually make four ties in one. The Fourtie is made of silk in Germany and decorated with classic designs such as dots, stripes, paisleys, and geometric patterns designed in Italy. They are both fun and handy on trips! Fourties can be found in the Netherlands at Oger Fashion and De Bijenkorf, and in a certain number of retail stores in the United States, England, and Germany.

SPAIN

GENE CABALEIRO
Head Office:
Corretera de Bayonne 95, 36213 Vigo
Tel.: (86) 20-00-00

The Spanish designer Gene Cabaleiro, a sworn enemy of the straight line, has been creating bold, wavy-edged ties (made of polyester) since the late eighties. His undulating creations are, like his clothing collection, at the forefront of fashion design. If you are searching for the most avant garde of neckties, Cabaleiro designs are available in Paris at 6, rue Vivienne and in Spain at the El Corte Inglès department stores. Gene Cabaleiro also has stores throughout Spain under his own name in Marbella, Vigo, Ibiza, Canarias, Grenada, and Pamplona.

RICHEL
Head Office:
Aribau 185–187, 08021, Barcelona
Tel.: (03) 200-1333
Richel combines the most exquisite Italian silk with flawless Spanish craftsmanship. The house does not sell from a store of its own, but in Spain Richel ties are available in El Corte Inglès department stores. In Paris they are sold at Cravatterie Nazionali (18, rue Marbeuf 75008) and Daimaru (Palais des Congrès, 2, Place Porte Maillot 75017). They can also be found in Rouen (Douglas), Caen (Camille), Rennes (Ascot), New York (Barney's), London (Harrods) and Tokyo (Wako). Richel also makes personalized ties on request, such as the "official" tie of the 1992 Olympic Games in Barcelona.

SWITZERLAND

FABRIC FRONTLINE
Dienerstrasse 16–18, 8004 Zurich
Tel.: (1) 241-6465
Silk suppliers for French *couturiers* such as Christian Lacroix, Olivier Lapidus, Pierre Balmain, and Christian Dior, this firm, founded by André Stutz and his two sisters Elsa and Maja in 1990, has developed a surprising selection of printed silk ties. André Stutz explains the Fabric Frontline effect: "If one wears a tie created by us, people will not exclaim: 'Oh what beautiful stripes!' They may however take a second look and ask : 'What is that thingumajig?' " The "thingumajig" could be a polecat, a multicolored butterfly, or even an illustration of how to knot a tie! Unbridled whimsy reigns, but with a refined grace due to the immense delicacy of interpretation and color, and the utilisation of the most magnificent silk. Fabric Frontline ties can be found in some forty fine retail stores in Switzerland; in France at Charles Jourdan stores (including 5, boulevard de la Madeleine, in Paris); in Germany at Mey & Edlich and Selbach stores; in the United States at Charles Jourdan and Saks Fifth Avenue; in London at Charles Jourdan and Robert Emmett.

M U S E U M S

These selected museums offer exhibits of either ancient ties or modern ties—and sometimes both. They often have displays that trace the history of silk-weaving techniques, and many even sell a few original models. Tie lovers, especially collectors, will be delighted to browse through the collections, or better yet, purchase neckties with hard-to-find labels.

FRANCE

MUSÉE DE LA CHEMISERIE ET DE L'ELÉGANCE MASCULINE
Rue Charles-Brillaud
36200 Argenton-sur-Creuse
Tel.: 54-24-34-69
This wonderful new museum features a collection of late nineteenth- and early twentieth-century cravats and bow ties, Sulka ties from the fifties, and a few sensational, modern articles such as Paco Rabanne's metal ties. The museum library has a large collection of books and publications with articles having to do with ties.

MUSÉE DE LA MODE ET DU COSTUME—PALAIS GALLIÉRA
10, avenue Pierre-Ier-de-Serbie, 75016 Paris
Tel.: 47-20-85-23
This lovely Paris museum focuses on the history of urban fashions from the early eighteenth century to the present day. Ties are not on display, but students and researchers have access, on request, to the reserve collection, which includes several hundred outstanding items from the earliest lace ties to the latest creations. A gold mine.

MUSÉE DES TISSUS
34, rue de la Charité, 69002 Lyon
Tel.: 78-37-15-05
This is a museum for people with a passion for textile history. There are no ties but a matchless collection of items is on display, ranging from Coptic and Persian fabrics woven in the earliest centuries of the common era to present-day materials. The museum's staff has had the excellent idea of storing information in a computer, making research, consultation and reproduction easier. The data bank is not yet completed, but it is open to the public and attracts designers and illustrators looking for old patterns to inspire new creations.

MUSÉE DU TISSAGE—MAISON DES CANUTS
12, rue Ivry, 69004 Lyon
Tel.: 78-28-62-04
This museum pays tribute to the techniques and achievements of Lyons' silk-making tradition. Exhibits show how the canuts, as silk-weavers were called in the local dialect, lived during the second half of the nineteenth century. There are also demonstrations of very old hand looms in working condition. The museum shop sells more than two hundred models of woven and printed silk ties bearing the "Maison des Canuts" label. Ironically, most of them are made in Italy, a clear sign that the Lyons silk industry is in decline. In any case, collectors will love the museum's original label.

GERMANY

DEUTSCHES TEXTILMUSEUM KREFELD
Andreasmarkt 8, 47809 Krefeld
Tel.: (2151) 57-20-46
Krefeld is Germany's silk capital and home of the Ascot company, which makes outstanding ties. The textile museum has several original items on display, including late nineteenth-century ties made in Krefeld; models by Gucci, Emilio Pucci, Yves Saint Laurent, and Christian Dior from the sixties and seventies; and a series of American ties from the fifties. A collector's dream.

GREAT BRITAIN

Craft Centre of Silk
Bourne Road, Crayford, Kent DA1 4BP
Tel.: (0322) 55-94-01
This museum designed by the much-acclaimed silk printer David Evans takes visitors on a highly educational journey through space and time. Exhibits include a reconstructed Victorian silk shop, a film about silk, and displays on silkworm breeding and old printing methods (for example, there is a magnificent group of printing blocks engraved with paisley patterns). A museum shop, duty free for tourists from outside the United Kingdom, offers a wide selection of silk items, including, of course, ties.

PAISLEY MUSEUM
High Street, Paisley PA1 2BA, Scotland
Tel.: (41) 889-3151
The patterns named after this small town, located fifteen kilometers east of Glasgow, have been woven and printed here for more than two hundred years. The museum does not have any old ties on display, but it does trace the fascinating history of paisley designs from their origins in ancient Babylon, and features a collection of exquisite shawls and clothing. The museum shop sells contemporary ties, many of which, of course, sport elegant paisley patterns.

ROYAL ACADEMY OF ARTS
Burlington House, Piccadilly, London W1
Tel.: (71) 639-7438
This illustrious institution sells ties designed by some of its members as well as an astonishing "Design-a-Tie" kit, which includes a cotton ecru tie and five magic markers.

THE SILK MUSEUM—THE HERITAGE CENTRE
Roe Street, Macclesfield, Cheshire
Tel.: 613-210
Macclesfield was a major nineteenth- and early twentieth-century silk-weaving center. One of today's most widely-used tie patterns—a small geometric design—was even named after the town. The Silk Museum, located in a former Sunday school for silk-weavers' children, has a permanent exhibition and an audio-visual program that trace the entire history of silk and silk production methods. Nearby Paradise Mill has been restored and turned into a "living museum" (tel.: 618-228). Guides, most of whom used to work in the mill, introduce visitors to silk-weaving techniques on a Jacquard loom. A few tie makers are still active in Macclesfield.

VICTORIA & ALBERT MUSEUM
South Kensington, London SW7 2KL
Tel.: (71) 938-8352
This famous museum's Textiles and Costumes department features approximately 300 ties spanning a wide range of historical periods, including a collection that has recently been donated by Sir Roy Strong, a former curator and great collector. There are some surprising items by major tie designers such as Turnbull & Asser, Zegna, and Prochownik, including extravagant cotton knit "kipper" ties and Liberty designs from the sixties to the eighties. There are "batik ties" dating from 1921 (printed using a wax process) and a striking woven tie from the thirties based on a Picasso drawing. One of the most astonishing items is the incredible wooden tie sculpted by Grinling Gibbons in 1669, which imitates the Venetian lace cravats that were so popular at the French court.

ITALY

MUSEO DELLA SETA
Via Valleggio, 3, Como
Tel.: (31) 30-31-80
Exhibits of objects and old tools trace the history of silk production methods in the Como

area. The museum regularly organizes tie exhibitions. The most recent one, Tie Fabrics in Como: Jacquard from the Late Nineteenth Century to the 1940s, was held during the winter of 1993–94. The next show will be an exhibition of printed silk that is manufactured specifically for ties.

THE NETHERLANDS

Kasteel Twickel
Stichting Twickel, Hengelosestaat 2
7491, BR Deldon
Tel.: 05407 61309
This museum is housed in the magnificent Twickel castle in Delden, located approximately 80 kilometers northeast of Arnhem. The lovely collection includes cravats and ties that date from the 1880s to the 1920s, most of which are of English origin.

TIES IN FIGURES

More than six hundred million men regularly wear ties. Around eight hundred million ties are sold every year all over the world. The Japanese buy almost one hundred million a year, and the Italians nearly twenty million. The overwhelming majority are made of synthetic fibers or poor quality silk. Today only 2.5% of all ties are made with the fine silk and highly-skilled craftsmanship worthy of collectors' interest.

In France prices range from around two dollars for a polyester tie at the discount store Tati—where a silk model costs only five dollars—to over 200 dollars for certain custom-made neckties from Lanvin.

UNITED STATES

THE METROPOLITAN MUSEUM OF ART—THE COSTUME INSTITUTE
1000 Fifth Avenue
New York, NY 10028-0198
Tel.: (212) 570-3908
The museum's Costume Institute, an integral part of the Met, exhibits a small but highly interesting collection of ties, including eighteenth- and nineteenth- century stocks and cravats with large bows, cowboy-style string ties, all sorts of bow ties, narrow ties from the fifties, and wide "kipper ties" by the trend-setting Michael Fish, who invented them in swinging sixties London. For the collector, the Met's shop sells ties that have been specially designed for the museum's blockbuster exhibitions, such as the Tutankhamun and oriental rug shows.

All-Over: A pattern that covers the entire surface of the tie with single or multiple motifs. Also called a repeating pattern.

Application printing: The dyestuff solution, thickened with printing gum, is applied directly to white or undyed cloth. Also called direct printing.

Ascot: A form of cravat, now worn only with formal attire, with wide ends that are usually crossed over to form a plastron, and held in place with a pearl tie pin.

Bandanna: Large brightly colored handkerchiefs, worn tied around the neck, originally imported from India in the early eighteenth century and made of silk.

Bandolier stripe: A diagonal stripe appearing only a single time, below the tie's knot.

Bar tack: Usually made of the same fabric as the tie's envelope. The small end of the tie is slipped through it so that it stays in place. In the absence of a bar tack, the tie's label often serves the same purpose.

Basket weave: A plain weave with two or more yarns woven together, resembling the weave of a basket or the squares of a checkerboard.

Bat wing: A bow tie with straight ends.

Bengal stripes: Stripes of identical width but of alternating light and dark colors.

Bias: Diagonal direction of the cloth. Fine ties are cut on the bias, which helps them knot properly and stops them from twisting round against the shirt.

Bola tie: A cowboy-style, leather string tie secured with a metal clasp and having metal tips. These fittings are often made of silver, sometimes with turquoise detailing.

Bottle-shaped ties: Ties with a marked narrowing that resembles that of a bottle. Placement of this narrowing can increase or decrease a knot's bulk.

Bow tie: Today, there are two types of bowties the "bat wing" with straight ends and the "butterfly" with curved ends. The butterfly or *papillon* resembles a butterfly in flight and was given its name in 1904 due to the success of the opera *Madam Butterfly*. Until that time, ties with bows were simply called cravats.

Cambric: A plain weave made from closely woven fine white linen, with a smooth, glossy finish. Along with muslin, cambric was used in the first cravats.

Carrousel: A machine that sews the linings into ties, six at a time.

Chenille: A fringed silken thread that resembles a *chenille*—the French word for caterpillar. This rare and complex weave is now being used at Ermenegildo Zegna for some of his finest neckties.

Club tie: Tie bearing the printed or woven emblem of a club, organization, or institution (stripes, repeating patterns, shields, symbols, etc.).

In principle it should be worn only by members, affiliates, or alumni. Some club motifs are entirely fictitious and can be worn by anyone.

Conversation-starter tie: A term used to designate novelty ties featuring amusing or unusual motifs that might spark conversation and so facilitate personal interaction—a Nicole Miller tie with an opera ticket motif is a tasteful example.

Cotton piqué: Figured cotton that is woven with a raised geometric pattern. It is used for white bow ties to be worn with formal evening dress.

Crêpe: A lightweight fabric with a surface that is more or less crinkled according to the method used (hard-twisted yarns, weaving in various tensions, etc.).

Discharge printing: The predominating ground shade is dyed first and then is overprinted with different colors mixed with a chemical that removes or "discharges" the dyed ground shade.

Engineered motif: A motif that appears in a particular position on a tie, and usually only once. These are often "underknots" (see entry for this).

Envelope: the entirety of the visible surface of a silk tie (sewn from two or three pieces of material) into which the interlining is inserted.

Faille: A silk weave with thin, tight warp threads and thick, loose weft threads, resulting in a surface with pronounced transverse ribs. Some manufacturers offer ties made from faille fabric.

Flecked fabric: A fabric whose weave produces a grainy or speckled surface texture.

Float: A weave in which each turn of the weft thread is crossed by at least three warp threads, or vice versa. This configuration produces satin and is responsible for the pliant hand of woven ties.

Focale: (Italian; from the Latin *fauces,* throat) scarf worn by Roman soldiers knotted around their necks. The ancestor of the modern necktie.

Four-in-hand: The modern necktie, which appeared in around 1870 and gradually replaced cravats with their large, loose bows, was named a four-in-hand because its knot with two long, trailing ends resembled the reins of a four-horse carriage. Early versions were shorter than those familiar today. Originally associated with sports and sailing, because of its practical knot, it is also known as a sailor or yachting knot (see these entries).

Grenadine: A loose weave using twisted yarns, resulting in a fabric that resembles a knit, which has an excellent drape and maintains its shape. Some men swear by their grenadine ties.

Grisaille: A fancy weave using black warp thread and white or silver weft thread. Grisaille ties are very dressy. Also known as pepper-and-salt weave.

Gumtwill: As its name suggest, a gummed twill with a velvety texture similar to that of real madder (see this entry).

Hand: Term used in the textile industry to describe a fabric's texture and consistency—the way the cloth feels to the hand. Sometimes called "handle."

Heraldic stripes: Stripes arranged either horizontally or vertically.

Interlining: The piece of material, most often wool or a wool blend, inserted inside the envelope to give a tie consistency and shape.

Jacquard silk: Silk woven on Jacquard looms, a technique allowing for the use of threads of various colors to weave a pattern or motif directly into the fabric. Also called "yarn-dyed" silk, or simply woven silk.

Kipper tie: A wide tie—from five to six inches across—that became fashionable in the 1960s and 1970s that was launched in London by the designer Michael Fish, and shortly afterwards was taken up in Paris by Pierre Cardin. Nicknamed the "kipper" tie by its inventor, because of its resemblance to a herring, it was often decorated with flowery or psychedelic patterns, but sometimes had more sober motifs.

Label: Small piece of fabric sewn onto the back of the tie's wide end, usually about seven inches from the tip, bearing the maker's name. The narrow end can sometimes be slipped through it in the absence of a bar tack.

Lavalière: A long cravat tied in a large, loose bow, similar to the one worn by the duchesse de La Vallière in the court of Louis XIV. It was the preferred neckwear of intellectuals and artists at the end of the nineteenth and into the twentieth century. Today it is most often worn by women.

Liba: A machine that places the interlining and sews the envelope around it. Its invention was crucial for the development of an automated tie production process, since it operates at thirty times the speed of a hand laborer.

Lining: Pieces of acetate or silk sewn onto the back of the tips of both ends of the tie. This fabric is sometimes woven with the designer's name or emblem. Also called "tipping" fabric.

Macclesfield: A tie pattern that was a speciality of the textile producers of Macclesfield at the turn of the century and derived its name from that town. It became particularly fashionable in the 1920s. Its small, geometric figures give an effect of marquetry across the entire surface of the tie.

Madder: Term designating a specific color range and texture in some silks, obtained by dying them with a madder-root extract, giving them an indigo bath, and then treating their surfaces. Madders are characterized by deep, muted colors and a soft, suede-like texture.

Mogadore: A very finely woven fabric (with as many as 124 warp threads per centimeter) of silk warp and silk, cotton, or linen weft.

Mogadore stripes: Stripe configuration often used on neckties, in which a wide stripe is followed by two thinner ones.

Moiré: Watered silk, with very thin transverse ribs, characterized by its constantly undulating reflections; obtained through a process in which the fibers are heated and crushed in such a way that it reflects light to produce a desired motif. "Moiré" ties currently on the market are made of a fabric with similar qualities but obtained exclusively through weaving.

Momme: Japanese term (pronounced mummy), now the standard unit for measuring the weight of silk fabric. One *momme* cloth equals 4.33 grams per square meter, or .127 ounces per square yard.

Muslin: A sheer lightweight fabric made with very fine yarns of cotton, wool, or silk. Cotton and silk muslin were, along with cambric, the first materials to be used in European cravats, ancestors of the modern necktie.

Ounce: Standard British and American unit for measuring the weight of silk fabric. One *momme* cloth (see entry) equals one square yard weighing .127 ounces.

Ottoman: Fabric with transverse ribs; silk ottoman is often used for neckties.

Panel stripe: A single horizontal stripe appearing below a tie's knot.

Pastille dots: Large dots that resemble round French candies called *pastilles.* They are usually multicolored and nearly an inch in diameter.

Pleated silk: Pleated or creased silk is sometimes used in making ties—most recently by Claude Montana. The pleats are secured in the silk through the use of a heat press.

Polka dots: Small dots arranged in a quincunx—four dots surrounding a fifth. Polka dots are the most often-used dot motif.

Poplin: Silk-and-wool poplin was introduced into Ireland two hundred and fifty years ago. The material has a silky feel (the warp is of silk) and is solid in use (the weft is of combed wool). Its name is said to derive from "papeline"—a silk woven in Avignon in the fifteenth century, at the time when that city was the seat of the papacy. The Irish company Richard Atkinson, founded in 1820, has always produced a line of ties in poplin bearing the label Richard Atkinson's Royal Irish Poplin.

Neckband: In ties made of three pieces of fabric, the segment positioned between the wide and narrow ends of the tie and which fits under the shirt collar.

Old school tie: Any tie bearing the insignia of a school or university, particularly in Britain. It should be worn only by alumni.

Paisley pattern: A design motif of ancient Babylonian origin, often used on scarves and ties, and long a staple of shawls from northern India. It consists of sinuous drop-like forms with intricate detailing, usually surrounded by stylized vegetation.

Pattern drafting: The motif of a patterned weave is broken down into warp and weft on a sheet of graph paper, which enables the weaving loom to be set up. Today, this procedure is increasingly carried out by computer.

Printed figured silk: A pattern is woven into the silk fabric, dyed a solid color, then printed with another motif. Figured printed silk ties are offered by numerous fashion houses including Armani, Léonard, and Hugo Boss.

Printed silk: Silk whose colored patterns or motifs have been printed onto (as opposed to woven into) the fabric. Also sometimes called "piece-dyed" silk.

Ready-tied: Any tie that is pre-knotted and is kept in place by an attaching system (clips, elastic, velcro, etc.). Some bow ties are simply pre-tied—their knots can be loosened; others have their knots sewn in place.

Regimental tie: Any tie with diagonal stripes in regimental colors. It should be worn only by members or veterans of the regiment in question. Imitation regimentals, however, which adopt this overall style, can be worn by anyone. The term regimental is sometimes incorrectly applied to club and old school ties.

Rep: Fabric with ribs running perpendicular to the selvedge. Silk rep is often used for ties.

Repeat: The size of a motif in an all-over or repeating pattern. The larger the size of the "repeat," the smaller the number of motifs that will appear on the tie (see repeating pattern).

Repeating pattern: A pattern that covers the entire surface of the tie with single or multiple motifs. Also called an all-over pattern.

Ribbed fabric: Fabric whose weave produces a surface with alternating ribs and grooves.

Ribbon stripes: Diagonal stripes that are isolated or widely spaced from one another.

Sailor knot: An alternative name for the four-in-hand knot (see this entry).

Satin Weave: A weave in which at least three warp yarns are floated over one weft yarn (or vice versa) forming a smooth, compact surface. The weave is frequently used in today's ties.

Screen printing: The design is first separated into as many colors as it contains. Each color separation is then stenciled onto a piece of silk or polyester stretched on a frame or "screen." The non-printing areas are then blocked out with a lacquered glaze and the fabric is unrolled on a long table. The screen is placed on the fabric and the dye is forced through the meshes of the unglazed areas of the silk and onto the fabric. The process is repeated the length of the fabric and for each color of the design. The number of screens used (one per color) is a key factor in the cost of a printed silk tie.

Seven-fold tie: A tie without an interlining. Its firmness and shape are assured by the silk itself, which is folded over seven times. Already expensive in the 1920s, this tie is quite rare today.

Shadow stripes: Stripes whose colors blend or shade into one another.

Slip stitch: The end of the thread, several inches long, deliberately left free in quality ties at one or both ends of the lengthwise seam in order to let the tie stretch, not break at the seam. This is indispensable if the tie is to maintain its shape and drape. The slip stitch usually is in the form of

a loop; some tie makers divert it to the inside of the lining, thereby rendering it invisible and thus safe from scissors wielded by wearer's unaware that it is their tie's "lifeline."

Solitaire: The *solitaire,* probably invented in England but very fashionable at the court of Louis XV, owed its rise to the fashion for tying one's hair back. The thin black silk ribbon, used to secure the hair was brought around to the front and knotted on top of cravat. It was called a *solitaire,* because of the effect created by the single filigree of black ribbon on a mass of white muslin.

Spun silk: Silk woven from the short, "waste" filaments generated by the silkworm, as opposed to raw silk—the longer filaments that are spooled directly from the cocoon. Raw silk is the more precious of the two products; spun silk is often used in printed ties, but it is less brilliant and less resistant than raw silk.

Steinkirk: A type of cravat in vogue in the seventeenth century. It was said to have been created on the morning of the battle of Steinkirk (1692) when French officers had no time to fashion their customary knots. It was simply wrapped around the neck and the ends of its flaps were passed through a buttonhole in the jacket.

Stocks: Cravats with high, stiff collar-like neckbands equipped with easily fastened hooks, and often decorated with a bow sewn on to the front. Stocks were popular in Europe from about 1715 to 1850.

String tie: A thin strip of cotton or velvet tied in a loose bow. It originated in the southern United States and was made popular in the 1950s by American rockabilly fans and British Teddy boys.

Titan stripes: Stripes arranged in chevron configurations.

Twill: A weave with fine diagonal ribs. Twill is the weave most often used for printed silk ties.

Underknot: A single motif, placed on the tie's face, so that it will appear only once the tie is knotted. The design motif of an underknot is usually positioned just below the knot.

Washed silk: Silk fabric whose gloss has been dulled by washing it with sand or pebbles. When used in conjunction with certain weaves and motifs it is often made to resemble wool—a technique employed by Ermenegildo Zegna.

Weave: The method of interlacing the warp yarns and the weft yarns that characterizes the texture of a fabric. There are three basic weaves: plain (the simplest and most widely used), twill (with diagonal ribs), and satin (smooth and glossy).

Windsor knot: Large tie knot made fashionable by the Duke of Windsor in the 1930s.

Yachting knot tie: This tie marked the final stage in the evolution of neckwear: it lies directly at the origins of our modern four-in-hand. Sportive and easy to knot, it was ideally suited for soft, turned down collars. It consisted of a simple band of woven material (usually silk), sometimes folded over onto itself and sewn. The yachting knot continued to be worn up until the 1920s (see entry for four-in-hand).

BIBLIOGRAPHY

Algoud, Henri. *La Soie: Art et Histoire.* Paris, 1987.

Ashley, C. W. *The Ashley Book of Knots.* New York, 1944.

Balzac, Honoré de. *Physiologie de la Toilette.* Paris, 1992.

Barbey d'Aurevilly, J. *Du Dandysme et de George Brummell.* Bordeaux, 1989.

Beaton, Cecil. *Photobiography.* New York, 1951.

Beaton, Cecil. *The Glass of Fashion.* London, 1954.

Beckett, J. V. *The Aristocracy in England 1660-1914.* Oxford, 1986.

Boucher, François. *A History of Costume in the West.* London, 1987.

Byrde, Penelope. *The Male Image: Men's Fashion in Britain, 1300–1970.* London, 1979.

Chenoune, Farid. *A History of Men's Fashion.* Paris, 1993.

Clark, H. *Textile Printing.* Aylesbury, 1985.

Cunnington, C. W. and Phillis. *A Handbook of English Costume in the Nineteenth Century.* Boston, 1970.

Cunnington, Phillis, and Ann Mansfield. *A Handbook of English Costume in the Twentieth Century.* Boston, 1973.

Darwen, James. *Le Chic Anglais.* Paris, 1990.

Doke, Donald. *The Consumer's Guide to Menswear.* New York, 1983.

Davidoff, Leonore. *The Best Circles: 'Society,' Etiquette and the Season.* London, 1986.

Dyer, Rod and Ron Spark. *Fit to be Tied. Vintage Ties of the Forties & Early Fifties.* New York, 1987.

L'Empesé, baron Emile de. *L'art de mettre sa cravate de toutes les manières connues et usitées, enseigné et démontré en 16 leçons.* Paris, 1827. Translated as *The Art of Tying the Cravat* by H. Le Blanc. London, 1828.

Favardin, P. *Le Dandysme.* Paris, 1988.

Geijer, A. *A History of Textile Art.* London, 1979.

Gibbings, Sarah. *The Tie, Trends and Traditions.* New York, 1990.

Greef, John de. *Cravates et accessoires.* Paris, 1989.

Harris, Jennifer (ed.). *5000 years of Textiles.* London, 1993.

Hecht, A. *The Art of the Loom: Weaving, Spinning and Dyeing across the World.* London, 1989.

Keers, Paul. *A Gentleman's Wardrobe.* New York, 1987.

Kempf, Roger. *Dandies : Baudelaire et Cie.* Paris, 1984.

Langlade, J. de. *Brummell ou le Prince des Dandys.* Paris, 1985.

Laurent, Jacques. *Le Nu vêtu et dévêtu.* Paris, 1979.

Larsen, Jack Lenor. *Material Wealth.* New York, 1989.

Laver, James. *The Book of Public School Old Boys, University, Navy, Army, Air Force and Club Ties.* London, 1968.

Mercier, Louis-Sébastien. *Tableau de Paris.* Amsterdam, 1781-1788.

Molloy, John T. *Dress for Success.* New York, 1975.

Mosconi, David and Ricardo Villarosa. *Les 188 façons de nouer sa cravate.* Paris, 1985.

O'Hara, Georgina. *The Encyclopaedia of Fashion.* London, 1986.

Pastoureau, Michel. *L'Etoffe du Diable. Une histoire des rayures et des tissus rayés.* Paris, 1991.

Schiaffino, Mariosa and Irvana Malabarba. *Eloge de la cravate,* Paris, 1988.

Stone, Jeff and Kim Johnson Gross. *Shirt and Tie.* New York, 1993.

Storey, Joyce. *The Thames and Hudson Manual of Dyes and Fabrics.* London, 1992.

Storey, Joyce. *The Thames and Hudson Manual of Textile Printing.* London, 1992.

Tolstoï, Tatiana. *De l'Elégance masculine.* Paris, 1987.

Walker, Richard. *The Savile Row Story.* London, 1988.

TIE CREDITS

PICTURE CREDITS

Cover: J.P. Dieterlen; **p. 1** R. de Seynes/C. Renonciat/Hermès; **p. 2, 3** J.P. Dieterlen; **p. 4, 5** J.P. Dieterlen; **p. 6** A. Eisenstaedt, Life Magazine, Time Warner Inc., Cosmos/Paris; **p. 7** Coll. S. Thull; **p. 8,9** Kobal Coll.; **p. 10** F. Kollar/Ministère de la Culture-France; **p. 11** J.P. Dieterlen; **p. 12** above: Giraudon/Château of Versailles; left: C.N.M.H.S./Spadem 1994; right: B.A.D./*Fit to be Tied*/Abbeville Press; **p. 13** above left: C.N.M.H.S./Spadem 1994; right: J.L. Charmet; below left: The Bettmann Archive; right: Nuova Italia Editrice/D.R.; **p. 14** Kobal Coll.; **p. 15** above: The Bettmann Archive; below: C. Beaton/Dunhill; **p. 16** above: B.A.D.; right: B.A.D./*Fit to be Tied*/Abbeville Press; below: Association des Amis de J.H. Lartigue; **p. 17** H. Cartier-Bresson/Magnum; **p. 18** M. Seliger/Stills; **p. 19** above: Kobal Coll.; below: Image Bank/Liberty Coll.; **p. 20,21** Giraudon/Musée du Louvre; **p. 22** A. Reffet/Explorer; **p. 23** Luisa Ricciarini; **p. 24** E. Lessing/Magnum/Musée du Louvre; **p. 25** above: National Portrait Gallery; below: Bulloz; **p. 26** above: Giraudon/Musée des Beaux-Arts de Valenciennes; below: B.A.D.; **p. 27** National Gallery; **p. 28** Phillips Auction; **p. 29** above and below: Bulloz/Musée Carnavalet; **p. 30** above: Archives Pictures/NYC; below: J.L.Charmet; **p. 31** National Portrait Gallery; **p. 32** above: Coll. S. Thull; below: B.A.D./photo: J.L. Charmet; **p. 33** above: Artephot/Musée Fabre; below: Bulloz/Musée du Mans; **p. 34** above: Roger-Viollet; below: National Portrait Gallery; **p. 35** R.M.N./Château of Versailles; **p. 36** C.N.M.H.S./Spadem 1994; **p. 37** above: J.L. Charmet; left: The Bettmann Archive; below: Roger-Viollet; **p. 38** above: J.L. Charmet; below: Roger-Viollet; **p. 39** E.T. Archive; **p. 40** above: Studio Editions; left and right: Museo della Seta, Como; **p. 41** above: Association des Amis de J.H. Lartigue; below: Explorer/Mary Evans Picture Library; **p. 42,43** J.P. Dieterlen; **p. 44** J.P. Dieterlen; **p. 45** above and below: J.P. Dieterlen; **p. 46** above: M. Walter; below: Atkinson; **p. 47** J.P. Dieterlen; **p. 48** above: Gessner A.G.; below: Donalisio/Ratti; **p. 49** J.P. Dieterlen; **p. 50** above: Ratti; left: Donalisio; below: J. du Sordet; **p. 51** above: Flammarion 4; right: J. du Sordet; below: J.P. Dieterlen; **p. 52** J.P. Dieterlen; **p. 53** above and below: J.P. Dieterlen; **p. 54** J.P. Dieterlen; **p. 55** J.P. Dieterlen; **p. 56** above: J.P. Dieterlen; below: Kobal Coll.; **p. 57** Kobal Coll.; **p. 58** above: U.F.A.C.; below: J.P. Dieterlen; **p. 59** J.P. Dieterlen; **p. 60** J.P. Dieterlen; **p. 61** above and below: J.P. Dieterlen; **p. 62** J.P. Dieterlen; **p. 63** above: Hilditch & Key; below: J.P. Dieterlen; **p. 64** above and below: J.P. Dieterlen; **p. 65** J.P. Dieterlen; **p. 66,67** J.P. Dieterlen; **p. 68** J.P. Dieterlen; **p. 69** above: Retrograph/M. Breeze; below: Ferragamo; **p. 70** above and below: J.P. Dieterlen; **p. 71** J.P. Dieterlen; **p. 72** above J.P. Dieterlen; below: Roger-Viollet; in margin: Flammarion; **p. 73** J.P. Dieterlen; **p. 74** above: P. Aprahamian; below: Museo della Seta, Como; **p. 75** P. Aprahamian; **p. 76** The Bettmann Archive; **p. 77** above: R. Talbott; left: P. Aprahamian; below right: G. Bavoillot; **p. 78** above: Retrograph; left: The Bettmann Archive; right: P. Aprahamian; **p. 79** J.P. Dieterlen; **p. 80** above: D.R.; below: J.P. Dieterlen; **p. 81** E. Watson Inc.; **p. 82** J.P. Dieterlen; **p. 83** left: J.P. Dieterlen; below: R. Talbott; **p. 84** J.P. Dieterlen; **p. 85** above: Deutsches Textilmuseum, Krefeld; below: Ascot; **p. 86** J.P. Dieterlen; **p. 87** P. Smith & D. Bailey; **p. 88** above left and right: J.P. Dieterlen; below: Keystone; **p. 89** left: J.P. Dieterlen; in right margin: Retrograph/M. Breeze; below: B.A.D./*Fit to be Tied*/Abbeville Press; **p. 90** J.P. Dieterlen; **p. 91** J.P. Dieterlen; **p. 92,93** J.P. Dieterlen; **p. 94** above: Museum Moderner Kunst Stiftung Ludwig/Wien; below: G. le Querrec/Magnum; **p. 95** above: J. Kudelka/Magnum; below: Fédération française de la Cravate; **p. 96** A. Dunhill; **p. 97** above and in the margin: The Bettmann Archive; below left: B.A.D./photo: J.L. Charmet; below right: Retrograph/M. Breeze; **p. 98** Retrograph/M. Breeze; **p. 99** above: L. de Selva/Tapabor; left margin: U.F.A.C.; below: Victoria & Albert Museum; **p. 100** above left: B.A.D.; right and below: J.P. Dieterlen; **p. 101** J.P. Dieterlen; **p. 102** T.M.R./Adagp Paris 1994/Coll. L. Treillard; **p. 103** Imapress/P. Lichfield/Camera Press; **p. 104** C.N.M.H.S./Spadem 1994; **p. 105** above: National Portrait Gallery; left: The Bettmann Archive; below: Coll. S. Thull; **p. 106** above: B.A.D.; right: J.P. Dieterlen; below: The Bettmann Archive; **p. 107** above: C. Steele-Perkins/Magnum; below: Coll. Blottière; **p. 108** J.P. Dieterlen; **p. 109** B.A.D.; **p. 110** above: Explorer/Mary Evans Picture Library; in margin: The Bettmann Archive; below: Deutsches Textilmuseum, Krefeld; **p. 111** above: Explorer/Mary Evans Picture Library; below: The Bettmann Archive; **p. 112,113** J.P. Dieterlen; **p. 114** J.P. Dieterlen; **p. 115** above: B.A.D.; below: J.P. Dieterlen; **p. 116** above: Flammarion; below center: J.P. Dieterlen; **p. 117** J.P. Dieterlen; **p. 118** J.P. Dieterlen; **p. 119** above: J.P. Dieterlen; below Charvet; **p. 120** above: J.P. Dieterlen; below: Ferragamo; **p. 121** J.P. Dieterlen; **p. 122** above and center: J.P. Dieterlen; below: E. Boubat/Hermès; **p. 123** Archives C. Dior/photo: W. Maywald/Adagp 1994; **p. 124** J.P. Dieterlen; **p. 125** P. Aprahamian; **p. 126** J.P. Dieterlen; **p. 127** J.P. Dieterlen; **p. 128** J.P. Dieterlen; **p. 129** above: J.P. Dieterlen; below: R. Talbott; **p. 130**: J.P. Dieterlen; **p. 131** Zegna/Il Punto; **p. 132,133** J.P. Dieterlen; **p. 134** F. Kollar/Ministère de la Culture-France; **p. 135** above: R. Gruau/D.R.; below: Kobal Coll.; **p. 136** above: B.A.D.; below: Stills; **p. 137** E. Hofer; **p. 138** above: Roger-Viollet; below: Sygma/*L'Illustration*; **p. 139** Springer/The Bettmann Archive; **p. 140** above: Gamma/Figaro Magazine; below: Coll. S. Thull; **p. 141** Kobal Coll.; **p. 142** above: Breuer; below: B.A.D.; **p. 143** Kobal Coll.; **p. 144** above: Loro Piana; below: Retrograph/M. Breeze; **p. 145** J.P. Dieterlen; **p. 146** J.P. Dieterlen; **p. 147** J.P. Dieterlen; **p. 148** J.P. Dieterlen; **p. 149** Zegna/Il Punto; **p. 150** above: C. Porchez/Kenzo; below: C. Dior; **p. 151** C. Porchez/Kenzo; **p. 152** Helen Drew; **p. 153** J.P. Dieterlen; **p. 154** Windsor Gmbh, Bielefeld/photo: D. Eikelpoth; **p. 155** above: T.M.R./Adagp 1994/Coll. L. Treillard; below: U.F.A.C.; **p. 156** Musée des Arts décoratifs/photo: J.P. Dieterlen; **p. 157** above: Driggs/Magnum; left: J.P. Dieterlen; below Coll. S. Thull; **p. 158** Doisneau/Rapho; **p. 159** above: Kobal Coll.; below: Rapho; **p. 160** H. Newton; **p. 161** J. du Sordet.

On page 161:
detail of an old-fashion plate formerly
used to print ties with paisley
patterns (Gandit, France).

INDEX

ACKNOWLEDGMENTS

The author would particularly like to thank Jean-Claude Colban of Charvet who transmitted his great knowledge and expertise with the patience and generosity of a true master, and who proofread the text with faultless attention. Gratitude for their precious help is also due to: Benoît Berthoux, Alain Blum, Stephania Caprotti, Farid Chenoune, Anne-Marie Colban, Luciano Donatelli, Jean-Louis Dumas-Hermès, Nathalie Gaillard, Gilles Ghez, Luciano Guggiari, Regina Hutet, Florence James, Tadashi Kinami, Michiel Lassche, Marco Nozeda, Fabien Ouaki, Karen Petrossian, Albertina and Vana Porro, Donatella Ratti, Christian Richard, Pia Ripamonti, Filippo Saladanna, Ivor Spencer, Yosuke Tanaka, Laurence Thibault, Stephan Thull, Georges Touzenis, and Alain Weill. Finally, the author extends his profound appreciation to Ghislaine Bavoillot and her editorial team for the successful realization of this book: Nathalie Bailleux, Laurent Breton, Sabine Greenberg, and Hélène Liard, as well as to Florence Picard and to the designer, Marc Walter.

The publisher would like to thank all of the fashion houses, the silk manufacturers and the museums for their precious collaboration, and more particularly José Alvarez, Bruno Berger, Bettina Borner, Jean-Marie Bossard, Pierre Brullé, Canale, Jack and Rogier Chapon, Deborah Gill, Antoine Hébrard, Véronique Manssy, Thierry Mugler, Virginia Murray, Bertrand Niaudet, Peter Nicholson, Marc Perron, Jean Ristat, and Andy Stewart.